Never Drive A Hatchback To Austria

(And Other Valuable Life Lessons)

R.A. DALKEY

First District Publishing, Vienna

Shopping and Loathing

In the spring of 2015, I very much wanted the cricket season to begin. It had been a long winter, painful and dark as always. And this particular summer, I was convinced, would be the one to finally see me conquer that most unforgiving, misunderstood and rewarding of games. I was going to play as many times as I could, and surely thrive. I was going to get good this time around. I couldn't wait to dust off my gigantic kit bag once again.

If you're not from England or some other cricket-playing country (there are only about a dozen of them: a motley collection of former British Empire places as disparate as St Lucia, Sri Lanka and South Africa, where I'm from), then you may not know exactly what game I'm on about. But please don't worry. I promise this isn't going to be a book about cricket. Although at this point I would like to clarify just one thing: cricket is not croquet. They might both have a reputation for Englishness, involve wearing a lot of white and feature a lot of men clubbing red balls with bits of wood, but they are not - and never will be - the same game. Croquet (albeit with a twist) is what they played in *Alice in Wonderland*, while cricket is, well, not known for being in any book or movie at all. It has to be seen to be understood. And I'll say no more on the matter.

If your concept of cricket remains hazy, that's okay. All you really need to understand for this story is that the sport attracts strange, nostalgic people who possess attention spans few millennials could hope to grasp. It's a throwback and anachronism that could never be invented in this day and age. And that by my mid-thirties, having now found myself saying things like 'this day and age' on a worryingly regular basis, I had become the game's target market. After a layoff spanning the 18 or so years that had gone AWOL since the end of high school, I'd rediscovered the joys of playing in a big way.

What really matters for this tale is that early summer was making its tentative presence felt, which meant - hooray! - that the first game of the season was on its way. The match, slated for a Sunday in the middle of April, was only to be a friendly warm-up affair. But it didn't matter to me. I don't need things to be competitive. Primarily because I'm not very good at sports.

But cricket, you see, can be as keenly anticipated by the weekend trundler as it can by the talented and prolific. I was impatient to hear the lambs bleating beyond the boundary fence. I longed to read *The Times* on the pavilion terrace - cricket, almost uniquely in sport, does allow certain players to read the newspaper while the game goes on. I pined to soak up the outdoors while getting mildly high on the smell of fresh-cut grass. But of course, along with all that excitement, I wanted to chase the occasional ball around too. I was straining at the leash like a walk-deprived collie dog.

An English winter holed up in a bland apartment without so much as a tiny patch of grass outside, much less any bleating livestock, will do this to you. You become obsessed with escaping your grubby sofa, racks full of clothes that won't dry and the awfulness of Radio One, whose model - which astoundingly seems to work - involves playing the same five current chart-toppers on an endless loop. You crave moving air beyond what the kitchen extractor fan can provide. When something approaching pleasant weather arrives, *Outside* becomes a must-visit. And that time had come.

But while the thought of Sunday's game had me going dreamy-eyed, there was still that one thing that had been niggling away at me ever since we'd locked down Shipton-under-Wychwood Cricket Club back in September. One problem I'd been meaning to get around to solving, but hadn't yet. And that problem was transport.

Shipton, as it was colloquially known, was a small town in rural Oxfordshire. It was a good few miles from Witney, the slightly bigger town in rural Oxfordshire I called home. And if Witney was a fiddly place to get to by public transport, Shipton was borderline impossible. If you wanted to get to a cricket match you had to hitch a lift with your car-owning team-mates.

Towards the end of the previous season, I'd begun to find this wearisome. Everyone was very generous, sure, but I'd simply grown tired of all the texting that catching rides seemed to involve. I was suddenly too old to want to fiddle about in WhatsApp groups that can never make a decision. So I'd vowed to get a car in time for the new season.

And now, with the first quarter of the year having done its usual vanishing trick, that new season had somehow snuck up on me. As a person who takes vows seriously (why make them, otherwise?), I *had* to get a car in time for the weekend.

And why had this become a matter of last-minute urgency? Good question. The answer to which is this: there's a *thing* with me and shopping. I abhor it so much that I simply can't do it unless there's a near deadline hanging over me. Some people need pressure to get started on their work; I need pressure to go and buy onions.

If you're the kind of person who is incapable of walking down the street alongside a companion without abandoning them for a shoe-laden window display (usually without a word of warning, so that they've covered the equivalent of three metro stops before they notice you've disappeared), this burden I bear might be hard to grasp. But let me try to explain it.

I'm a minimalist, more interested in buying practical things that won't break than something that merely looks good on that table in the study. This makes shopping fraught with difficulty. There's always too much choice and too little information. I don't even begin to know what I'm doing. How does one buy motor oil or pairs of secateurs without mistakenly picking up the viscosity that cooks your engine, or the blades that do roses instead of geraniums?

Even buying something to trim my own beard is a trial for me. I'm positively brand-blind: I simply have no memory for any of them. How anyone makes space in their head to remember that the razor stick they've got in the bathroom is a Wilkinson Schick FineLiner or a Gillette Sword MellowShave, is beyond me (what lengthy debates they must surely have about these nonsensical names over at Gillette and Wilkinson...). If I do find myself in a shop and actually remember that I need blades - quite the alignment of stars in itself - I usually end up having to slink home empty-handed. Where I'll almost certainly fail to remember to get out my phone and take a photo of my current shaving installations for the next time I'm staring gormlessly at the shelves in the men's hygiene section.

Even if I do have some inkling of what the item might be that matches my requirements, the spartan budget I allow myself often leaves me worryingly vulnerable to the Chinese. They know perfectly well that once we decadent Westerners have bought their low-cost crap and it breaks, we'll just shrug and buy it again. We'll do that because it's easier to spend another five bucks than it is to call Xiamen City and try to complain about your faulty toaster in Mandarin.

I'm actually not against spending more money to get a quality, longer-lasting product. In principle, I'm all good with this. In practice, though, we don't actually have any information with which to make such a call. For all the smart searches, chatbots and algorithms out there, how is one to know where exactly the tipping point at which rubbish turns to quality can be found? I'm pretty sure a $20 suitcase will be junk. But how *much* more am I supposed to spend? At what price do suitcases actually start lasting longer than one holiday? $30? $60? $200? And then, is it going to be two holidays or five? Nobody tells us this - probably nobody really knows - and I don't like spending my money on guesswork. So I may as well just buy junk.

Speaking of crap that falls apart, I blame this new phenomenon one hundred percent on the anonymity of globalisation. When we all lived in villages, and you knew your cobbler by name, surely he didn't even *think* of selling junk? Because he'd be well aware that all the townsfolk would know exactly whose windows to break when their shoes started leaking. Bakers would have lived in fear of somebody getting an iffy baguette, lest they get whacked on the head with it later that afternoon. But now it's all changed: our artisans are many thousands of miles away. I don't think the Chinese lie awake thinking 'Ye Gods! What if that ballpoint pen I made today runs out after five words!? Do you think they will come for us tonight, Xi?'

If these horrors and difficulties stalk even the most basic items, shopping decisions get even more vexing with more technical things. This is especially true when they're second-hand. You either have to do a lot of research or hope you have someone in your family who can spot a faulty carburettor. With the former, I can't be bothered. People less grumpy than I might be happy to come home from a day of doing things on a screen and continue doing things on a screen after dinner, but this is something I actively seek to avoid. And as for savvy snag-spotters, my family is generously thin on streetwise, practically-minded people. I did have an uncle who succeeded in working illegally in America for six months of the year throughout most of his adult life, and moreover he spent them doing all manner of DIY for Floridians. But he's sadly no longer with us.

Without any truly useful relatives, I tend to assume I'll get hoodwinked when it comes to buying anything much more complex than an apple (I don't buy these second-hand, but I *have* been known to mistakenly pick up those rascally, sour Granny Smiths instead of sensible, sweet Golden Delicious). I convince myself I'll be led astray by some crafty so-and-so who's selling that item on Gumtree (or Craigslist, if you prefer) precisely because they've seen early indications that its time is nigh.

You might say I ought simply to avoid second-hand shopping, but the agony of choice remains either way. Let's return to the supermarket. You're still expected to take a wild guess when the packaging answers every question *except* the one on which one's purchase depends. I mean really *big* questions, like 'can I put this pot in the oven?' Critical ones like whether the bottle you're holding contains shower gel or shampoo, shaving cream or deodorant. (This really is a thing with modern toiletries. It's become a trend just to sell bottles that tell you plenty about the Baltistani Jemimawood aroma and all the women who are going to swarm in your direction if you buy the mystery item, but don't think to mention what the thing actually *is*.)

And it's not as though that 15-year-old shop 'assistant' is really going to know what's what either, is he? All he does is stack shelves full of poorly-manufactured stuff that came from Xiamen City, occasionally stopping to croak at customers, who quickly remember that the age of the specialist shopkeeper can't come back soon enough.

Buying new stuff is also massively wasteful. It's a real burden having a conscience about humanity's obsession with throwing things away and making new stuff instead, but one I'm lumbered with. Because I've seen the plastic bottle dumps of India, the grim television graveyards of Hampshire and the paradise beaches piled up with flip-flops that floated in on the tide from Java. I try, though I know I'm doing terrible things to China's economic growth figures, to give ironing boards, rugs and kettles a second chance where I can. That means shopping on Gumtree and eBay, which I don't enjoy at all. It's a long, fiddly and mighty dangerous business, made infinitely harder by not being able to pick up the item and shake it around.

By now I hope you've gotten a feel for the reasons why I can put off buying just about anything for months on end. And why buying a second-hand car was just about the scariest project I could ever imagine undertaking. But now I'd reached my deadline. The pressure point I needed had come.

Only by deliberately creating a false narrative of hectic urgency would I overcome my loathings and actually go out to buy the damn thing. So I'd convinced myself that acquiring my own vehicle in time for the weekend was both critical and non-negotiable. If I had to get a refurbished military Jeep from the 1920s, so be it. But I would get to Shipton under my own steam for that game.

And I knew precisely what the result of deliberately creating a panic would be: I'd rush off and throw my moderate budget at something with no thought whatsoever. It really *might* be an army throwaway. But it simply had to be that way. If I had too much time or reflected too much, I'd never buy anything at all.

5

There was another explanation for the fact that I'd waited so long. It was my annoying sense of social responsibility again. I didn't want to become a lazy, thoughtless person who polluted the atmosphere when they didn't need to. And outside of cricket season, without the need to transport an enormous kit bag to a remote village, I could cope just fine on foot and with my bicycle.

I did live in the Witney town centre, after all. And Witney was one of the most harmless, feel-good sort of places anywhere in the country. It lay in Oxfordshire no-man's land: neither famous university city nor officially within the bounds of Cotswolds. Its once-famous weaving industry had died out, but the town remained pretty affluent. It had become a walkable sort of overgrown village where various people got born, grew up, lived and worked. It wasn't a particularly bad place to die either, I imagined.

Few from outside the area will have heard of Witney, although if you've ever followed British politics you'll no doubt recognise the name as that of then Prime Minister David Cameron's constituency. In which role it routinely attracted some of England's more committed and creative protesters, who knew exactly where in the High Street the Conservative Party's tiny local offices were to be found.

Cameron was known to pop into Witney on Friday afternoons. You knew he was there when three black cars with tinted windows were pulled up next to the sidewalk. It always struck me as ludicrous that after a week of talking Iraq, North Korea and Brexit, the PM was then supposed to come back to Witney and concern himself with the zebra crossing outside the chemist. Why pretend?

But Witney was quite the appropriate place for the Prime Minister to call home. It was about as English a town as it was still possible to find in modern-day England. It had pubs so posh that they were borderline restaurants. It had a cathedral and a green. Its school kids didn't yet make you want to cross the street for your own safety, and it was home to a specialist teddy bear shop so famous that people flew over from Japan to visit it.

It also had to be one of the biggest settlements in the United Kingdom without a railway station. There'd been one once upon a time, but they closed it down in the sixties, so now you had to take an extortionately expensive double-decker bus to Oxford if you wanted to get to or from anywhere else in the country. The only homage left to its flirtation with rail was Station Road - halfway along which you could now do your shopping at Waitrose.

6

I tended to side with Marks & Spencers for my rare successful grocery forays, if only because their branch lay at the bottom of my apartment building. Just another reason why I didn't need a car in Witney for more than just this summer. Anyway, negotiating the town didn't look like much fun in a car. There were so many of them roaring down bumpy Bridge Street that even crossing the road on foot could take 20 minutes.

And what had this stupid combination of trying to do the right thing and shopping phobia left me with? Precisely a day and a half in which to buy a car. Where would I even start? I briefly considered giving up cricket in order to avoid buying myself some wheels. But then I pulled myself together.

Who could help? I might not have had any family who could give me the slightest bit of useful advice, but I did have a lanky mate from Middlesbrough who bought and sold used cars on a pretty much annual basis. There'd been - to name a few - a 1990 Ford Fiesta that he'd crashed after six days, a 1989 Fiesta 'with holes in it', a 1996 Nissan Primera, a 2001 Audi Cabriolet, an Isuzu Trooper (an impulsive buy to tow our co-owned racing car, which he never actually bothered to race), a Mazda RX7, a Skoda Fabia VRS and, more recently, a Mitsubishi Shogun that had exploded on an icy night near a lake outside Witney and forced us to walk home in shorts. Even more recently, Steven had finally settled down into a long-term and committed relationship with a Nissan 350Z.

None of our acquaintances understood why constantly replacing his car made him so pleased with his life, but the petrolheads among them - including Simon, another mate who'd spent just about all of his money on a souped-up Subaru Impreza - often seemed moved to poke fun at his choices. I didn't know enough about the apparent lunacy of these to mock them, but I figured he must at least know where to start shopping. The occasional dud purchase didn't much recommend him, but I knew he knew how to navigate the car sites on the Internet.

That, and he was conveniently nearby. We'd been house-mates until about ten days earlier, in fact. We'd shared a flat at number 50 Mandrill Lane. I'd only just moved - not making this up, I promise - to number 49 Mandrill Lane, where I was now living with a Lithuanian girl I hadn't known before. Doing that was already beginning to look like a big mistake: more on her later.

"Get this one," said Steven, jabbing his finger at a burgundy Peugeot hatchback on the Autotrader search results screen he'd ordered me to pull up on my laptop on Friday evening. It was a 306 Meridian of 2001 vintage, priced at 600 Pounds.

"That one? Aren't there any others?"

"*That* one."

I should mention at this point that he was quite the fan of *Little Britain* - or at least the Lou and Andy sketches, in which the wheelchair-bound hero's favourite line is *'that* one'.

"Will it break down?" I asked, with about as much confidence as I might reserve for questions to those teenagers stocking shelves at Curry's.

"No, it looks solid. It's only done 120K."

"Why aren't there any others in my budget? I thought there'd be dozens to choose from."

"Because you're being cheap. And because we live in small-town Oxfordshire. This isn't London."

I nodded thoughtfully. In my consideration 500 Pounds was more than enough to spend on anything - especially if it was only going to be for one cricket season - but I was willing to stretch to 600 for something 'solid'. That price still qualified as reasonable, I supposed. Not that this would stop me from grumbling: the car wasn't going to have to ferry three kids to school for the next 20 years, after all. It was only going to be in use for the summer, and then only a couple of times a week. When winter came, I was going to sell the thing and be an environmentally responsible citizen again.

"What about these ones?" I asked, indicating a few significantly cheaper cars further down the list.

"No, those ones *will* break down."

He hadn't actually looked at the results for very long, and now had his attention firmly back on the television. I knew perfectly well that Steven didn't actually know an awful lot more about what went on under the lid of a car than I did. But he *had* been the brains behind buying a quite similar car once before, and that had gone alright.

By which I mean that race car - okay, an '86 Ford Fiesta that you could race against people who also couldn't afford the real thing - which we'd co-owned for a couple of years in our distant youth. I should have been the one who knew about cars now, though. After all it was me, and not Steven, who'd actually taken the engine apart and put it back together again. I'd done a surprising amount of mechanical things during that time, actually, but always under complete supervision and instruction from Iain, another friend of ours. Now he really *did* know about cars. I'd not taken much on board for myself.

But our Fiesta, despite the shifty racer/mechanic who sold it to us making his best attempts to hoodwink us on various levels, had been a fundamentally good purchase. I guess it was this success, along with his inability to ever utter the words 'I don't know' that made Steven my first port of call for advice. I should probably have asked Iain, now that I think of it. But he, having made the mistake of marrying into an Irish Catholic family, had sired about seventeen children since our amateur pit crew days. So he was out: he'd be far too busy preventing them from constantly trying to kill themselves to talk to me about cars.

I looked at the pictures of the Peugeot once more. I had to admit that the car looked okay. By which I mean it had four wheels, a colour I didn't hate and was currently parked at a dealership within cycling distance. I was in dangerous territory now. It was just like running out of patience in the salt grinder section and buying whatever I like the look of, even when none of the grinders categorically state that they *are* the kind you can refill. I'd now obtained a satisfying and straightforward directive - you could always count on Steven for one of those - about this Peugeot. Suddenly, in my mind, I already owned it.

My personal shopper had spoken, and spoken well. My self-imposed deadline bearing down on me, the test drive would have to involve multiple fatalities and explosions to put me off. My reckless shopping moment had well and truly come.

"Oh, one thing," said Steven as I shut down my laptop and got ready for a good night's sleep ahead of the scary shopping trip that lay in wait the next day. "Offer him cash. I bet he'll knock the price down."

Fierce Negotiations
and Sunday Driving

"You want to pay cash? Alright. For cash, I can let it go for five hundred."

Negotiations were going as planned! But I nodded at the ruddy-faced dealer in front of me without showing any sign of being pleased. I wanted him to think I did this kind of wheeling and dealing all the time.

And anyway, I wasn't going to get overly excited. I'd expected the cash discount even before I discovered that nothing sparked into life when you turned the Peugeot's radio knob. And before I learned that the air conditioning didn't condition any air whatsoever.

Positives from the test drive along the A40? The Peugeot started. The Peugeot went where it was told. The Peugeot didn't break down. And - a deal-maker, this - there were neither fatalities nor explosions. I returned from the short blast both alive and convinced.

"What about four-fifty? I mean, I'm taking a car with a radio that doesn't work. And the aircon…"

"I can't do that," he said, without so much as glancing up from the paperwork he'd already started filling out. Smart. His salesman's intuitions surely told him that I needed the car urgently for an impending cricket fixture. I'd probably told him so myself when we did the test drive, come to think of it. I often blurted out things about cricket, even if they might have been detrimental to negotiations. After all, you never knew when you might be talking to one of those rare people with an appreciation for the game. But on reflection, I don't think second-hand car dealers out of Middle England are very often to be found within the cricketing demographic.

"Very well," I sighed politely, although I longed to say 'Screw you, your broken radio, your 500 Pounds, and all your mum's cats and dogs too. I'll take my money elsewhere, Buster!' That was always the problem with my last-minute strategy. Last-minute strategies leave you no time to go elsewhere. You give up all your negotiating power, and worse still, any chance to say 'Buster'.

He might have won a small victory over me on the price, this great pheasant-shooter of a fellow. But he, on the other hand, would have to come to terms with something far more existentially troubling: the fact that he was a second-hand car dealer on the outskirts of Brize Norton.

The man's life was terrifying and incomprehensible to me. He'd voluntarily established a business for which Saturday mornings were key to success. It required him to spend these Saturday mornings - which God made, let us not forget, for far better things - surrounded by the kind of people who like looking at second-hand cars on a Saturday morning. And he'd evidently done it for many years, without appearing to be obviously suicidal. I almost had to take my hat off to him.

What sort of reaction do people who sell second-hand cars get when they reveal their occupation, I wonder? Is it the sort of 'Oh, right...' that one reserves for people who tell you they work in acquisition enterprise scalability systems engineering? The tepid grunt that says you'd love to be interested enough to ask something further, but can't quite manage it. Maybe not. Maybe some of their interlocutors - small children, perhaps - jump up and down with excitement, yelling 'I want to be one of those when I grow up!'? I suppose we'd better hope so. I presume we always need a robust next generation of used-car dealers.

My new friend had gone into a line of work that had zero prospects of scalability and could never propel him into early retirement. Maybe he did have such a project on the side, mere weeks away from changing his life. Or maybe he didn't. I think about these things. What else are you going to do while you watch a portly chap in a visibly sweaty blue shirt fill out the VL5C form for the six hundred and seventeenth time in his life?

Papers completed and a wad of notes handed over, I drove the car away. Immediately the hurried vehicles of Oxfordshire started whoosh-whoosh-whooshing past my right ear. That I was a long way from any city of substance made no difference to the relentless stream of traffic. England never stops being crowded, wherever you go on the map. You're rarely more than about 300 yards from a settlement of some description.

These were RAF wives taking their kids to football matches, rich people from the small villages around Witney heading for a spot of boutique shopping for shabby chic lamp-stands, and other assorted stony-faced types off to do whatever they thought necessary and important. One of them might even have been Cameron in weekend stealth mode, hiding in a Vauxhall Astra and wearing dark glasses. Whoever, they were entirely indifferent to the fact that they were passing a new member of the motoring public. It was Saturday morning, after all. Whoosh-whoosh-whoosh.

But I was a little delirious behind my new steering wheel, and wouldn't have said no to a working radio on which I could blast *Ode to Joy*. Still, there was no ceremony. I just got in it and drove, and was thrilled because I was actually driving myself about. And no more than that: I'm not somebody who's going to get sentimental about an actual car. I understand this kind of thing if a vehicle has been with you for a lifetime, or if it's the one you drove from London to Vladivostok. And you can love your racing car too, as every member of Scuderia Banana surely did our bright yellow Fiesta. But a cheap street car? Nah. That's for taking you places. Be happy and thankful when it works without giving you grief. End of story.

These opinions already had deep roots. This may have been my first road-going car in Britain, but I'd had such a thing once before, in South Africa, my homeland. I guess, given that you're never too far away from the pleasures of an armed hijacking there, that it's a good place to learn not to develop too fond an attachment to your vehicle. Even in a best-case road piracy scenario, where you finally get to press your door-mounted highwayman incinerator device into action and turn your assailant into a pile of ash with gun laid neatly on top, surely your side panels are going to get a little singed.

Driving my Volkswagen Polo around Cape Town for a couple of years had taught me that I really didn't give a monkey's about scratches or dents. I'd never been able to understand why people whose car begot a scratch made clucking noises (or worse, flew into rages) and immediately rushed off to a paint shop. I'd wondered if owning my own machine would enlighten me, perhaps in the way that becoming a parent apparently makes seven hours relentless squawking, all the way across the Atlantic, take on the quality of a symphony orchestra performance led by Herbert von Karajan. (When would someone launch a guaranteed baby-free airline service?)

But the first time I involved an unwitting lamp post in my attempts to park neatly up against a kerb, I'd realised I wasn't going to get parentally sentimental. I'd gotten out of the car and noted a foot-wide, metre-long strip of destruction where once there was paint. Then I'd shrugged, and walked off to where I was going. Would my car still take me home? Yes. Was there a problem? No. Why would I ever take it to a paint shop? I simply couldn't think of a reason.

Maybe there's something wrong with me, but I think people are very odd about all this cosmetic stuff. And not just with cars. Consider walls. A mark on a wall is a major event for a lot of folks. A teeth-grinding, froth-inducing, sleepless-night kind of major event. Landlords, I have noticed, are particularly passionate about marks on walls. And there I was thinking that a wall's job was to hold up the ceiling and stop the wind from blowing your bed away in the night.

And then, just when you learn that a little black smudge from your bicycle's tyre is a terrible thing to happen to a stairwell, you watch on in amazement as these same people then *pay* to have somebody come round and splash great cans full of coloured liquid all over the wall. How does this make any sense?

For me, the best thing about owning something had been that I could put my money where my mouth was and rail against this nonsense. When I'd first bought that Volkswagen, I celebrated by inviting friends to give it a good kicking. After so many years of having to be careful not to scratch, dent, chip or mark other people's stuff, that was the true pleasure of ownership for me. You should try it sometime.

And so I hadn't gone looking for superficial perfection with my second car. Cosmetic 'flaws' were welcome, in fact, because these kinds of things made the price go down. In the case of the Peugeot, yellow, sponge-like stuff poked through the faux leather around the edges of the seats. The steering wheel was a bit worn. There was one of those scent-things on the dashboard, which I'm quite sure hadn't smelled of anything much since Tony Blair was running the country. And there was a two-penny piece wedged in an utterly inaccessible nook beneath the handbrake's hinge.

None of these things mattered to me. Why should they? You could sit on the seats, the steering wheel turned the car, and smells (or lack of them) didn't really stop you getting anywhere. Okay, the coin did nag away at me a little bit, but the engine started and the boot was big enough for a cricket bag. These, as well as the petrol consumption figures I awaited with bated breath, were the important things.

Nothing, in short, was a problem until it threatened to cost me money or prevent my car from starting up. On this front, I was quite sure something would go spectacularly wrong soon enough. I'd undoubtedly get stranded in the middle lane of the country's biggest motorway, without AA membership,

13

and that would be fitting punishment for my long list of extraordinary oversights in the research process. But for now I was happy.

The thrill of independent driving came flooding back to me. The pleasure of being able to decide to get in the car and go, and then, well, get in the car and go. It's many times better than having to wait for your ride to finish netball practice, feeling your bones freeze while your nose starts dripping sleet as you cycle, or standing in the teeth-chattering rain at the mercy of a bus while your violently heavy supermarket bags try to tug your arms and your shoulders asunder.

I remembered that I was also a big fan of being able to leave various sports equipment in the boot on a permanent basis. Why do parents and other assorted grown-ups always insist on unpacking everything when they get home, only to bring it out again for the next game? You cannot defend these kinds of antics.

My cricket bag was going to live in the Peugeot, because I was its Lord and Master. Selfish, one-man motoring may have its drawbacks on society and the planet, but boy, there's something swell about grabbing the keys and simply taking off. Something beautiful about being boss of the trunk, too. Self-drive cars and enforced sharing may be coming, and they surely have to. But let's enjoy the pleasures of independence while they last.

If driving in general was a treat I was relishing again, then I was even more excited about the route to cricket. I'd seen it as a passenger enough times. But now, I could enjoy the stunning landscape north and west of Witney whilst haring along some marvellous country lanes. Roads I'd also cycled many times, huffing and puffing up the hills, then freewheeling carefree between the stone walls whenever gravity could do the work. The way from Witney to Shipton was somehow made for gliding down hills, one-handed and slow, on epically long summer evenings.

But right now wasn't the time for cycling. I went to sleep with the smugness of the first kid in high school to get a car, feeling more than satisfied with my day's work. The cricket season would begin the next morning, and I'd be driving to the club.

Around lunchtime the next day, I heaved a cricket bag into my newly-acquired Peugeot. As is perfectly standard, the kit included a bat, helmet, gloves, leg pads and, most importantly, the protective guard every gentleman cricketer about stuffs into his trousers before squaring up to any leather projectiles that might come his way. Then I hit the road. I wanted to be at the club early, hopeful of getting a session in the practice nets before the match started. I also wanted to soak up the drive itself.

It wasn't all that beautiful a day, but off I went, full of the joys of spring and vehicle ownership. Past the edge-of-town BP service station I drove, as fast as the speed limit and my aversion to hundred-Pound fines conspired to allow. I was too excited even to stop at the Madeira Fish Bar across the road and gobble down a fat-fuelled heap of Britain's favourite take-away. Not that any jolly British people actually make fish and chips any more. The folks who cooked in this one were Portuguese, if I had to guess. And there's every chance you could order in Polish, Kurdish or Cantonese at any British chippie these days.

A few doors up from the Madeira lurked the grim remnants of a pub, boarded-up and bearing a 'for sale' sign ever since I moved to this town. It always looked like it must have done a good job of being a rough sort of establishment in its heyday. The kind of place where you'd find men drinking pints not long after nine in the morning. But I guess a true dive just couldn't last in a town as gentrified as Witney.

I bet that by now somebody has decided to try and bring the pub back to life. And probably led it to a second death already. Because one of the few certainties in life is that taking over a pub in England never works. The fact that some optimistic soul almost always comes along and tries to succeed where sixteen previous landlords have failed is testament to the human spirit. But it takes a certain type of business brain to look at a boarded-up establishment that rolled over and died while trying to sell food and drink in Town X, and then try to make a go of doing that same thing, on the basis that serving lattes and having a quiz night is going to make all the difference.

I left the pub to rest in temporary peace, and drove on towards the fluffy green hills that awaited me. Witney ended suddenly, just as it did when you cycled this road out of town. One minute the street was flanked by row upon row of identical houses (no country, with the possible exception of Belgium, is less imaginative when it comes to architectural diversity than Britain, unless you count satellite dishes in differing shades of grey as diverse), and the next you were in a forest. A little further on, I followed the road to the right at the rugby club, resisting the temptation to plunge down the aptly-named Foxburrow Lane. The route through Crawley village, with its electrifying descent, was more of a bicycle thing.

15

The main road took me past the junction with Poffley End Road. Which leads, in case you're wondering, to a tiny settlement called Poffley End. And the most marvellous thing about Poffley End is that the good people of the village are able to say its name repeatedly without breaking into fits of mirth. But they too would have to wait for a non-cricketing day. I pressed on, the forest giving way to a village called Hailey, which has a pub called the Lamb & Flag. On the sign outside, there was a picture of a forthright young sheep bearing an England flag.

That sign was possibly the reason why neither I nor anybody I knew had ever seen fit to stop and explore Hailey, much less that particular pub. Because England flags had strangely negative connotations. Largely because the nation's infamous pot-bellied, table-tipping football fans were the people most likely to hang this flag in their windows. And these thugs were, rightly or wrongly, the kind of people I would have expected to turn around and glare at me upon walking into the Lamb & Flag.

I once met an American who was (understandably) puzzled to be turned away from an English pub, in England, for the simple reason that the polo shirt he was wearing happened to sport an embroidered England flag. Something to do with attracting the 'right crowd', they had explained apologetically.

Was there any other country that could identify with this odd phenomenon? Forgetting nations like North Korea, where you'd be shot if you didn't get a tear in your eye as you contemplated the flag, I'd always assumed that the Brazilians, Bulgarians and Botswanans were proud enough to see their national banner. Americans were seized by the spirit of Abraham Lincoln whenever they laid eyes on the Stars and Stripes, that much was certain. And when I'd travelled around the Scandinavian countryside, I'd noticed that every other house had the cross of Sweden, Norway or whatever flapping in the wind outside. Which to me seemed rather nice. Such touches give the traveller a sense of place.

I couldn't imagine that wealthy Norwegians living on a farm 120 miles outside of Oslo were fierce football hooligans. The nice lady who refilled my water bottle at one such flag-bearing dwelling hadn't struck me as one. In England, though, I'd think twice about walking up to a farmhouse with a red and white cross fluttering in the yard. At best, I'd expect to find a snarling Staffordshire Bull Terrier lurking about.

Although not an especially popular thing to do, flying a Union Jack in your yard wouldn't inspire the same sense of dread. That was the complex thing about England. You could choose to fly either the complicated United Kingdom flag or the simple English one. But largely because Britain didn't play football as one united country, none of the morons who take the game seriously had ever waved the British flag. If you had a Union Jack, therefore, you were considered a liberal, inclusive sort of person who didn't believe in Scottish referendums, Brexits or the primacy of football. Waving an England flag marked you as the opposite.

In Scotland or Wales, they didn't have this problem. They had their football thugs too, to be sure, but their flags were symbols of nationhood to be enjoyed. The difference was that Scotland and Wales were considered oppressed by the dominant English. Their flags were thus innocent, rare and not-to-be-persecuted expressions of their nation-within-nationhoods. And for the Celts, the English flag was an unnecessary reminder of chest-thumping domestic colonialism.

You may have noticed I like to pick on football. Having grown up on rugby, I simply cannot take seriously any sport where people have to *pretend* to be injured all the time. Moreover, this is a game in which one score can be enough to win. Which seems to leave far too much down to a fluke moment deciding matters.

Above all, football is too simple. It demands none of the patience and subtlety of cricket, nor the multi-layered decisions called for by rugby. Everyone can understand it and play it - which is exactly its problem. It attracts too many stupid people who like punching things. It's the only sport I know of in which, pretty much wherever you go in the world, the fans of each team have to be divided into special zoo cages within the stadium. I rest my case.

As I passed the Lamb & Flag (of St George), I was still only about three minutes out of Witney. Indeed, you could complete a car journey between any combination of Witney, Crawley, Hailey and even Poffley End in four minutes or less. So small are the gaps between settlements that I'm quite convinced all of England will be one big city called London in fifty or a hundred years.

After traversing about three minutes of roller-coaster country road out of Hailey, I took a left turn and headed westwards. The woods closed in again and the road became straight and flat. This is where Steven and Simon would always gun their engines like crazy, burning gallons of fuel as they showed off why their cars were so worthwhile. You had to be a nerveless passenger if you rode with them. Or at least desperate for a lift to cricket.

My Peugeot wasn't anything like their cars: my run through the trees was dull and slow. After all, I had no reason to believe that my wheels weren't about to fall off. I was already beginning to notice a strange clunking noise every time I went over a bump. If I'd heard it on the test drive, I'd clearly ignored it. To my mind, agreeing to take a potentially killer vehicle was the lesser evil in comparison to returning to my laptop and having to start choosing cars all over again.

I emerged from the woods, passed a Chinese restaurant and wound my way slowly up the hill into the middle of Leafield, which I'd heard was the highest town in Oxfordshire. From what I'd observed passing through, it seemed fair to say that nothing ever happened in sleepy Leafield. This was despite the fact that it was actually home to a Formula 1 team. Which is not as odd as it sounds: this part of England is pretty much the centre of the world motorsport industry. They might be relatively rural, but Oxfordshire and neighbouring Northamptonshire are full of high-tech factories that lurk among harmless-looking meadows. In a world in which industrial espionage is not unheard of, I suppose sheep make for good neighbours.

I could see the (now-defunct) Caterham team's factory away to my left as I left Leafield, its flat white roof peeking above the sheep and the stone walls. Now the road unfurled along a hillside, and a chocolate-box vista opened up to the right. The green hills and four-minutes-apart villages rolled on for miles to the north. You could see all the way to Charlbury on a clear day. If you were on the way to cricket and you saw that view, it was impossible not to feel content with the world, perhaps even with England. I knew this because I'd been a passenger along here before, my guts lurching as my boy-racer chauffeurs looped the loop over the humps and dips along this fine stretch of road. Right now, I could only sneak the odd peek. With its blind rises and hairy drops, admiring the scenery wasn't a good idea if you were behind the wheel.

And finally, Shipton-under-Wychwood. It sat in a valley and was every bit as idyllic as it sounds. The first house you saw was a posh one. And the second. And the third. It was the kind of place where people too rich to need to be near a town with jobs chose to live. Nestled in gorgeous countryside, it had a couple of pubs, a cricket club, a station. If you lived here, I'm not sure you could ask for much more out of life. (Although I'm sure people did.)

The station, by the way, was about a five-hundred-metre walk from the edge of town, along a busy road without a pavement. It was like this at many of the train stops around here. I suppose the railway planners of yore must have had their reasons. Perhaps, back then, people balked at the notion of having trains steaming through the middle of their villages, and preferred the walk. Which is understandable, and perhaps a reason why some of these places have remained villages and didn't become London. It might even be seen as a remarkable bit of foresight in preserving rural England, and I have no problem with that.

The only thing they never thought of was that one day there'd be hundreds more cars whizzing down the road between the station and the town than there were back then. Which makes the walk, especially with a hefty cricket bag that makes sudden changes of direction tricky, something of a suicide mission. Nowadays you really wanted to be *driving* from the station to town. Which kind of defeats the point of public transport.

Anyway, there were only about three trains a day that could bring me to Shipton (via the overpriced Oxford bus). All these were factors in my decision to buy a car. A decision that made me want to give myself a hug as I edged the Peugeot up the fiddly gravel entrance to the cricket club. I was one of the grown-ups who turned up to the match in a vehicle of their own! The parking area (basically the patch of land near the gate that wasn't cricket field, clubhouse or practice area) was my oyster. The sound of my own tyres on its crushed stone and dirt was a fine one indeed.

There's not much going on here yet, I thought as I pulled into the prime spot behind the clubhouse. There was only one other car about, but it hadn't thought to take the one space where your car was thoroughly protected from anybody who smashed a cricket ball (they're not soft) out of the field during a match. *Must be an opposition player,* I chuckled.

I got out of my car and sauntered over to the unfamiliar gentleman in his fifties who was leaning up against his own vehicle. Opposition player, most definitely.

"Hi, do you fancy a warm-up in the nets?" I asked after introducing myself.

"Wooi not?" he murmured in a sombre monotone, adding a curious trilled hiss to the 't' on the end.

Then I remembered that the team we were playing against was from Birmingham. His strange way of speaking suddenly made sense. They talk funny there.

We batted and bowled for a while, dusting a few winter cobwebs out of our respective games. Meanwhile, I couldn't help noticing that the car park wasn't filling up as I had expected it to. We were now twenty minutes from the scheduled start time, and not another soul had yet arrived.

"Er, you've come for the friendly match today, right?" I asked my practice buddy. I'd just kind of assumed that's why he was here, leaning up against his car at a cricket club over an hour away from where he lived.

"That's rrroyt," he replied. "I'd have thought the others'd've been ear boy now..."

"Hmm," I murmured, starting to get worried. "Let me text our captain."

This was most curious. I could understand one person on one side getting the wrong end of the stick. But the fact that a guy from the other team had travelled here proved I wasn't going nuts all on my own.

A minute later, a message from the captain pinged in.

Sorry mate, we called the game off on Thursday.

I blinked a few times as I stared at the message. Very slowly, I broke the sinking news to the one poor bastard on the visiting team who hadn't got the memo either. He shrugged, muttered something about how he really ought to get a mobile phone, and climbed into his car for the 90-minute drive back to the Midlands.

And then I climbed into mine, closed my eyes and tried to come to terms with the fact that I'd bought a car for a cricket match that wasn't happening.

Living with Satan's Sister

Two or three weeks later, we did start playing cricket matches that didn't get called off without my knowledge. And since I had a car, I drove to them.

Sure, with hindsight, I hadn't needed to jump into my car purchase as quickly as I had done. But since it was a mostly made-up sense of urgency that had gotten the job done, it didn't matter all that much that the supposed cricket match turned out to be kind of made-up as well. I'd gotten the whole business out of the way. And that was a good thing.

The Peugeot was treating me well, too. That weird noise was still happening over the bumps (and there were a surprising number of potholes in David Cameron's Witney at that time, let me tell you), which was gradually convincing me that the thing had no suspension whatsoever. But, importantly as far as I was concerned, this didn't seem to affect the thing's ability to get me to cricket. The engine always started and ran strong. The wheels always went where I pointed them, although I have to admit I was stalked by images of them all detaching at once, leaving the car's body skidding belly-first along a tranquil country lane in decidedly untranquil fashion.

Sure, I was nervous, mainly because I didn't know how much attention the car had had before, and because I *did* know that all I'd done from a maintenance perspective was dust down the back seats. I didn't think about deadly scenarios for extended periods, however. It boiled down to me being a bit cavalier about these things. Or, if you want to put it another way, I preferred to take my chances with a gory accident than go to some mechanic and try to fathom whether he's ripping me off or not. My concession to safety was merely to drive much less expressively than both Steven and Simon. If you make sure you're always going slow enough, then wheels can fly off as much as they like, can't they? So I became the sort of driver the police might fine for being too far *under* the speed limit.

(Going too slowly in my Peugeot *did* eventually lead to me getting in trouble with officialdom. But we'll get to that later.)

Pootling around Oxfordshire's roads on my way to Shipton, or various away matches in places with fantastically English names like Great Tew and Stokenchurch, seemed like the perfect way to spend the summer. Clearly my car was the most awesome decision anybody had ever made. And that was *before* it saved me from my appalling new house-mate at 49 Mandrill Lane.

As if to balance out the glory of buying myself a car and making my life easy, my life at home was becoming difficult and burdensome. Fate had dealt me a terrible hand on the house-mate front: it was fast becoming clear that Karola was quite impossible to live with.

I hope that wherever she is now, there's a measure of solitary confinement involved. Because no human being should have to share even a medium-sized and abundant tropical island with such levels of OCD. She'd always be coming over to re-arrange your coconuts in a neat pile and chastise your adopted monkeys for some made-up crime against order. In time, swimming to the horizon without a hope of survival would emerge as the only viable option.

The only time this woman should share a small space with anybody is if that person has committed a terrible crime and been sent to a particularly cruel corrective facility, in which she would be assigned as your roommate. But I must stress that it would have to have been a truly heinous sin.

I'd had my suspicions about Karola the moment I'd gone around there to view the room she'd advertised on Gumtree.co.uk. As we'd sat in the gleaming open-plan lounge/kitchen area, I'd noted that there was no evidence of any cooking (or eating) having been done. Ever. No plates in the sink, no loaf of bread on the side, not even a half-cooked onion slice stuck to the stove plates. I'd even commented on it.

"It's very...*neat* here," I remembered saying bluntly. "I don't think I would live quite like this. I don't wash every plate immediately after I finish eating."

I hate it when people insist on washing every plate immediately after eating, whose number includes my parents. It's not like I make a point of *not* doing it, given the choice, but I just don't get why it's so critical if you wait a while. Being thoughtful for the next person means not leaving sticky rice in the pot they might need to use later in the evening, or vast quantities of goo in the sink. But unless you live in a house that shares a single plate, simpler items like that can wait for a day or two if you're busy. And nobody will catch cholera.

"Oh, it's not always so tidy," she'd said with a dismissive wave and a reassuring smile. I should have noted the manner in which she then glanced away. And perhaps that the smile was a fake one.

Oh yes, I really should have noticed.

"Why did the last person move out?" I probed cautiously.

"Oh, she was really a bit crazy," replied Karola, still avoiding eye contact. She spoke with a convincingly world-weary air. "She couldn't share..."

When I came back for a second viewing - for I had become quite careful about house-mates and rooms generally, and learned not to decide purely on first impressions - I noticed a few lightly soiled plates stacked up next to the sink. It was the first and last time I saw such a thing. I later realised that this was a cynical attempt to prove that she could be as casual about such matters as the next person. But like the busy, happy classrooms they show you in Pyongyang, it was an illusion. And I should have known better.

Obviously in dire and urgent need of some help with the rent, she addressed my various concerns with what appeared to be easy-going reasonableness. She let me pay the lion's share of the rent and kick her out of the giant main bedroom, while agreeing to leave all of the essential furniture in it. She allowed me to move my tasteless chest of drawers into the lounge. She didn't even ask for a deposit, saying she trusted me. And all of this made the little voice of warning in my head pipe down.

A few days later, the month of April had begun, I'd paid my share of rent and picked up a key. I'd also provided the good folk of Witney with the amusing spectacle of a man wheeling his clothes-rack-on-wheels across the main shopping drag in what must rank as one of history's shortest and simplest house moves.

While I certainly enjoyed not having to phone up any removals men or badger friends with cars, this particular home switch would also go down as one of my life's greatest mistakes. Time to find a room had been running out, though, and there seemed to be precious few of any description on offer.

Yes, my flat-renting strategy was just about as frantic and flawed as my car-buying strategy. But I think the former is easier to explain away. With rentals, you've got the added complication of lining up your move-out and move-in dates, unless you're particularly fond of paying double-rent for a month. They force your hand a little more than a car purchase does - you don't even need a made-up cricket deadline to rush into signing a lease.

And finding a room for rent in Witney was even more do-or-die than it would be in other places. Sharing was the only financially viable option, but Witney wasn't the sort of town where much house-sharing went on at all. It was full of families and people who had mortgages. It was also too far from Oxford for any students to want to live there. So when I saw a room on offer, the need to claim this rare beast swiftly pressed hard.

The room was very nice, it had to be said. I might have been sharing a flat, but this was the biggest room I'd *ever* had. I had myself a double bed, ample closet space and a sizeable desk at which one could write. If I wasn't sensible enough to keep my cricket gear in the car, I could quite easily have stored it in my bedroom too.

This part was good. As for how things might play out in the common areas, I watched and waited. Karola worked from lunchtime until late at night, so we didn't actually see much of each other. But even ships passing in the night leave a wake - and I was hoping she would too. I *wanted* her to make some tiny hint of a mess. It would ease my suspicions that I was trapped in a flat with a neat-freak.

But after just a handful of days, I hadn't noticed so much as a dirty knife in the kitchen or a misplaced remote control in the lounge. I began to get unnerved.

I could do what I wanted in my own room, but all this pristine order made me uneasy about disturbing the perfection of the bathroom or kitchen. Unfortunately, there wasn't a lot of choice: I *did* need to wash and cook. In other words, actually use the place for living.

I had a nasty feeling in my gut that Karola saw this arrangement not as two people sharing the rent - and thus the common areas in friendly spirit - but rather as me renting my room off her, the grand Lordess of the apartment. While she never said such a thing out loud, it was obvious that any plans I might have to prepare food or observe daily washing rituals were only going to be put up with grudgingly. The idea of a flatmate who left traces of his existence was clearly at odds with the apparent priority of ensuring the apartment was always ready to receive a crew of photographers from *Modern British Interiors* magazine.

Let me confess here that I actually have a little bit of OCD myself. I'm not one for living in a pigsty, believe it or not. I am a great fan of reasonable cleanliness, and do not particularly adore cobwebs. I also see value in being tidy enough to be able to find my things when I'm looking for them in a hurry (which is whenever I look for something. Because we only look for things we need *now*, don't we?). But, moderation in all things. A stray jumper on the sofa or a coffee mug by the sink is what makes a place a home rather than a made-up hotel room, not so?

In those first couple of days, I began to take on board a number of things my two exploratory visits hadn't quite revealed. There was the fact that the electricity for *every* device - kettle, toaster, microwave - was always switched off at the wall plug. (Easy for her, really, since a glance at the fridge confirmed my suspicion that she never actually cooked or ate anything at all.) I noticed that the front door would always end up double-locked, even when I'd not left it so. And, most astoundingly, that there was not one single bottle of gel, soap, shampoo or any other bathroom confectionary around the combined bath and shower area.

This strange washroom phenomenon was the first thing to really get on my nerves. I don't know about you, but I'm quite a big believer in keeping my soap and shampoo somewhere within reach of where I'm going to be using them. I mean, this is quite standard procedure, isn't it? So that's where I put these items when I moved in. But when I returned for my second shower in my new lodgings, they'd migrated all the way across the room, landing up on what appeared to be a special shelf near the door. A shelf designated for shower gel and shampoo storage, apparently.

Considering myself within my rights as an adult and (more than) equal sharer of the rent, I moved the bottles back to where I wanted them. On the occasion of my third shower, I was well and truly soaking under the hot water before I realised that they'd been whisked away once more. Apoplectic, dripping and not altogether dressed, I had to hop across the room to retrieve them. Was I really paying five hundred and fifty Pounds a month for *this*? What had I *done* in my past life?

"Can you stop moving my soap?" I asked as politely as I could once I'd finally managed to take care of washing myself and thrown on some clothes. "When you do that, I have to run across the room to go and fetch it. Apart from not being much fun, it means I drip water everywhere."

The last bit was an attempt to get on her wavelength. Disorderly puddles of water on the floor, surely, would be the one thing that would make her see reason. But here she surprised me.

"Oh, that's okay," she said, carefully avoiding my eye as she went about tidying her room, probably for the sixteenth time that morning.

I was a little stunned by this response. She thought I was asking *permission* to drip across her floors.

"Well, yes, but it's not something I want to do," I went on, turning up the heat a little as I stood there in her door frame. "I am paying rent here too, and unless you're proposing to let me live here for free, I don't see that you get to make all the rules."

"Well, I clean the bathroom all the time," she said, the atmosphere turning ever less pleasant. "And I can't clean the bath with bottles on it."

We hadn't discussed the question of cleaning duties yet. Not that I was at all against doing so in principle. It's just that I felt I'd be on a hiding to nothing if I tried to share any of this with one of such mighty perfection. No flick of the duster nor wipe of the cloth would ever be good enough for her. I was quite sure of that.

Still, I knew a thing or two about sharing houses. One was that it's fair for everyone to share the cleaning, too. Unless, of course, you could cut some kind of deal, such as I'd done two houses ago. Then, to put it bluntly, my lazy house-mates had *paid* me to do it. It was still fair, though. Everyone was happy.

Now, despite my increasingly bad mood, I wondered if I was being offered a face-saving deal.

"Wait, so you're happy to do all the cleaning?" I ventured.

"Yes, I would do it anyway," she replied. And I totally believed her, too.

I'm deeply averse to conflict, and wasn't much enjoying this. But clearly, I couldn't let her have her way on this without some kind of rational justification to myself. In the heat of the moment (this is where people with tempers really lose it), I decided to accept that I had one, and could walk away.

"Well, if you're saying you'll do all the cleaning, and I don't have to do any, then fine, I'll do it your way," I muttered, unsure that I'd really gained anything except a clear conscience on the cleaning front. Which is, I suppose, a good thing in a house share.

"Fine."

"Goodbye."

"Bye."

It was one of the last conversations we had in the two months I survived in the apartment. Because it wasn't long before I ran out of ways to justify caving in to her ridiculous demands, and concluded that some people just shouldn't ever, *ever*, share their living space with other people.

I couldn't find any reason to suppose I should slink around the kitchen trying not to leave a footprint anywhere. While I always stacked my dishes neatly and got rid of anything too gross right away, I most definitely did not make every dish disappear within seconds of swallowing my last morsel. Nor did I see why she should take 550 Pounds a month off me and still expect me to jump through hoops with respect to switching off every device at the wall, replacing everything just-so in the 'correct' cupboard and replacing the chairs at right angles to the dining table every time.

Yes, much of it was her stuff, and she could expect me to look after it - even ban me from using it if she wanted. But her owning everything didn't mean some kind of absolute authority of the spatial interactions of objects within shared living space or cupboards, which I was also renting, thank you very much. Nor the ability to expect automatic compliance (without tabling a discussion or requesting nicely) on double-locking the door, which - correct me if I'm wrong - would also fall under the category of jointly-rented items.

If you want that level of dictatorship, don't ask someone to share the rent with you. Alternatively, have children. You can tell your kids what to do and where to put things, or so I'm told. If she does choose to reproduce one day, though, I'd like to send heartfelt prayers to those poor young people. They did nothing to deserve such a mother.

Quite remarkably, Karola did have a boyfriend. He seemed like a decent, well-rounded sort of guy. I couldn't find fault with him. She was good-looking, to be sure, but I absolutely knew she would make his life hell the day he made the mistake of moving in with her. I wanted to take him to one side and offer some sage, considered and quiet advice along the lines of *GET OUT WHILE YOU CAN, SHE'S NUTS AND SHE'LL RUIN YOU!!!!*

I didn't do that, though. It wasn't my business, and besides, I didn't think he'd listen to me. I probably wouldn't listen to me either, if some madman was asking me to give up the prospect of sleeping with her. He only stayed over one night a week, you see, so didn't quite grasp what a traumatic and impossible experience actual co-habitation would be. I was quite sure he wouldn't last five minutes.

He did get at least one sneak preview of what it might be like. One morning, following his weekly napover, I overheard her having a go at him for some or other object being in the wrong place in the bathroom. I remember this well, because I was pretty sure I'd actually been the one to commit the crime. He was protesting his innocence, and she wasn't having it. I heard the whole thing while lying in bed, half-wondering if this madness was all a wacky dream.

But no, I really *had* stumbled into an apartment where the other people were mad. I'm not sure how it works in Lithuania, or in OCD-land, or Control-Freak-land, but it's not normal house-share practice to put your pile of ready-to-iron clothing in the middle of the sofa and expect it to stay there for days on end when people might want to, oh, I don't know, sit down? Maybe I should have seen it as some kind of territorial statement, but when I had the occasional wish to park my posterior on the sofa, I would simply move her pile of stuff to the far end of the couch, giving not another thought to the matter. Little did I know that this was an act of war.

Not much of this ever came up for direct discussion. We rarely crossed paths, and clearly neither of us wished to. She went away for ten days, and then, rather nicely, I went away for a week. My trip was to Budapest, where I met up with Monique, the Dutch girl with whom I'd fallen into something approaching a long-distance relationship in January. But it could have been a solo trip to Baltistan, and I'd have been happy. A week far from Karola was bliss.

No, the anguish and irritation between her and I was savoured privately and alone. She'd no doubt well up with fury to find I'd left the kettle plug switched on, while hours later I'd smile insanely to myself as I discovered that she'd gone to the trouble to switching it off after me. I'd go to bed with the door single-locked, shaking my head and chuckling in the dark when I heard her come back from work and try to unlock the part that wasn't locked. She kept on doing it: more than anything, this mindless key-turning summed up her inability to process the notion of someone else being in the house.

The *last* thing I wanted to do was move again. I wanted to hang on there until the end of summer and cricket season at least, somehow establishing a workable home life. Even if 'home' was the last thing this apartment felt like. There's nothing less homely or welcoming than the feeling that your every move might be a contravention of some or other pointlessly authoritarian directive from somebody more than a decade your junior.

But six weeks in, the letter came. That's when I knew I had to go.

I'd thought she might have been happy to let things go on in moody silence, as she fixed all my mistakes behind me. Instead, she was storing everything up like a nice passive-aggressive. I woke up one morning to find, attached to my door, the most unforgettable piece of written communication I've ever received. It was so off-the-charts mental that I took it into my office, where it was laughed at and ridiculed by people who'd never met her.

Though it's frankly a rather disturbing text for me to have to revisit, I feel it's worth quoting the contents of this handwritten A4 page verbatim here:

Hey,

Can you please do the following?

*Put dry items away where they belong in the kitchen.
*Switch oven & kettle switch off [this was double-underlined] when you [sic] done using them.
*Clean the oven from crumbs as I do not use it at all and feel tired of it being dirty 24/7.
*Do not move my pile of ironing on the sofa (it has my personal items and I do not feel great about you moving it).
*Lock the door on both locks
*Keep your shampoo and other cleaning items where they belong in the bathroom and not around the shower bit.

Thanks

It was all there. Every last obsessive niggle. And no, I could not please do any of the above. The letter confirmed everything I had already decided about this strange person: that where she thought things should go corresponded to 'where they belong', and that crumbs behind a closed door that she only ever opened to check for signs of food preparation (gasp!) were immensely fatiguing for Her Worship. In short, that she was the boss was not even up for discussion.

There wasn't even so much of a whiff of compromise or let's-talk-about-it where this amazing piece of text was concerned. Clearly there wasn't any point in trying to sit down and come to some sort of solution with somebody demented enough to leave her undergarments bang in the middle of common area furniture (instead of in, let's think for a minute, her *room*?) and be outraged that some other rent-payer might move it so that they could sit down.

I was done with the place. Just done. I was damned if I was going to live like that at the age of 35. I texted her a blunt 'no' to her frothing demands, and resolved to be gone by the end of the second full month I'd paid for. Thank the stars I didn't have to worry about getting a deposit back off her. It meant I could just leave - in the dead of night, if I wanted - without saying a word. And I wasn't going to, either. I was a little concerned she might be the sort of person who might throw my personal items out of the window once she realised she wouldn't be getting my rent money any more.

I didn't know where I was going to go, but this time it was probably going to be further away than the other side of the road. And the one blessing that was going to make my escape easy as pie? I had a car!

The Pug to the Rescue

With my Peugeot 306 poised for getaway, I started to plot my escape from Karola's oppressive regime. And this, let me be clear, was precisely the opposite of what I wanted to do that summer. I wanted to work as little as possible, write as much as possible, and drive my car to as many cricket matches as I could find. And with a part-time office job that didn't follow me home in the form of emails or calls, I thought I'd set myself up to do exactly that.

But none of that was going to plan. I was looking at a second move of house before the summer solstice. And this move was going to be complicated and time-consuming. Perhaps I'd been overly smug about how smooth and easy it had been to shuffle across the road with all my belongings, and this was comeuppance.

Deserved or otherwise, I felt absolutely determined that this *stupid* girl wasn't going to ruin my summer. I had a job in Oxfordshire, I had boundless cricket possibilities in Oxfordshire, and I'd bought a car for the express purpose of exploiting them. So wherever I went, I wasn't going to allow myself to be hounded out of Oxfordshire. If she was going to spend her summer doing the things that made her happy (making sure that the permanently-laid placemats were always square to the edge of the dining table must have featured prominently), which I was sure she would, then I, the innocent victim forced to flee his home, felt more than entitled to the same.

The plan was to get the move over and done with as painlessly as possible. Whenever she wasn't looking, then, I started packing boxes. I made sure to shut the door on the obvious signs of an impending move whenever I was out of my room. Leaving without notice was an important part of my plan, and not just because I feared a maniacal reaction. It was a matter of principle too. She'd made my life a misery for several weeks; the least I could do was ensure that she wouldn't have time to find some other poor bastard to share the following month's rent with her while being made to live as if in a detention centre.

While the packing process inched along, I was scouting around for more house-shares. Now, at this point, I wouldn't blame you for asking 'why not get your own place?' Oh, believe me, I *wanted* that. But England is a very expensive place to try living alone. And places like Oxfordshire, while very good for cricket, are particularly pricey. And while I might have been earning enough per hour to stretch to solo accommodation if I worked a full week, I wasn't. The part-time thing had its benefits when it came to writing books, but it meant that sharing was my only option.

Besides, I'd almost always found sharing a positive experience. I'd had something like eight co-habiting arrangements in three different countries up until that point. Sure, it wasn't great when London housemate Hannah fell in with a fifty-something roofer boyfriend from Wellingborough, who kept turning up at my place with a ring in his ear and a barking Alsatian at his side. In Wimbledon house-shares, as toilet rolls ran low or even critical, I'd be treated to fearsome shouting matches about whose fault it was. Or I'd be jolted awake when the door slammed shut at whatever terrible time teachers set off in the morning, shaking the house to its very foundations: no amount of imploring could make Laura understand that closing it gently was also an option.

More than once, I'd been obliged to share my space with a hamster without strangling the little rotter (is it weird that hamsters running on their wheels drives me, an animal lover, to the brink of violence?). I'd also had house-mates who would insist on watching *soccer* - a pastime on which I've already made my feelings perfectly clear - when South Africa had an important rugby match on. Or, worse still, would just be randomly flicking through channels for no good reason - when South Africa had a rugby match on. Then, despite the fact that they had no particular show in mind that they wanted to see, they'd grumble about my wanting to watch something around which I'd carefully planned my entire weekend. ('I say, would you be terribly put out if I interrupted you mindlessly whiling the hours away in front of whatever the box shows you, having no original thoughts whatsoever? Ever so sorry!')

But these had all been small niggles, really. Until now, house-sharing had by and large been a good thing. A high number of my best friends - people I still see regularly to this day - have come out of house-shares. It can be a good way to not be lonely, especially if, like me, you're always moving to new places where you don't know anybody. And believe it or not, I'm quite good at getting on with most people. As long as you're not manic-obsessive and we treat each other as equals, we'll probably have a good time.

Having grown up watching *Friends*, I always rather liked the idea of a bunch of young folks coming and going from each other's homes, no invitations required. Just, you know, hanging out all the time. I'd never been in a house share quite like that (I'm sure I'd have noticed if Jennifer Aniston had been present), but I'd had a flavour of it more than once. I liked the convenience of having friends in the lounge when I got home. It meant not having to send texts or, worse yet, watch your life slip away in WhatsApp groups, just to plan the simplest thing. If you wanted to go surfing, sing a song or build a fire in the garden, you could just look around the room and (in a fun house at least) doubtless find some takers.

With an imaginative group of house-mates, one could make a party without even having to put your shoes on. You could hijack their friends without having to go to the trouble of making your own. And if the stars aligned as they (very) occasionally do, you might even find yourself falling into bed with one of them. All very practical.

I pondered my house-sharing memories at length as I got ready to escape Karola's lair. And there were so many good ones: from Australia, from London, from up the road in Witney.

I recalled sitting in the back garden of the house I'd shared with Suz and Glen in Sydney, soaking up the Coldplay concert taking place across the road. Practicing my French and making crepes with Aurelie and Pierre, my Breton house-mates in Perth. Destroying light fixtures during late-night indoor cricket matches with Simon and Steven in Witney. Learning how to make a proper *roux* when I shared with Hannah, who happened to be a chef. Long Friday nights in the garden shed with Iain, a stack of fish and chips, and a Ford Fiesta engine block.

The list went on. Hosting random couch-surfers. Watching *Geordie Shore* after nights out. Coming home to find a Frenchman playing the piano blindfolded. Watching your home's semi-wild rabbit hop about in the garden. Being enthusiastically offered tea by Sarah (another door-slamming English teacher, come to think of it) and then having to make it yourself when she forgot about it. Spider-catching episodes. Coffee. Late-night raps on the door from angry young people who'd somehow got the idea Simon was a drug dealer. Birthday celebrations for which you didn't need to leave the house. House-share gold.

For every time I'd had to battle for the television with ignorami who thought *Hollyoaks* was important, there were just as many occasions on which I could enjoy watching sport with somebody else who knew what was going on. And it was nice being able to latch onto shopping trips with girls, who would usually be able to give me some advice about what clothes I should buy. (I haven't got a clue about dress sense, and quite frankly find it puzzling that anybody does. Why don't they teach practical things like that in school? After all, wearing a bad tie to an interview could lose you a job as fast as full marks in geography might gain you one.)

It was with house-mates or former house-mates that I'd travelled to places as far-flung as Venice, Budapest, Estonia and the Nullarbor Plain. And also to Hereford, where we'd witnessed another former house-mate get married to a gentleman who'd made his first 'overnight visit' whilst she was living at our place. The more I thought about it, the more sure I was: my years between the ages of 20 and 35 would have been infinitely poorer had I not shared my home for much of that time.

This had been my first truly awful experience. I'd never even *thought* about moving out of a place because of my house-mates before. I suppose, on reflection, that I'd been quite lucky in that regard. Sooner or later, this comes to everybody who makes a habit of renting a room in a shared space. But at least my one big disaster was out of the way for me now. I would need some extraordinary misfortune for the next place to be a disaster too, right?

Judging by the Internet, it didn't look like I was going to have a lot of choice when it came to picking the next place. Witney was still a bare cupboard when it came to rooms to rent, unless I wanted something that was 'Monday to Friday only'. There seemed to be quite a lot of those about, oddly enough. I'd never actually come across such a thing until this particular house search. Personally, I couldn't imagine anything worse.

What kind of a life are you living if you leave for work on a Friday morning with a landlady hovering in the doorway making sure you're clearing out? I pictured her murmuring, 'Now remember, I don't want to see you until Monday, do you hear me? We want our private time! No itinerant lodgers intruding on our Sunday roast! Get lost! And while you're at it, the rent's overdue. Oh look, you've made me shout, you stupid man! Now you've woken the cat up! Why must you be such a burden on us?'

Alright, perhaps I have an overactive imagination: not all landlords actually breathe fire. And I know that such an arrangement makes sense for those people who live in one place, where they spend weekends, and travel during the week to work in another. I had a colleague who did just that, actually. Still, as someone rather unimaginatively traditional about the idea of having a home to come home to 24/7, there was something highly unsettling about the notion of a five-day rent. That could *never* be a real home. And I didn't even think the atmosphere could be all that nice for the weekdays one was there. Think about what sort of people are willing to give up rent money in exchange for the assurance that their lodger will *not* be there on the weekend. It struck me as the sort of thing the very housemate I was fleeing might do in her grown-up future.

Since everywhere else around was even smaller and more devoid of viable options than Witney, only Oxford was left. And that fiercely competitive rental market wasn't going to be easy. Another generation of students would soon be graduating, though, which I'd hoped might mean a flood of new leases becoming available.

But that didn't appear to be the case. There was next to nothing on the Internet. And with such demand for a room in a house-share, you were up against seventeen other people jockeying to take it. And if one of them was a juggler, Jennifer Aniston or could teach guitar, you knew the current house-mates weren't going to pick you.

A stressful few days followed. I only managed to line up three or four viewings. More than once I got messages saying the room had been snatched even before I could do the actual visit. And when I *did* venture into Oxford (always by car, because I was too pissed off to worry about the environment for the moment), I could never find parking. Distracted and feeling the pinch of the month running out, I got a speeding fine on a road I will argue until my dying day should never be a 30-zone. Sorry, Oxfordshire, but you've got it wrong: Botley Road is like a six-lane highway when you go past Aldi. It's impossible to do 30 there.

Part of the reason I didn't see speed limit signs was that I was usually driving around lost, and thus concentrating primarily on being found. Like most of England, Oxford is a fiddly town with very few straight roads. It's also got a very curious, lopsided shape. The train station is way over on the left side of the map, which is also where the 'centre' is. Then, as you move to the right side of the map, the city splays out wide and sprawls endlessly up massive hills like Headington. It's the last place anybody could accuse of being a planned settlement.

With about three days until the end of the month, I finally hit gold. A certain Azalea, half-Spanish but basically from Germany, was advertising a room over in - you guessed it - the eastern part of Oxford. Azalea and her three house-mates were all German interns, over in England for six months honing

35

their engineering skills at the BMW Mini plant in nearby Cowley. I called this young lady up and went to see her room.

Sure, the only cupboard space was out in the hallway. And yes, this single-bed affair was a third of the size of the last one. But it would do. I was quite desperate by this stage. That bargaining power thing again.

"I'll take it," I told her whilst holding my breath for the announcement that I would now be advanced into an interview process. Unable to do a very good Brad Pitt impression, I gave her my best I'm-a-juggler-smile.

"Okay!" she said, as if a weight had been lifted from her world. I should have registered that it didn't matter to her if I was a juggler, actually, because she was the one moving out. She just had to find someone to take over the lease. I'd seen the rest of the house-mates in the kitchen, briefly, and they had seemed nice enough. And if they weren't clamouring to see my repertoire of party tricks and weigh them up against other interested parties, I wasn't going to insist.

"Alright then," I said cautiously. "What about contracts? And money? When can I move in?"

"Oh, there's some papers to sign at the agency," she said vaguely. "But I'll be out by Thursday. You can pick up the key and move in then."

Thursday would be the last day of the month. Perfect alignment: leave one apartment and move straight to the other. It seemed slightly too good to be true.

And it was.

The next morning I received a message from Azalea, who apparently hadn't really *had* the discussion with her house-mates about the sort of person they'd be sharing with.

Hi, sorry, the guys say they would like to meet with you before you can move in. Are you okay to meet at the Cape of Good Hope on Thursday night? Then if they are happy you can get the key from me on Friday.

Brilliant. I wasn't too worried about showing them I was a good guy - because I am one - but now I was going to have to move out of my Witney premises with no guaranteed place to rest my head that night. My fond memories of good house-shares were rapidly fading. I was more aware than I wanted to be that this wouldn't be nearly as complicated if I was renting solo. But I still couldn't *afford* renting solo.

I was at the office when that particular message came through. I buried my face in my hands, not even trying to pretend to do the work I was meant to be doing. I wondered if I should just sleep where I was currently sleeping until it was all sorted out. It wasn't like I'd given notice. But I was slightly too honest for that. I had only paid Miseryguts until the end of the month, and painful though she was, I didn't think it fair to steal extra accommodation from her, especially as she'd trusted me by not asking for a deposit.

Yes, I could also have simply paid her some extra money for some extra days. But if I was certain of one thing by that stage: I'd rather sleep in a field strewn with horse manure and lashed by wind than give her a single extra penny. So I ploughed on with packing up my car when she wasn't home. My chest of drawers, which she'd agreed to let me place in the lounge, would have to wait till the last moment, lest the secret of my impending departure escape.

But that Thursday morning, with my immediate future looking decidedly uncertain, I set off for work in a car bursting with all my worldly possessions. Which, thank goodness, just about fitted. It would have been a breeze without the drawers, which were a decidedly sweaty job for one person. (Unless you're a proper grown-up unlikely to face sudden accommodation upheavals, it's always a good idea never to own more stuff than you can fit inside a hatchback with the seats down.)

Once I was safely out of bazouka range, I sent her a text message.

I left. Your key is in the letterbox.

She never replied. I imagine she danced a jig. What could be better than to have complete control of the shower gel bottles once more? And I don't think I'm necessarily overstating the case to suggest that this might have been worth more to her than five hundred and fifty Pounds of rent money every month.

After work, I proceeded to the Cape of Good Hope, which sits on a roundabout called The Plain, right in the middle of the map of Oxford, just where the great centre of learning starts to do its thing of sprawling upwards, downwards and eastwards. It's the point where green spaces squeeze the city down to almost nothing and four major roads meet. Pretty much every vehicle trying to move along an east-west axis has to pass through here. That night I was one of them, and mighty glad about it. I dared not even imagine trying to do all of this by bus. The car was the one thing I had going for me.

I'd been to the Cape of Good Hope once before, and took it as a good omen that the place was named (more or less) after my hometown in South Africa. But I didn't need a good omen, really. Meeting Mischa and Klaus for a cider was pretty easy. They were nice guys in their twenties. I liked them, and they seemed to like me. The fourth housemate, Frank, wasn't there, but was apparently happy to go along with their judgements. Azalea was conspicuously absent.

There was no doubting that Klaus and Mischa were decidedly European. You could tell that from the fact that each of them did a most un-British thing by standing up to get their own drinks, one by one. I thoroughly approved of this. One of the worst things about England is that people insist on buying you drinks, then other people buy each other drinks, and then someone says 'Oi, it's your round mate!'

The whole culture of buying rounds, annoying as it is, perfectly fits the phenomenon of fake niceness that pervades modern-day English culture. It's the same false politeness that results in people on British streets apologizing to you when you bump into them, or asking 'How are you?' when you've answered the question once already. Why pretend you're being nice to each other by buying a bunch of beers for people you don't even know, when you're really keeping score in the hopes of getting one back later?

There might be an argument for the efficiency of round-buying in a world where everybody drinks the same drink at the same rate all night long, and nobody goes home early. In fairness, English men do try their level best to make this utopian dream a reality, with the result that everyone has to drink beer as quick as the fastest drinker, staying out far later than they should. This in turn results in boorishness, fisticuffs and puking.

I myself am not very good at drinking once I'm finished being thirsty. (People think this is very weird, but never have an answer for me when I ask them if they keep eating when they're done being hungry.) Which means I drink very little over a night, and quite slowly too. I'm much better off paying only for what I consume. Much as one does with postage stamps, pears, socks or whatever.

On that night's evidence, Germans agreed with the logic of this. If you wanted to drink something, you went to the bar, bought it, brought it back to the table and started drinking it. And miraculously, no-one would give you a funny look or whisper about what a selfish bastard you were.

When I told the guys the reasons why I was currently seeking new lodgings, they laughed out loud. I thought it a good sign that they didn't shake their heads and start tutting about how my moving in wasn't going to work. Apart from a few cultural differences, these were just normal guys in their twenties. Mischa was actually Russian by birth, but had been living in Bavaria since he was in his teens. Klaus, who was about eleven feet tall, was born and bred in the city of Nürnberg.

Not wanting to appear completely nuts and desperate, I thought better of mentioning the car parked just around the corner, which contained everything I owned. Nor the fact that I didn't exactly have anywhere to sleep that night. They said, more or less, that they were happy with me as a new housemate. But that I would have to sort things out with Azalea before I moved in.

This didn't seem unreasonable. I spoke with her again, and she assured me that she would call the agent the next day, that we'd sign whatever papers we needed to sign, and that I'd be able to pick up the key. It sounded great. In theory, that left me only one night in which to figure out where to sleep.

As it happened, my inability to say no to a little moonlighting on my days off meant I had a solution at my fingertips. I was booked in to man a certain office in a co-working space in Cornmarket Street. And I had all the keys I needed to get from the street to the desk.

All I had to do was find somewhere I'd be allowed to park my car overnight, and where chances of someone smashing the windows and looting the bounty inside were low.

After locating a place that ticked both boxes - no mean feat in Oxford, believe me - I undertook a long walk back towards the centre. Sleeping bag under one arm, blow-up mattress under the other and laptop case in my hand, I'm not sure any passers-by knew what to make of me. I wasn't sure *I* knew what to make of me either.

Cornmarket Street is the main shopping drag in Oxford. Closed to traffic, this is where you'll find all the same shops you find in every other town in the United Kingdom. From Santander to Lush Cosmetics to McDonalds and WH Smith, it's wall-to-wall chain stores. Despite this, it's always full of people. Students, mostly, if only because they knew that by ducking up a side-alley they could reach a university bar called the Purple Turtle, where they could get beers for about a Pound.

Anyway, none of the people milling about seemed to object when some kind of digital-age hobo used a variety of chips and codes to let himself into a small office building wedged between, I don't know, Vodafone and Flight Centre.

That night I slept under the desk at which I would officially start work at nine the next morning. To call it an extraordinarily depressing experience would be to do 'understatement' a huge disservice. I might go so far as to say it was the low point of my life. Going to bed with a photocopy machine as your nearest companion is pretty soul-destroying at the best of times. Doing so at the age of 35, while temporarily homeless due to the tiresome antics of some random Lithuanian girl, really gets you thinking.

Did I really have no friends who would take me in? Well, I probably could have gotten someone to give me a bed that night. But only in Witney, really. I didn't know anybody in Oxford, except the guys I'd just met that evening. I had a car-full of stuff to worry about, and needed to be back in Oxford for work and house agent stuff the next day. The office floor seemed the easiest solution. And something about it appealed to the part of me that takes a cynical pride in system-beating resourcefulness.

Ever since a cash-strapped mate and I camped rough in Siberia on our post-university travels, I've always taken elaborate satisfaction in sleeping places that grown-ups and other assorted authorities wouldn't approve of. And I dare say Britain's legendary Health & Safety killjoys could have referred me to a thick book full of reasons why I wasn't allowed to sleep in an office. From that point of view, it was a satisfying sleep. But on every other front, it was dead miserable.

I lay awake for many hours, watching the green lights of the Internet router bounce off the bottom of the desk, and thinking about how I wanted the village back. You know, the one where you knew your cobbler, and, in fact, everybody knew everybody else? You wouldn't go homeless in such a place, would you? You couldn't sleep on the street even if you wanted to, because unless you were a completely terrible person, you'd keep getting woken up by great-aunts saying 'My goodness, Terence, whatever *are* you doing out there? Come in and have a hot bath at our house!'

(My name's not Terence, as you've probably surmised. But it has a ring to it, don't you think?)

But we've come a long way from the village, haven't we? I had no great-aunts and no doors to knock on. Nobody in Oxford knew me or cared. I was alone under a desk in a cold, heartless modern city where everybody looked out for themselves. And I was pretty lucky even to have that desk - I'd noticed the usual gathering of presumably homeless beggars gathered just a couple of hundred yards down the road outside McDonald's. And there'd be more up on the corner with George Street, too. I guess this was how they felt all of the time, only colder.

After rising early enough to ensure I didn't get caught by keen sharers of the office space, I bought a coffee and a bacon baguette down the road at Taylor's. I suppose the chance to try the breakfast special at this Oxford-only chain of cafe's was one positive to emerge from this darkest of nights. It was a good baguette, and moreover the weather was fine. It was with renewed optimism that I returned to my desk and prepared for the day when everything would start looking up. In between pretending to work, I'd get this house paperwork sorted, then pick up the key and have somewhere new to call home by sunset.

I struggled for some hours to raise Azalea. I wasn't quite sure what she was up to. Wasn't this priority for her as much as me? What was she *doing*? But in the early afternoon I finally got a message.

Hi, I can't get the agent to give us time to do the papers today. We can do it on Monday. But don't worry, you can get the key from me today still and move in!

Well, that was fine with me! I was happy to pay the rent from today when the time came. If everyone else was happy to sort it out next week, I sure as heck wasn't going to complain, was I? Having mostly rented informally or from friends in the past, none of this was all that uncomfortable or unlikely. For most of my life I'd pretty much managed to avoid ever having my name anywhere near a lease at all, actually.

All I had to do was go over to meet her at BMW Mini, where she would hand over the key. And as soon as my obligation to be at the Cornmarket Street office was out of the way, I sought out my (thankfully unmolested) car and drove around the ring road to the gigantic concrete wasteland of a car park that surrounded the factory.

Beaming in just the way you'd expect a person who's just been relieved of their rent to beam, Azalea came bounding over the sun-soaked asphalt to meet me. She thrust the key into my hand.

"So we're going to do the paperwork at the agent next week, right?" I asked her, just to make sure.

"*Ja*, I'll call her and get back to you about when we can meet at the agency," she declared gaily, flashing me another smile.

"And it's really fine for me to go over and move in now?"

"*Ja ja*! You have the key. Just go over there."

"Are the guys there?"

"I think so, sure!"

Well, that was that: I was about to move into a house entirely on trust. Woohoo! Goodbye OCD! I'd rediscovered the reality I was used to: a world in which people were faithful, relaxed and open-minded. And it looked like the house I was about to call home really *was* a cool, chilled sort of place. It had been a harsh and sad night, but the bad dream was over. I'd lay down on my own sheets again this evening.

I gunned the motor back into life, still mildly surprised that it started every time after my stab-in-the-dark purchase. It was another moment in which I would have made full use of a working sound system. My new digs was pretty much just across the road, but the streets were such that it would take a five-minute drive to get there. There'd have been time enough for two happy-day songs.

I pulled up in front of the house, jumped out of the 306 and walked over to the front door. I briefly considered whether I should use the key Azalea had just given me to let myself in. But I didn't see the need to give the guys a fright by suddenly appearing in the kitchen. I decided to knock.

The ludicrously tall Klaus opened the door. He seemed happy to see me. Albeit a little surprised that I'd rocked up.

"Er, hi," I said, trying to reproduce an Azalea beam while slightly uneasy about the fact that Klaus didn't seem to be expecting me. "I'm here to move in!"

"Are you?" he asked, his forehead creasing in perplexedness.

"Yes, Azalea just gave me the key," I explained, holding it up as proof.

"Did she? Well, I'm afraid I need to take that from you."

He was holding out his hand for the shapely piece of metal that would open the front door. For my prize, so hard-won and so very treasured. For a split second I wondered if he was joking. But then I remembered that Germans never joke. I swear the sun went behind a cloud at that moment.

"What...why?" I was beginning to panic.

"You're not on the lease yet, are you? We have no confirmation from the landlord that you should move in. We like you, but we can't let you move in yet."

Oh Lord. I wasn't done with this struggle.

"Ah, but…" I stammered hopefully. "But…Azalea has moved out and she said I could take the room and we'd sort the paperwork out on Monday. I thought you guys didn't mind?"

He looked a lot like he minded right now.

"Sorry, this is a typical Azalea move. She didn't check any of that with us. Moving in already would not be correct."

A Prolonged Devonian Pitstop

My spirits sank to a deep, dark place I never knew existed within me. In the space of a couple of seconds, I'd gone from overjoyed and relieved - my days of sleeping under desks were behind me! - back to a state of homelessness and dejection. Why was this strict and uncompromising interpretation of German *Ordnung* making my life a misery on a fine Friday afternoon, in a place so far removed from central Bavaria?

Thinking about it, I guess they asked themselves the same question in Dar-es-Salaam in the 1890s. Back when the Germans were running the show in what later became Tanzania, and the locals were understandably getting a bit fed up with it.

I handed over the precious key with a slack jaw and no words to say. My fight had drained away. All I felt like doing was giving up and moving into a cave, where I could engage in some light reading on, say, the Maji Maji rebellion of 1905 in German East Africa.

Why was this being so *difficult*? I had money. I needed a room. All I wanted was somebody to take my money and let me move into a room. Preferably someone who wouldn't make it their core business to write me letters about the precise placement of shower gel bottles, thereby making my life a series of torments. Was this asking so much?

I knew I couldn't really argue with Klaus. And not just because he was about six feet taller than me. I'd paid no rent, nor been anywhere near a lease agreement. Beyond general goodwill, I didn't have any palpable claim on a key. If he and the other rent-payers wanted it back, I couldn't put up a very good argument in my favour.

I also knew very well that having a massive set-to right now would see me back to trawling the 'Rooms to Rent' section of Gumtree.co.uk in no time. I was unofficially first in line, but the next twenty hopefuls in this were only a phone call away. I had to play it cool.

After a short conversation in which I tried to show just how chilled and reasonable I was about this little hiccup, Klaus and the guys said it was okay for me to move my things in while the paperwork got taken care of. I did so immediately, pondering why my pillows, pencils and the giant stuffed duck I'd won in a customer contest at the ice cream shop in Witney could start sleeping in the house, but my status as a living organism meant I wouldn't be extended the same privilege. I guess a relatively unknown human is much more of a concern than a pair of underpants.

Now *I* was the one who had to be trusting. I'd left the bulk of my belongings in a house full of people I barely knew, without any legal framework in place. But then, so what? Paperwork was causing me enough trouble already, and when things went awry it never got respected anyway. If you were from the 99% of the population that couldn't afford a lawyer, the ability to judge people on gut feeling counted for more than any contract – and my gut judged these to be good guys. Besides, the law of averages said I was due some sanity in the people around me.

Anyway, with at least a weekend without lodgings ahead of me, the danger of having my stuff held for ransom was a relatively minor concern. I couldn't think what else to do but drive to my parents in Devon. At least my trusty Peugeot would be light for the journey, now that I'd unpacked the car into my (hopefully) new room.

"So, I'll talk to the agents on Monday," I said to the guys after I'd heaved the last of my belongings up the narrow flight of stairs. "And hopefully see you next week…"

"Okay, sorry about this," said Klaus sympathetically. "We just don't want to get in trouble."

"Keep us posted, we'll see you soon," waved Mischa.

And then I set off for the other side of England.

If sleeping on an office floor is about the most depressing thing that can happen to you in your thirties, having to crawl back to mom and dad in order to have a roof over your head must come a close second. Nothing does quite so well at making you feel like you've gotten nowhere at all since leaving high school. But it does, on the other hand, give you a new appreciation for family.

It's almost worth getting in situations like this just to find out who your real friends are, too. The more I thought about it, the more I felt like I didn't have many phone-up-in-a-crisis mates in England just then. Sure, I had a few such people scattered around the world - but folks in South Africa or Australia couldn't do much for my little situation in Oxford. Even Monique was in another country.

Once I'd driven a few minutes away from the house, and was thinking a little more rationally, I remembered that it *was* still Friday afternoon. The agency hadn't quite shut for the weekend yet. Azalea had been supposed to get in touch with them, but it was obviously time to take things into my own hands. I didn't trust her and her vague statements anymore. In fact, a new reality was slowly dawning on me: Azalea thought that giving me the key automatically meant she wasn't paying rent any more.

Well, she could think what she liked: if I wasn't going to be allowed to use the room, then I most definitely wasn't paying rent either.

It was yet another unsolicited problem. On days like this, I did tend to wonder if the world had woken up with the sole purpose of figuring out what would annoy me the most, and then making damn sure it happened. And one of those things was talking to estate agents.

From what I'd heard, all these people did was take large sums of money from you in exchange for doing practically nothing. But this would prove to be untrue. I couldn't accuse Martin & Co in Oxford of doing nothing. They were actually quite proactive in making life difficult for me over the next week. As I discovered when I pulled into a petrol station and called them for the first time. After explaining who I was, I was put through to a certain Sally, who was in charge of this particular property.

Azalea, of course, had been conveniently optimistic when she'd said that we could sort out the paperwork in five minutes at the agency. What actually needed to happen, Sally informed me, was that I would have to go through a 'referencing process' before we could even get to contract-signings. She told me this would take at least 'three or four days.' When I heard this, I heaved a miserable sigh, unable to hide my frustration.

"But...where do I sleep in the meantime? In my car? Why can't we just do this now?"

But Sally was either without compassion or completely numbed to this kind of reaction: she remained firm and humourless in equal measure. Giving up hope on finding any human side to her, I asked if I needed to be able to pop into their office during these 'three or four days'. If so, then perhaps I shouldn't go to Devon. I really needed to know which way to point the car right now.

"Oh, you can do all the referencing remotely," she said breezily. "You don't need to come and see us."

This sounded distinctly like a silver lining. But I'd had previous with misinformation about this kind of thing.

"Are you sure?" I enquired. "Because I'm about to drive five hours to Devon. You're positive you're not going to tell me on Tuesday morning that I have to present myself at your desk with photographic identification?"

"No," she said flatly. "You can also sign the contract remotely."

Sally didn't see the funny side to anything, it seemed.

Well, at least I could go and stay with my folks for as long as was necessary to make myself an official renter. That was something.

On the way down to Devon, I called my boss and told him that I'd be 'working from home' indefinitely. It wasn't really a case of asking his permission, since I was already on the road. I didn't think he'd believe the whole story about the keys - it sounded made-up, even though it wasn't - so I just told him there was a delay finding anywhere to live in Oxfordshire.

"It's really hard to find anything affordable around the office, as you know," I hinted. "That's just the way it is, unfortunately."

He didn't bite on giving me a pay rise.

I was in a pretty vile mood all the way to my arrival in Devon late that Friday night. My mind kept spinning towards the fact that if it weren't for having to share with impossible people and the heartless bureaucracy that comes with renting, I wouldn't be in this situation.

Suddenly I wanted to become a homeowner.

Well *this* was a new feeling!

Sure, I'd been loosely drawn to the idea of property for over a decade - not even the most independent of spirits could fail to find the notion of rent-free life (or rental money funding one's treks across the Altiplano) a seductive one. Moreover, my knack for saving meant I'd long since had enough in the bank to cover a deposit. But I'd never quite twisted my brain around the idea of paying vast sums in interest each month. Like, really, *really* large sums. Not a penny of which even went towards repaying your actual loan. I simply couldn't understand how people were okay with this.

The last several years had been spent watching an ever-growing number of responsible friends and acquaintances get on the property ladder, gaily signing up for these terrifying interest payments. No matter how many times they patiently explained to me that it made more sense than renting, and that this system was supposed to be perfectly reasonable, I couldn't see it as anything other than a racket.

'You're just paying somebody else's mortgage as long as you rent,' they kept telling me. But if you had to pay 300 Pounds a month to a bank for lending you money, I thought, then it looked to me like you were still renting, in a roundabout sort of way. You were just renting money instead of a home.

And while you might not be paying somebody's mortgage, you'd be paying a bank executive's salary. Same difference?

(Isn't 'interest' a funny word? I see a banker momentarily distracted from his newspaper-reading by the dull thud of a wad of fifty-Pound notes landing on his desk, raising his eyebrows and saying 'oh, *interesting*,' before returning to the racing results. Anyone else would be quite excited by getting free dosh every month. If it were me, I'd be far more than *interested*. I'd be fist-pumping. But of course, banks want this kind of business to seem credible, necessary and entirely in the order of things.)

Maybe the maths made sense, if you were a thorough disciple of the system and content to commit to working a day job for 30 years in order to end up too old to enjoy the benefits of a paid-off home. I never did bother to sit down and work it out rationally. But intuitively? Paying a bank for a roof over my head and paying a landlord for a roof over my head *both* seemed like renting. Bigger picture, maybe not...but the thought of taking three decades to be debt-free was more depressing than growing old in abject poverty whilst living under a bridge. Not kidding.

For me, being in debt was like an itch I had to scratch. I was always chasing people around trying to pay them back piffling sums they'd usually forgotten about. A thirty-year loan was unthinkable. I would have ruined every minute of those years scrooging pennies to try and pay the bank off early. And three decades is a rather significant chunk of one's life to ruin.

All told, the pay-as-you-go approach to accommodation had always just made more sense to me. Or at least, it certainly had more merit than people claimed.

Until now. Because the world of renting and sharing was giving me a seriously rough ride. Rough enough to make me want to do anything - maybe even pay *interest* - to have my own space. One where the keys would be mine, the rules would be mine, my choice of co-habitant (if any) would be mine, and from which I couldn't be thrown out.

But while I brooded over these revolutionary thoughts, I knew that right now I needed a quick fix. I still had a job and summer of cricket to play in Oxfordshire. I couldn't mope around in Stoke Gabriel indefinitely.

Stoke Gabriel was actually an uplifting place. It perched on the edge of a millpond that swelled and shrank with the tide of the adjacent River Dart. When you looked up at the little town from the river and beheld the medieval Anglican church (its yard boasted graves dating from the 1700s) that dominated the hillside, you just wanted to wrap up the view and take it with you.

The place had once been a true village, with a post office, a general store, two pubs and no more than a few dozen houses. The amenities and road system - in essence a single-track loop that swooped down to the centre and back - were once just fine for its needs. Now they were hopeless. Stoke Gabriel had become the sort of town to which people from Surrey moved for a quiet retirement, and then complained about how all the other people moving from Surrey were spoiling the peace.

My parents, who'd moved from Surrey a couple of years earlier and were now heartily complaining about the new arrivals, had a posh house and garden in the upper part of town. Outer Stoke Gabriel continued to sprawl over the top of the hill, marching ominously in the general direction of Paignton. But there were still plenty of nearby spots in which you could contemplate nothing but the fluffy green hills, laced with stone walls, that instantly told you that you were somewhere in the British Isles. I spent much of that weekend enjoying all of this and pondering the complexities of life.

When Monday morning came, it was time to try and make peace with the idea of 'referencing', at least for long enough to get myself a home. And that was going to be hard.

Look, I don't have an issue with a landlord paying an agent to check that they're not getting a python devotee, lightbulb-stealer or rent-dodger moving into their property. It's also fair enough for the agent to charge the landlord for this, which is after all a labour-saving service. But I have an enormous issue with agents charging the *tenant* a referencing fee. Wherever this happens, it ought to be stopped by act of parliament.

I mean, come on! If I make a conscious move to ask you for a pie, you're entitled to ask me for cash in exchange for it. Same thing if I request satellite television, a gallon of petrol, or a trip to Barbados. Supply and demand. But when exactly do I as a tenant make it known that I wish to be 'referenced'? I don't. No demand. It's the agent and the landlord who insist on referencing. So then, how about *they* pay for it? Why should I pay for someone else's pie?

Not only was the principle perverted, but that Monday morning also revealed that we weren't talking pocket change. We were talking - wait for it - *two hundred and ninety-five Pounds*.

And for what, exactly? Two hundred and nine-five Pounds' worth of man-hours? The same amount of work and time I'd spent to earn the equivalent sum in my job? Tell me another! Martin & Co actually *outsourced* this job to an external 'referencing agent', and so did precisely nothing. And did the 'referencing agent' pore over hot papers for hours on end? Again no! All they did was brainlessly punch a couple of things into a computer, and wait for it to say yes or no.

Just another completely made-up industry, if you asked me, in which large sums of money flowed from one company to another and not a lot happened. And now *my* large sum of money was being dragged into this sordid business, with the lunacy actually sanctioned by regulation. Somehow a situation had arisen in which a landlord engaged an agent to work for them, but the tenant ended up paying a share.

As you get older, you become more aware of these little ways in which the rich stay rich. And I'd felt myself getting a *lot* older in the last few weeks. I really needed a hammock and Barbados. But for now, Stoke Gabriel would have to do. I had to get this business sorted out as soon as possible.

Already seething about the cost, I set about the homework involved in my 'referencing'. It turned out I was a nightmare for the computer. I was always switching countries, bunking with friends, working multiple jobs and couldn't remember the last time I had a 'utility bill' in my name.

It turned out that 'referencing' really meant showing that you'd been a good little drone and conformed to the local system, by means of providing contacts for respectable upholders of said system - landlords and so forth - who'd vouch for you. But if you didn't have paperwork to that effect, then a law-abiding and debt-free track record didn't seem to help at all.

The whole thing was a bloody joke. I realise now that I was far too honest in my answers. Telling a bunch of lies would have made it much easier for everyone. As it was, when asked about landlord references, I couldn't think of *anyone* to whom I'd paid 'official' rent in the UK during the specified previous three years. I'd lived with a girlfriend and just given her cash every month. I'd flung Steven a few hundred each month too. Same thing with Lithuanian nutcase. Bills were invariably included.

On which point, when would the people who insisted on utility bills - clearly the sort of people who owned their own homes - understand that billions and billions of us poor serfs lived in shared houses. And that under these kinds of living arrangements, quite sensibly and I think quite legally, just one of the four or five people was usually responsible for the electric bill, collecting a share of cash from the others each month. None of which should cause the others to be considered non-persons by some soulless computer a few years down the track.

Confounded by the form I was expected to fill out, I eventually got the lad at the 'referencing agency' on the telephone. I wanted to see if I could make him understand that I hadn't been living as a highwayman, but nonetheless couldn't complete his form.

"So you haven't had a lease at all in the last three years?" he asked incredulously.

"No, I've been sharing rent with friends," I repeated.

"Okay...that's dangerous...renting illegally..."

I nearly flipped. How was it *illegal* to share rent with my girlfriend and not feel the need to draw up a cotton-picking *contract* about it? Had I wandered into an episode of *The Big Bang Theory*? And *dangerous?* To work on trust and decency with people you know well? What if I was eighteen and seeking my first abode, and had forgotten to sign a lease with my parents whilst growing up? Would I be eternally forbidden from renting?

Either the world had gone mad, or I had.

I decided it wasn't worth mentioning further 'illegal' rentals in Australia, which would also have squeezed into the magic triennium.

"I did have an official lease in South Africa," I replied drily. "How about that?"

"Oh no, Sir, they do have to be United Kingdom addresses."

Was this guy for real? I tried to stay calm.

"Tell me then," I begged. "What do all the people who've been so bold as to live outside the country for the last three years do in this situation?"

He made a sort of shrugging noise down the phone.

"I can't be the first person who has lived in house shares and occasionally outside the country, can I?"

"Well..."

So, as per usual, it looked like I *was* the first person with this problem. It was still real news to me that I'd lived such an extraordinary life.

This referencing guy and his faceless cronies became the bane of my existence in the days that followed. They morphed into a symbol of all that was wrong with a deeply unsympathetic world in which common sense would never again be allowed to prevail, and ticking boxes mattered more than people did.

It turned into a long week. Not only did I have to wage battle with various uninterested bureaucrats as I failed to fit into any of their drop-down menus, but Monique broke up with me over Skype on the Wednesday. "I'm just not in love," she said with typically Dutch directness. Maybe she just didn't fancy the idea of a long-distance relationship with a homeless guy. Whatever, it said much about my situation that I was too wound up to care about the dumping.

Finally, after I chased down various references from employers past and present, common sense prevailed. Basically it boiled down to the fact that my referencing friend didn't care all that much. So although I wasn't going to complain, they didn't, according to the strictest rules, reference me properly. Which meant both the landlord and myself were paying top whack for a questionable service. But it was enough, of course, to make a few people richer and avoid litigation.

But now, at last, it looked I might actually be permitted to move into the house in Oxford.

The referencing hurdle cleared, we moved onto the lease. I made so bold as to ask Sally if there would be an inspection and inventory upon moving in. I'd had previous bad experience of landlords retaining deposits from me. Specifically one Mr Johnson of Woking, who several years earlier had judged it his tenants' fault that his 60-year-old radiators had spontaneously erupted brown goo all over his South London carpets.

I wanted assurance that I wasn't going to get punished for something Azalea had done to the room weeks ago.

"No, there's no inspection," emailed Sally in reply, articulating my worst fears perfectly. "You pay your deposit and Azalea gets hers back."

"Yes, that's the issue," I replied, scarcely believing I had to explain this to somebody whose full-time business was renting property in a city heaving with shared houses. "What if she's done something and I end up paying for it? I should get an all-clear that the room was fine when I moved in!"

"I'm afraid we don't provide an inspection mid-tenancy," came the crisp reply. "But they're a lovely group, and I don't imagine there being any problems."

Lovely? *Lovely?* How freaking *lovely* was the agency going to be when they found that Azalea had been practicing her squash against the walls and I had to pay for it? Reading between the lines, I saw Sally's real sentiments as follows:

As long as we've got someone's deposit, we're not really going to bother checking out the room to protect you as a tenant. Because when we get to the final inspection and there's a problem, it's all the same to us whether we take the money off you or Azalea. The landlord will be happy either way, and we'll keep getting our cut from him. Have a nice day!

Whatever. I didn't care anymore. The fight had gone out of me once again. Like any peasant who wants to wring some enjoyment out of his existence, I just had to accept my lot. If I paid hundreds of Pounds in agency fees and still got further screwed by the whole rotten system down the line, well, that was just *life*. In peasant terms, it was like a drought or a thunderstorm, which would come and spoil things no matter how much tax you paid. You could only stay sane by taking a fatalistic view.

Am I overstating the case to use such feudal terminology? Well, just think about the very word *landlord* for a moment. It's basically the same one they used in the days when a rich man sat in a hilltop castle stuffing his face with chicken legs all day, while dozens of serfs toiled on the surrounding land. And as far as things being skewed in his favour were concerned, I didn't feel like much had changed in the intervening centuries.

But careworn as I was, at least I'd finally succeeded in getting somebody to take my money and let me have a room. By the end of the week, I had an 'electronically-signed' lease sorted, a deposit paid and a written assurance from all stakeholders that I was now free to sleep at my new lodgings. The pleasure of a home would only last until the entire house lease ran out in September, mind you, which meant I was going to be in the same position in about four months' time. But that was a summer's cricket and a lifetime away.

I drove the 306 back up the M5 and the A40 with a certain determination to put all these painful learnings to some kind of positive use. I wanted to make sure this would *never* happen again. I couldn't carry on living like this. I wanted a home that I wouldn't have to keep on shoving into the back of a car at a moment's notice.

If the world was incorrigibly tipped in favour of property owners, then clearly I would have to find a way to become one. Enough was enough: I had to reinvent myself as a grown-up.

Screeching Brakes and Dreaming Spires

I might have reached a landmark life decision, but the annoying reality was that getting a home of my own wasn't going to happen overnight. Securing a mortgage would not be the work of a moment - or so I was given to believe. And while I figured out how on earth I was going to get one, my short-term goal was to restore some semblance of sanity to my existence. For the next few weeks, that meant trying to live a smooth life in Oxford.

I'd secured my short-term survival essentials, and it was time to enjoy things for a while. Spent from my travails, I didn't want to think about the challenges that lay after September until I really had to. It was the start of June, and my simple plan for the summer was to surprise my boss by returning to work, to gorge myself on cricket and attend philosophy and comedy workshops all over Oxford. I was also looking forward to living with normal people again.

Some of this even went to plan. By the end of the cricket season, for example, I'd played matches for no less than five different cricket clubs. While I still played in the local league for Shipton-under-Wychwood, my primary club was now half an hour further away from home. This wasn't saving my petrol nor the planet, so I moved my Sunday friendly operations to Cumnor Cricket Club, which lay in a small village just west of Oxford. On weekday evenings I also turned out for the Oxfordshire County Council Cricket Club. Thanks to a general lack of enthusiasm for cricket amongst the local public servants, the club took anyone. You didn't actually have to work for the council to play for them.

Lacking a home ground, the OCCCC (for short...) played all over the place, touring the local villages. One highlight was the incredibly picturesque field at Cuxham. You actually walked through a forest and crossed a brook to reach the ground: all very Enid Blyton.

It was at Cuxham that I took a catch that was, if I do say so myself, quite wonderful. I know I promised not to write too much about cricket, but it would be wrong not to mention such a rare flash of brilliance. Fielding in the point position, I dived full-stretch to my left, somehow getting two hands to the ball and holding it. It was moments like that for which I'd gone to such lengths to stay in Oxfordshire for the summer.

Well, those, and not wanting to let Karola win.

My conscience about being a car owner hadn't dissipated. I was still cycling to work, and more from duty than pleasure. Cycling *per se* is fun, but this was a largely grim 13-mile route involving Oxford's choked ring road and various other smaller ones on which cars and trucks tried their level best to bash you into the blackberry bushes. The 'economy' bike I had at the time was no ally on such missions. Riding that thing (made in Xiamen City, I'm quite certain) probably did me permanent damage. But hey, at least my carbon credentials would be better.

(Why did I even bother? What difference would my efforts make against the multitudinous varieties of swill produced by the Asian industrial machine?)

But sometimes a bike just isn't fit for the job, and at times like these my Peugeot opened up whole new worlds of possibility. Take, by way of example, the time I discovered a second midweek cricket team while cycling past Jordan Hill in North Oxford on my way home from one particular half-day's work. I'd never seen anybody playing there before, but here, indubitably, was a group of decidedly unsporty-looking men spanning about fifty years in age, standing largely idle and wearing white. They looked like my kind of guys.

Better yet, when I asked if they needed another player, they said 'actually, we need two.' They were just about to start, but I had no gear with me at all. Back in the bad old pre-Peugeot days, that would have been that. But knowing that I had a car in the driveway back home made all the difference. I cycled to my new house-share like the wind, jumped straight into the 306 and was back in forty minutes for a bonus half-game of cricket. That, right there, is the kind of freedom money *can* buy.

If I'd begun to notice one drawback about the car, apart from the front half of the thing still making rickety sounds whenever the suspension moved, it was that she was a thirsty little thing. Pretty good on the highway, but in any other environment the gauge needle kept dropping like Wall Street on Black Monday. I only had to breathe in the direction of the accelerator, it seemed, and petrol would fly out of the tank.

When I thought about it, this was probably because the car was a 1600cc. Even *I* knew that this wasn't ideal from an economy point of view. But had I carefully considered engine capacity during the three-and-a-half minutes I'd spent weighing up the purchase? I'll let you have a wild guess on that one.

Apart from paying the price - quite literally - for my failure to appreciate the difference two hundred cubic centimetres can make, I was apparently driving around Oxfordshire with a lethal set of brakes. This came to my attention some way into the summer, when I gave my colleague Christopher a ride for the first time.

A little background on Christopher. Born in Spain to English parents, he'd decided to try out working in the land of his roots. But having spent most of his existence thus far living just outside Barcelona, he found British life endlessly perplexing. And I could rarely find fault with his rants.

"This is the worst train service in the world, man!" he recounted after arriving late for work twice in his first two weeks. "I took the early train, which was supposed to get me in 45 minutes early. And four Pounds for 10 miles? It's a f***ing pisstake!"

And if that didn't make him angry enough, then there were the run-ins with the station staff. "I went up to them and asked if they had some kind of proof document saying the train was cancelled, so I could hand it in at work to prove the train was late. This is quite common in other countries, you know! But this guy? First he looked at me as if I was mental, then he had a good laugh about it with one of his colleagues right in front of me! This is supposed to be the land of punctuality and manners? Hah!"

Unsurprisingly for a man who grew up on good *tapas* and regular helpings of *jamón ibérico*, Christopher found the British culinary experience more than a little disappointing.

"Where the hell are the vegetable and fruit shops in this country?!" he'd rage to colleagues in the office kitchen, who could only shrug as they lined up to put their baked beans in the microwave. "A city as big as Oxford, and it literally has *one* vegetable shop! What's wrong with you people? Don't you realise fresh fruit at the supermarket sucks? Oh, right, of course you don't. Your knowledge of food is nearly as pathetic as what I saw in Holland. And another thing...actual grown-ups eating baked beans, pot noodles and spaghetti hoops for lunch in the office? As if that is an actual meal. Disgusting!"

Town names were another mystery to Christopher. He was more or less a native speaker of the language, but he hadn't a clue how to speak of settlements like Long Hanborough, which was home to our office and pronounced 'Long Han-bruh'. "Who decided to spell it one way and pronounce it a totally different way? And then the locals laugh at you if you mispronounce it! Well, how am I supposed to know, you baked beans eating t***?"

"And what are 'bank holidays'?" he'd ask, quite reasonably in my opinion. "This is a country with such a rich culture, but hardly any traditional celebrations. In Spain, when it's a holiday, it's due to historical or religious events. And you eat a certain food, dress a specific way or buy particular presents. But here? When I ask why it's a holiday, people say, 'Oh, just because.' Well, that sucks, you boring farts!"

But as rough a ride as he was having with general life in England, none of that compared to the first one he had in my Peugeot 306.

"F***ing hell, man!" he cried the moment we slowed for a corner. "What's wrong with your brakes?"

"Nothing," I replied calmly. "Look, I pressed the pedal and the car slowed down. What more do you want?"

"But didn't you hear that *screaming* sound?"

I shrugged. I'd never been anything more than peripherally aware of the little squeal that accompanied my car's retardation process. I suppose many years of cycling in the rain had dulled my senses to the noise of pigs being slaughtered when I squeezed a set of brakes. But Christopher seemed convinced that if I tried slowing for any more corners, *we* were the ones who were going to end up butchered. And quite passionately so, when you considered that the software salesman knew as little about cars as I did.

Within a few miles, I'd at least managed to convince him that he didn't need to jump out of the window. And I'd promised him I'd get the brakes checked out at the first available opportunity. Which meant, in reality, whatever time it would take to find a mechanic I actually trusted not to shaft me. I was, as ever, willing to drive a possible death-trap for many months whilst awaiting such a miracle.

Thankfully a colleague's partner happened to be a mechanic, and he offered to take a look at my car. I accepted happily. My co-worker was a nice person, so I felt confident James wasn't going to screw me over.

That's why I meekly accepted another round of reprimands following his first glance at the brakes. Christopher had been right to scream. And James probably had a point when he told me I ought to take maintenance more seriously. My pads (or maybe they were discs...how should I know?) were worn to the very brink of non-existence. I made no protest when he told me I needed new ones - £220, since you ask - if I wanted to pass my roadworthy test. Or carry on living.

I had the work done, and more or less sailed through that MOT (as the English lovingly call their annual roadworthiness test) when it came up for renewal at the end of summer. The authorized garage in question did charge me for some minor required changes without phoning to check with me first, even though I had said 'phone to check with me first'. Why is it so *hard* for these people?

If my car was starting to give the occasional expensive hiccup, living with Mischa, Klaus and Frank was no trouble at all. Thank goodness. If I'd had to deal with any more meddling co-habitants, I think I'd have flung myself from one of those church spires for which Oxford is so renowned.

Being in their mid-twenties, the guys did like to go out and drink until four o'clock in the morning. A couple of houses ago, back in Witney, I'd gotten used to (and sometimes joined) my English house-mates doing much the same after the occasional night of Oxfordshire small-town revelry at The Red Lion in Witney. To me these homecomings could only mean food-fights, a variety of other indoor sport contests, MTV on full blast and a great deal of shrieking and shouting. If it was a night on which I'd optimistically turned in early but forgotten to push a chest of drawers across my door, it was also pretty much a given that a merry Simon would burst into my room with the sole intention of cartwheeling his posterior into my face.

But the German way of coming home drunk at 4am seemed to be quite different. It involved going directly to the kitchen, considerately closing the door and talking quietly, then going to bed. They never woke me up once. It was a breath of fresh air, albeit not one that did much to deconstruct stereotypes.

Speaking of which, poor Mischa was regularly to be seen going about his business in socks and sandals. In this sense, he was more German than the guys who'd actually been born in Germany. Even as we stood about openly snickering at him, he wouldn't have a clue what the joke was. He almost never did. Sweet as a teddy bear and eternally amusing, whether for his own unique brand of English or his earnest interest in the latest TEDx talk, Mischa became my best friend in the house.

All my new house-mates had a curious obsession with protein. I'm not sure if it was a German thing or a guys-in-their-twenties thing, but the trio seemed to live for the stuff. I'm talking about those ginormous bottles of powder that you might find in shops dedicated to bodybuilding. Apparently the good stuff was hard to get in Oxford, so the Germans would actually send away for it. And they loved mixing it up into a disgusting slosh - this was the recipe, apparently - almost as much as they loved going to gym.

The powder wasn't always enough for Mischa, who also swore by the triangular 'protein rolls' you could buy at the local Lidl. This piqued my interest more, since I had to admit these were pretty good. Especially nice with jam on top, it filled you up in a way British bread never could. It must surely have been sent over by the chain's German owners.

British 'bread', if I may be permitted an aside once more, is simply an insult to the name. I believe whole documentary films have been made about how it's 90% air and 10% freakish, nasty chemicals that shouldn't be allowed near true foodstuffs. The UK (and I suppose Ireland too) is surely the only country in Europe where you can eat twenty slices of toast and still be hungry an hour later. Come to think of it, it's also about the only country where deliberately cooking your bread is actually something people do, which tells you everything you need to know about how fundamentally appealing the raw stuff is. When you go to a country where they sell the kind of fresh bread you just want to tear apart and devour with a little butter, your first thought isn't usually 'Hey, how about I hold this close to a heat source?' Bread, after all, has already *been* cooked once. If you have to cook it again, then you don't have a very good baker.

Ours was also a pizza-loving house. The guys taught me how much potential there was in buying a plain base and adding your own goodies. It didn't have to involve anything clever. Mushrooms, ham, extra mozzarella and lashings of olive oil could make a delicious feast. None of which is anything revelatory, I know, but you've got to understand that my default when confronted with a home dinner decision is to go blank. On a more Teutonic note, Klaus also showed me how to make *Rostzwiebel*, which is simply chopped onions dipped in flour, salt and pepper, before being plunged into hot oil. Crispy and marvellous.

Being millennials (or as good as), the guys also collected 'experiences' with great relish. They wanted to make the most of living in an exotic foreign land for six months, so you'd rarely catch them sleeping or watching TV. Working at BMW Mini meant they could book company cars for weekends away, so they were forever cruising off to different corners of Britain. Bath, Newquay and Scotland were all trips I could understand. The one to Swansea, on the other hand, left me gasping for a valid explanation. But they seemed to like it, and that's the main thing.

Sometimes they invited me on their escapades, but I always declined on the basis that I had moved heaven and earth to play cricket this summer. Which meant sticking around on weekends, usually to play all afternoon both Saturday and Sunday. Socially speaking, I was content enough to know that I was getting on well with multiple house-mates once more. That clearly it wasn't *me* that had been the problem in my last place. But I didn't feel pressure to become best buddies with anyone here, since we were only going to know each other for a few weeks anyway.

I quickly learned that relations with Azalea hadn't been good at all. I wasn't particularly impressed by my dealings with her either, especially when she inevitably declined to pay rent for the days between her giving me the key and my signing the lease. When the money-chasing woman at the agency emailed us all about a certain missing sum of rent money, I wrote to her and told her why it was nothing to do with me. To her credit, I think she must have chased Azalea down. Because I didn't hear anything about it again.

While cricket remained the priority and going to work remained a constant thorn in my side (how those with full-time jobs get anything else done still eludes me), I made sporadic attempts to make the most of living in Oxford. It was a city to which tourists from around the world flocked in droves, and as such had to be considered a privilege to be enjoyed. It's also the place where my comic hero Rowan Atkinson, who read electrical engineering at Queen's College, found kindred spirits such as Richard Curtis, with whom he went on to do the sort of work I'd very much like to do myself.

Where better to find smart, motivated collaborators who'd co-star in side-splitting sketches? No doubt there were plenty of restless, arty souls in the city - I just had to find them. I wasn't sure how to get invited into the Oxford University Dramatic Society, but I thought I'd start by joining a Meetup group to do with improvisation. From there, I'd man-about-townishly get to know people who knew people, and I'd finally find a kindred spirit of my own. That elusive comic foil.

That was the plan, anyway. As it turned out, I kept shifting these plans down the priority list and never did free up a single night to go to the Meetup. Probably because deep down I know I'm not a man-about-town, and I'm far too afraid of squishy fruit projectiles to try and take comedy ideas on stage. Call me a defeatist if you will. And never hire me as a motivational speaker.

My only successful foray into evening brain exercise was to join one group discussion on moral philosophy. It wasn't bad, although - perhaps inevitably - my abiding memory is of a pontificating buffoon named Norman making forceful yet utterly irrelevant contributions, using the sort of booming, pompous delivery only a witless 'senior student' with zero self-awareness could come up with.

I learned a lot about how I construct the pecking order of my hopes and dreams during my time in Oxford, actually. While tough things like developing a comedy network always slipped to the next week, I spent a lot of time trying to tick off 'play tennis on grass' from my bucket list. That doesn't require any brain power, you see. Although it still turned out to be a mighty challenge.

Lawn tennis is a posh man's sport in England. And since Oxford is the place with poshness coded into its DNA, I wasn't much surprised to find that grass courts abounded in my new temporary home. I eyed them up, licking my lips at the prospect of playing a familiar game on such a soft, growing and living surface. The idea of grass beneath one's tennis shoes had never stopped being an exotic attraction for me.

As a youngster, I used to sit glued to Wimbledon for two weeks every South African winter, filling out one of those round-by-round wall charts they included with the Sunday newspaper ahead of the tournament. I remember the cast like yesterday. Ivan Lendl, the Czech who was somehow also American. Martina Navratilova, the only sportsperson I'd ever seen wearing glasses. The ginger-haired Boris Becker, whose name was impossibly funny if you were nine. There was John McEnroe, for whose tantrums you absolutely lived if you were nine. And Stefan Edberg, the straight-up Swede whose role my best friend Matthew always insisted on playing when we'd re-enact events in south-west London on the quiet residential streets of Cape Town.

I remember Pat Cash with his bandanas, Andre Agassi with his *Beauty And The Beast* impressions and Steffi Graf with her legs. Not to mention Monica Seles, who managed to get stabbed during a match in Hamburg, and

Jennifer Capriati, who hit the big time at some crazy age like eleven. Somehow the cast of characters seemed broader and more colourful than it is today, but that's probably just because I was at that age when impressions stick for life. I suppose there must be kids out there right now who find Rafa Nadal, Venus Williams and Novak Djokovic impossibly exciting. Or maybe it was like that for everyone in my country: 1980s South Africa was an isolated place, where anything beamed in from this grand place called 'overseas' was like a trip to wonderland. We didn't have names like Gabriela Sabatini in our neck of the woods.

While my interest in tennis had long since diminished to zero, that dream of playing on a freshly-mown lawn court had never quite gone away. I didn't want to take up the sport. I just wanted to feel what it was like to play on grass. One match would suffice. And you'd think it might be reasonable to assume that some tennis facility in Oxford would hire me a court and a racquet for an hour or two.

But the problem with posh sports, it turned out, is that nobody is interested in your stinking twenty Pounds. Half of the tennis courts - always empty, by the way - belonged to the university colleges. They didn't *do* court rental. The other half were private member clubs. I was welcome to apply for membership, I was told.

"But I only want to play once!" I pleaded on more than one occasion. "I don't want to take up tennis and pay an annual subscription! Can't you just rent me a court for an hour? Don't you give interested newcomers a free trial? What about growing the game?"

The responses were always in the negative. If anybody from the Lawn Tennis Association - and no doubt many other tennis bodies around the world - is reading this, I hope you know that it's very hard for an interested passer-by to try your sport. If you have no players left in a couple of decades, snooty member clubs and Oxbridge-style exclusivity will be the reason. Even *golf* is more welcoming to visitors. And believe me, that's saying something.

While lawn tennis didn't work out, I found cricket to be very democratic. On almost any afternoon or evening I could go down to the public nets in the park in East Oxford, and simply join in with whoever was there. There would invariably be a few guys having a practice session, and they would always be of Pakistani descent. I was always the only white person there, which was interesting because one does not, it's fair to say, see one white chap hanging out with a group of Asians on the streets of Britain very often. I was proud of cricket for being the one thing that could make such a thing happen. Lawn tennis it was not.

Midsummer came and went. I spent the longest evening in Headington Hill Park with my office pal Sara, waiting rather pointlessly to see if a pixie might come out. I've always had hazy and gloriously inaccurate ideas about what Midsummer Night in Europe involves, and I cling to them with a hope that will probably only die when I do.

I've yet to see a saucy ritual spontaneously erupt, nor any magic woodland creatures emerge from the bushes to play shrill tunes on the piccolo beneath the rising moon. But when the twilight's at its most magnificent, you can't help but dream a little. It helps if you can find a spot that's deserted and miraculously free of abandoned Stella Artois cans. We managed it that night, but as usual, those nymphs and fauns simply refused to play ball.

When you're living in the same town in which Lewis Carroll came up with jabberwockies and the like, I think you may be forgiven for having a hyperactive imagination. I made sure to read *Alice in Wonderland* at least once during my time in Oxford, and also tried with limited success to imagine Christ College as it would have been in Carroll's day. He didn't have to contend with swarms of Spanish schoolkids waving selfie sticks, it's safe to say.

I read a couple of Carroll biographies, too, hoping I might glean something from the master of madness that might help my own writing. All I could really conclude, apart from that the Reverend was quite a lot cleverer than myself, was that being born in a time before television and Twitter was probably a tremendous advantage. So much more came down to your own imagination and observation, and when you went from child to grown-up, this didn't change to quite the same extent as it does in our content-saturated age. All the same, I rather hope it's true that Carroll was regularly sampling some wacky intoxicants. If his Cheshire Cat or hookah-smoking caterpillar were truly the creations of a sober mind, then my jealousy as a fellow writer is far harder for me to bear.

I've often wondered just how many greats of the arts genuinely did their best work 'clean'. If it turns out that everyone from van Gogh to Hemingway was on a mind-altering substance, then something really ought to be done. I'm not suggesting the International Olympic Committee step in and start locking up this performance-enhanced work, but we should at least have special galleries and museums for those who did it the hard way. Because dreaming up the Mad Hatter when you're high isn't nearly as impressive as doing it with a cup of Yorkshire Gold and a digestive.

Another advantage to taking drugs as an artist is that you don't have to keep stopping for meals. The right sorts of stimulants, in my limited understanding of such things, allow you to go for long periods of time without having to raid the fridge or frantically google what time the corner shop closes. Other drugs keep you awake for days on end. Both of these are very good for getting into a flow. I can't think why I don't try it. But, silly thing that I am, I still write my books sober.

As I continued to read up on Carroll, I learned more about his controversial extra-curricular photographic work with inappropriately young models, and marvelled about the innocence of his time as I read. I was also able to glean a fairly accurate idea of where exactly that hazy summer boat ride - Carroll and the three Liddell sisters, alone - that supposedly inspired *Alice in Wonderland* actually took place. As such I rapidly became obsessed with (at the very least) having a picnic next to the River Isis at Godstow, right on the edge of the vast common they call Port Meadow.

Probably spurning a comedy workshop, I found a fine summer evening to do just that. The friends from London who joined me (a pair of sisters, as it happened) watched on in bemusement as I made a point of looking for white rabbits and calling out to the jabberwocky. But, like those pixies in the park, the wockies and bunnies simply weren't going to heed me. That being so, all one could really do was go for a dip in the dark waters of the fairly small river, and marvel at how this could possibly turn into a great big thing called the Thames further downstream.

On the whole, though, the city never quite drew me in. Somehow the unique and old, like the scattered university buildings, didn't blend very well with the featureless and new, like the Sainsbury's Local shop on the corner or the monstrous (and thankfully now demolished) Oxford Central Library. Nor did the tourists and students seem a natural mix. University life, to me, doesn't involve several nosy Korean men poking their mobile phone lenses through your dormitory window. Mine certainly didn't.

Basically, Oxford had outgrown itself and lost the charm a student town ought to have. The size of it never ceased to irk me. If its weird shape wasn't awkward enough, so too were the distances. Caught in a twilight zone between large town and proper city, everywhere was far away enough from everything else to be a sweaty walk, but not quite far enough to justify getting on a bus.

A perfect cycling town, then - except for the fact that anybody living in the east had to slog up the unrelenting Headington Hill to get home. Needless to say, I was one of those unfortunates.

As the cricket fixtures began to dry up, the days got short enough that we could no longer expect to play until eight in the evening and the number of fingers needlessly fractured by cricket balls grew to a brace, my attention turned to the future roof over my head once more. After several weeks of sane living, my resolution to be a property owner had lost a little of its spark. Even though I was again about to suffer a renting-related upheaval, certain not-very-grown-up alternatives to buying a British brick house bubbled around my head. And the regular eggings-on from Sara did nothing to simmer them down. On dull afternoons in the office she would email at length about moving into a disused shipping container in the wilds of British Columbia, which made me feel like my mortgage resolution was a bit lame.

One daydream involved moving to Sri Lanka, where I'd discovered on a visit the previous year that I could buy a good house outright for less than the savings in my bank account. It would be halfway up the escarpment between Colombo and Kandy, in that happy in-between climate that was neither oppressive coastal heat nor the chilly mists of the highlands. They even played cricket in Sri Lanka. The only problem was that I thought I might starve inside my tropical palace. I didn't quite know where I'd get day-to-day food money from, you see. Writing, after all, is a fickle business.

I really liked this idea of living in a country where the weather was good and the currency wasn't. And where they didn't care about irritations like referencing. But I really didn't believe I had the small but steady stream of passive income I needed. A little flow that didn't depend on book sales or the vagaries of the remote-work job market I kept hearing was out there. For that, I would need a house in a rich country. This I could rent out to sustain me in a life of sloth somewhere in tropics. Alternatively I could just live in it. In that case I would have to work, but at least I could enjoy not having a landlord.

Another appealing possibility was going completely off-grid, finding myself a nice cave and becoming a bearded hermit. After the fun and games of referencing, this plan appealed to my flogged and beaten principles. But I had to be honest with myself: I had become far too much of a wimp in my old age. I didn't much like snakes or cold. And while the caves warm enough to live in year-round would inevitably be in places with many snakes, those without legless reptiles that would crawl across me in the night would be far too chilly for comfort.

Besides, even if I *could* figure out how to skin animals or grow crops faster than my vast appetite would demolish them, where would I watch rugby internationals and the golf Majors? I had far too much interest in following international sport to move into a media-free cave. I was, without being materialistic in terms of possessions, nonetheless a slave to 21st-century comfort and convenience. It had taken only a brief visit to India - which is nothing like Sri Lanka, believe it or not - to work that one out.

However I looked at it, it seemed I was going to have to be a grown-up after all, at least temporarily. This implied all sorts of things. One, given that nobody who isn't a banker can earn the kind of cash you need to buy outright in the UK, was getting a mortgage. Two, I'd have to scale up to a full-time job, because half a salary wasn't going to get me anywhere on the loans calculator. Three, I would have to move to a new company. My current employer would gladly take me for full hours, but they'd never consent to pay me what I needed to secure a loan on a habitable dwelling.

What I needed was a new, five-days-a-week job, and to keep it for at least the three months you needed to satisfy a mortgage lender. I also needed a new home to rent, at least for those three months and however long it took to find a place to buy. All rather daunting, but it was a real plan and it felt good.

With the cricket season just about gone, there was no particular reason to stay in Oxfordshire. I was tired of the effort of trying to find a room there. I could look for jobs anywhere I liked, although I was quite sure I didn't want to move into London itself. I'd been there and done that long ago, and in the intervening years the metropolis had become more of a bloated monster than ever. I couldn't understand why anyone liked it.

When people talk about why London is better than other places in Britain, they say things like 'there's so much more going on.' That's true, but I've never quite understood why this is supposed to be a good thing. If, like me, you tend to suffer from Fear Of Missing Out, then the last thing you want is too much choice. What's the point in a city with six hundred theatres? Only a millennial would fail to realise that you can only be in one of them at any given moment. Is a lifetime enough to eat at every restaurant in London? And do you really need nineteen million neighbours, and to share a train carriage with a third of them every rush hour?

I think London is only really cool for children. At a certain age, it got me as much as it gets any other youngster: red buses with two decks, a palace with an actual queen inside, soldiers with huge bearskin hats and an endless supply of amusing names, like Piccadilly or Wapping. As a kid, you willingly believe it's full of friendly Beefeaters and posh English people drinking tea. No six-year-old could fail to love it.

Maybe that's exactly London's problem. You grow up, and you notice with dismay that the colour of everything there is actually grey. Even the red buses somehow seem monochrome. You look around and find that there are no English people drinking tea. In fact, just like in Oxford, most people seem to be speaking Spanish. You discover that the queen, quite understandably, spends most of her time at some other residence. And then melancholy seizes you, as you start to think too much about how and why a double-deck bus no longer seems the most awesome thing you can possibly imagine. You're reviled by your own jadedness.

Or maybe that's just me.

I didn't want to live in London, but I was, however, open to ideas just about anywhere else. Especially if they were in a part of the country where property was cheap. And I was going to stick to the UK on this one, if only because I knew the rules and knew the system. Plus, Europe and its economy at that time looked like a mess. In those heady pre-Brexit months, I liked the idea of my future rent money being Pound-denominated.

So I gave notice at my job - no hard feelings, just economics - and started to hunt for a new one. But - wait for it! - I wasn't going to rush into something. I needed the right salary: this was paramount for once. Given that my goal here was to get a big enough loan, location and job satisfaction were of minor importance. If I didn't find something before the lease ran out, I could always go back to Stoke Gabriel for a while. Or go travelling while I waited for the interviews to roll in.

I especially liked the latter idea. It had been a while since I'd donned my backpack, and as always I felt almost duty-bound to travel between jobs. And since I also happened to be between houses, and therefore not paying rent anywhere, I considered a trip of some description pretty much compulsory.

Then two things happened that made hitting the road an absolute no-brainer. The job I'd just quit said they'd rather like to keep my services in some capacity, and offered me the chance to work remotely for a dozen or so hours each week. It was a world-first! The dream! Work from anywhere with an

Internet connection for a regular paycheck! If it had only been something more concrete than a three-month trial, I'd have started packing my bags for Colombo.

The other great development was that I had some social travel possibilities coming up. Suz, my former housemate from Australia, was heading for Europe and keen to nose around Venice and the Dolomites for a few days in September. I hadn't been to either of those. And then I would have another cool opportunity: my Cypriot colleague Anthony had invited myself and Christopher to stay in the house his family owned in a small village outside Agia Napa.

Suddenly things had fallen into place, and I had a rough plan for the autumn. It would kick off with Venice and some North Italian mountains, followed by a three-week stint in some (hopefully) cheap former communist countries, after which I would join the guys in Cyprus. Those job offers could most definitely take their time flooding in.

Selfies with Bears

I bade an emotionless farewell to Oxford. It's difficult, after all, to fall in love with a city when you only ended up there by dint of a madwoman forcing you out of your home. And in which your first night was spent on an office floor. Nor, come to think of it, is it easy to feel comfortable in a town in which everyone is either richer than you or cleverer than you. Sometimes both.

Still, it had turned out to be a very good summer, especially considering how terribly it had begun. Over a 24-hour period, three Germans and one South African said goodbye to each other one by one. The rest slipped off westwards towards Germany, a load of life experience under their belts. I loaded up the Peugeot with more or less the same goods I'd brought in May, and took a drive in the opposite direction.

My immediate destination - again - was Stoke Gabriel. But I wouldn't stay long. The plan was to dump my stuff at my parents and book that flight to Venice. The car could stay on the driveway until I knew what my next move would be in life. The move that would take me a step closer to home ownership. The future was suddenly looking bright on all fronts.

Venice (they call it the Amsterdam of the south, I'd heard it said) and the Dolomites would take care of the first week, that much I knew. But where and how would I fill the month or so between that and meeting up with Anthony and Christopher in Cyprus? I pored over the atlas - parents still have those sorts of things - drooling onto the possibility-laden pages. What strange freedom was this remote working? It still sounded far too good to be true: all I needed was an Internet connection, a desk, and not to be too many time zones away! Wowee, where to start?

I scoured the map of Europe for somewhere that was both cheap and missing from my travel list. That meant looking towards the eastern half of the continent, where I still rather hoped one could live like a king for a hundred Pounds a month or so. Why not find a country that used the Euro, which was still languishing in a Greek-induced slump against the Pound? It seemed the perfect time to hit up such lands. I'd already been pleased to note that the Cypriots used the European Central Bank's problem child; now I just needed another enthusiastic member state to host me till I got there.

Once I'd dismissed countries I'd already visited, I was left with Lithuania, Slovakia and Slovenia as my geographically viable Eurozone options. I ruled out the former on the basis that it would be much nicer in summer. I'd visit there when there was a chance that pagans (if not pixies) might come out and jump over bonfires. And Slovakia didn't grab me much: would it really be much different from the Czech Republic?

So for perhaps the first time in my life, I had a really good look at where exactly I might find Slovenia. I'd always been a bit hazy about it, unwilling to really engage with its existence. Maybe that's because its name and its flag were so hard to distinguish from those of the aforementioned Slovakia, neither of which had existed in their own right when I first learned the countries of the world. Or maybe I just didn't want to take on the challenge of trying to pronounce the name of its capital, Ljubljana. Now, as I looked at the map, I could see that it was the first thing you got to if you went to the top of Italy - where I was starting my travels - and headed east. Also, it was shaped like a chicken.

I started reading more about Slovenia. And it turned out that Slovenia had bears. More than a few, actually. The former Yugoslav Republic had a healthy 700 or so European Browns roaming its wooded mountains. And according to the books, they'd still be awake at this time of year. I'd never seen a European bear in the wild. This was a very good reason to go to Slovenia.

It turned out, too, that Slovenia had a curious tradition of hunting for dormouse on one night of the year, and that this night would fall during my visit. Fresh from all that *Alice in Wonderland* immersion in Oxford, I was down for all things dormouse. It came as a pleasant surprise that it was a real creature, actually. The book's sleepiest character is probably the one I identify with most closely, but I'd always thought the 'dor' was an addition from Carroll, rather like the 'mock' in his rather sad turtle.

Everything about Slovenia seemed to have to do with animals. At Lake Bohinj, in the far north-west of the chicken, something called the Cow's Ball took place every year. This was an autumn celebration in which the herders brought their beasts down from the high summer pastures. And would you know it? The Cow's Ball would occur during my window too.

These sounded like proper traditional events, which had a real cultural purpose beyond than impressing tourists. My kind of thing, since for me, travel experiences ought to go beyond eating, drinking and looking at monuments.

Invite me to join the locals in actually *doing* something - dormice or no dormice - and I'm there.

If nothing else, at least the photos you get from such experiences actually capture a moment in time; something happening. And in my book, those are the pictures worth taking. Maybe this is the fault of my father having had a *National Geographic* subscription throughout my childhood, but I want to come away from my travels with the kind of pictures I used to find in those yellow-bordered magazines, the weight of which always left one or two shelves in our house teetering on the brink of collapse.

And so I've always wanted to fill my camera with wizened Nicaraguan hags resting their chins on the handles of their walking sticks and staring into their uncertain futures, blocks of graffiti-riddled concrete set against the backdrop of dysfunctional Bulgarian factories and decorated natives drinking gourds of blood in Kenya. Nature counted too, of course. Brown bears munching on their dinner would fit the bill nicely.

This kind of photo is much harder to take. Without the benefit of the long zooms the guys from the National Geographic Society presumably had, I fear camera-shy hags spotting me and threatening me with their canes. Or far worse, an offended Masai warrior coming after me with a spear. And as for bears at dinner-time, well, they come with their own set of challenges.

One way or another, these are also the kinds of pictures that will lead you to unexpected adventures. In a best-case scenario, you might be offered a free sip of blood or an invitation to the hag's church. You might equally get arrested for espionage, which did actually happen to me in Mongolia once. More often, though, you'll just make a new friend or learn something.

On the other side of the travel photography coin, there's not one part of me that understands people taking pictures of famous sights. Bring an entire tour group to, say, the Great Pyramids of Giza, and every last one of them will whip out some sort of device and start taking snaps.

What are these inspired folks thinking they're going to say when they show the folks back home? "Wait till you see this next one, Rita...*pyramids!* Pyramids in the desert! Three of 'em!"

And then poor Rita will have to do a fake 'ooh'. Because this photo, of course, is no surprise at all.

It's not that pyramids and the like aren't worthy or beautiful. That's another debate. But if you want a terrific photograph of the pyramids, chances are that a professional has done a better job at some point in history. So buy the coffee table book, or a postcard if you're on a budget. Unless there's a comet flying above the Sphinx's head, the likelihood is very slim that you and your iPhone are going to add anything to the existing body of work.

Of course, once the pyramid photos have been done, everybody then takes pictures of the great edifices with themselves in the foreground.

I'm still waiting for someone to tell me the purpose of this exercise. How exactly does my ugly mug enhance the view of a global icon? What are we trying to say with these pictures? Do we take them in case we forget we were actually there?

"Well tickle me pink, Rita, would you believe this one? That's *me* in the photograph. I must have actually *been* there! Completely slipped my mind! I must ask Desmond if he remembers."

I jest, but actually I think there might be something in that. Watch the next group of tourists at a major sight. They do the round of photographs, then they turn around and walk straight back to the bus. At less major sights, when the rest of the group is getting ahead, you'll often see them do a snap without even stopping. People fly right across the globe to see a place - and then they don't even *look* at it.

Maybe travel really is just about making people jealous. People think putting yourself in a photo is something that only began with the selfie generation, but of course it goes way back. Our parents were at it for decades.

"Oh look, there's Desmond and I. *Man*, were we happy on that trip! We were smiling like that all day long, let me tell you. Did I mention we'll be in Cancun next year?"

I can only think of one really good reason to take a smiley-couple picture while you're on a trip, and that's if you're travelling with a boy or girl who is way out of your league. It's probably not going to last, right? So capture it. And you probably *were* smiling like that the whole time. I speak from experience.

When it comes to random pictures of oneself in particular locations, I think these ought only to be allowed if you can answer the question 'Was your presence at this place an arduous achievement worth documenting?' with a hearty 'yes'. If you hiked all the way across the Sahara to reach the pyramids, I want you to have a picture. If you're standing next to a hungry bear during the shoot, you deserve the shot. If you jumped the fence and got into Stonehenge for free, be my guest and have a photo.

If, however, your only success story was getting down the steps of the bus without breaking an ankle, and then waddling across the car park, please be so kind as to get out of the frame.

But I digress. Slovenia would be my filler destination. Bears, lakes, activities and cultural events. Proper photos. And there could be no more logical a place to go after a week or so in northern Italy. I was going to go and live in Slovenia for a while. First, though, it was time for *La Serenissima.*

Gondola? Mine's a Kayak...

The moment I saw that first gondola slipping through the canals of Venice, I knew I did *not* want to see the city that way. To enjoy Venice from the water would be superb, make no mistake, but not if it meant being punted along by a bored man in a stripy shirt and silly hat. If I was going to get onto the waterways, it would be as captain of my own boat.

Trying to find a vessel in Venice is not, I think, something most visitors would dream of. But once the idea came to me, I couldn't shake trying to make it happen. Perhaps being in a city built on water had redefined the bounds of what was possible. The place had definitely grabbed me.

Yes, Venice was full of heaving crowds, but they were there for good reason. Unlike some other places I could name - Oslo springs to mind - you don't need a guidebook to tell you that the city is breathtaking and special and spellbinding. It's bleeding obviously so.

It came as a pleasant surprise to find that Venice was so big. I'd always assumed that building a city on water was a rather difficult exercise, and that they'd have retired for a good *tagliatelle* once they'd proved they could do it. But the original Venetians had more dedication than I gave them credit for. The main island is a substantial four kilometres long, and made up of a vast labyrinth of backwaters and alleyways. Which means that if you can muster a modicum of imagination, you can very easily get to places where there's no crowd at all.

And once there, you're quite likely to find actual Italians. Among my hazy preconceptions lurked one that Venice would be nothing but an open-air museum for tourists, but I was pleasantly surprised to find that people did actually live there. While the locals surely avoided St Mark's Square (which is special both for not being square and for one of its sides backing onto water) and riding the jam-packed *vaporetto* water buses wherever possible, you could spot Venetians everywhere if you took a few steps back. You'd overhear their strange-sounding dialect as they shared a miniscule espresso while standing at a cafe counter. You'd see old ladies walking about with shopping, washing hanging out of windows and Italian names on the list of residents posted beneath every building's ornate brass doorbell. You might even hear a local shamelessly practicing their opera in their living room.

And if you ignore the silly gondolas, you'll see working boats by the hundred. Cars in Venice can go no further than Piazzale Roma, where the causeway to the mainland ends and buses dump bumbling tourists by the dozen all day long. *Real* life still happens by boat here. Humble vessels that deliver sugar, take dogs for rides, bring you to your friend's place in Ghetto, and do whatever else makes the world go round.

It was noticeable that none of these workaday boats were gondolas. Which is exactly why my stomach turned at the thought of signing up for this supposedly 'Venetian' experience. Maybe ordinary locals travelled this way once upon a time (although given how impractically regal they appear to be, I have my doubts even on that), but now the only people sitting in gondolas were Indian tourists. There's no value in that for anybody, except to gondolier wallets. I can only imagine what gems the boatmen must trade on their WhatsApp group.

Giuseppe@Gondolieri ~ Hey, Luigi, just saw you out with those fat Sri Lankans. Are you crazy? They sank my boat yesterday! Get them out quick!

Luigi@Gondolieri ~ Haha, suuure they did mate! It's okay, I survived it. Bastards didn't tip though.

Enzo@Gondolieri ~ Neither did the Russian honeymooners I just took out. Probably coz the guy was holding his phone so far out over the water I just couldn't resist giving the boat a wobble...

Carlo@Gondolieri ~ Splash?

Enzo@Gondolieri ~ Haha, yeah. Six for the summer now.

Luigi@Gondolieri ~ LOL. Who's leading?

Giuseppe@Gondolieri ~ Must be @Fulvio. What you on now chap?

Fulvio@Gondolieri ~ 23.

Luigi@Gondolieri ~ Decent!!

Fulvio@Gondolieri ~ Need to up your game boys!

Enzo@Gondolieri ~ I'm gonna step up, don't worry. On another note, has anybody made up any good stories this week?

Carlo@Gondolieri ~ OMG yes!! I was telling these Americans about this ghost that lives on Rialto bridge. They believed everything haha!!

And so on.

It only took a couple of hours wandering around Venice, having all these thoughts, for the practicalities of my latest crackpot travel adventure to start taking shape in my mind. Surely I could find a boat. And in Suz, the crazy New Zealander I'd shared digs with in Sydney, I probably had the perfect partner in crime.

Suz was the sort of person who'd drag you out of bed at five in the morning to shoot pictures of sunrises on Bondi Beach. Always eager to live life and learn, she'd teach herself to make macarons and grow new plants in the garden, just because. When I'd needed someone to drive across the Nullarbor in Australia with me, she'd put up her hand immediately. She was always in a good mood, would talk to anybody and try out anything once.

"What do you think about getting a kayak?" I wondered out loud as we lingered over the first of many nondescript pasta dishes we'd be served up on this trip. (Italian cuisine has a terrific reputation around the world, but when you go to the actual country it's decidedly hit and miss. Some of the chefs could do with watching a bit of Jamie Oliver, if you ask me.)

"A kayak? I'm not sure...is that allowed? I haven't seen any around."

I shrugged. "That's the point, really. No tourist has the imagination to try and get their own boat, do they?"

"Okay, it sounds better than a gondola ride. I like the idea. But where would we find a kayak?"

"Not a clue, but I guess we could start at the tourist office."

The information centre on Piazzale Roma evidently wasn't used to handling queries for kayaks. But luckily we were served by a lady who relished a new challenge. I guess when you spend all day telling people what time the last bus to Mestre leaves, the chance to spend ten minutes phoning around about kayaks is to be savoured. More so when it gives you licence to ignore a growing queue of bus time enquiries.

"I have one possibility for a kayak," she told us after a couple of calls. "You can try this address, but it's in Mestre. It's three kilometres across the water, you know?"

I loved the way she left the possibilities hanging in the air. It was so... Mediterranean. Further north in Europe, she would have wanted to know exactly what I was planning, then launched into a hundred and one reasons why it was all illegal and impossible. Instead, she gave us a sort of good-luck cock of the head and handed us a printout with the details for *Canoa Club Mestre* on it.

We thanked her and left the building, thrilled that she'd not only given us an address for what sounded like a decidedly non-touristy canoe club, but hadn't mentioned any injunctions or bans on tourists paddling themselves around the canals of Venice. There may have been several which applied, but one got the feeling the law on this hadn't really been tested yet.

I volunteered to go over the water to Mestre and find the canoe club. Mestre is the major settlement across the causeway on the mainland. Ugly, run-down and a little squalid in places, it's where people who aren't millionaires stay when they visit uber-expensive Venice. It's where *we* were staying, that is to say. We'd bagged a room in one of many Airbnb offerings along the Via Piave drag that led up from the station. Ours was just above an optician's shop.

But I was trying to find the canoe place right now, so on this occasion I thought it would be clever to take the train towards Mestre and get off at little Porto Marghera Station. It looked a shorter walk to the canoe club harbour than Mestre Station would be. Nonetheless, it still turned out to be a bloody long way. In fact it took me the rest of the day, walking through the desperate wastelands between Mestre and the Venetian Lagoon, to get there.

When I arrived at the marina and asked around for the canoe club, it turned out to be nothing more than a wooden hut with a few incomprehensible bits of paper stuck to the outside walls. It looked very much like a place that existed solely for enthusiasts, and it was all locked up. No wonder there hadn't been a phone number on the printout.

One of the nearby boating-type people spotted me sighing, wailing and gnashing my teeth (possibly all three) and came to my aid. You won't be surprised to learn that he was wearing a white polo shirt and white shorts, had a deep tan, bright teeth and three weeks of stubble. Fortunately the guy spoke English, and explained that everyone knew everyone in the Mestre boating community. And so he was able to give me an email address for Diego, who was apparently the guy I needed.

This kayak ride was definitely going to have to happen now: I was seriously invested. As I started the long, dull trudge back towards Via Piave, I knew my knackered legs would never forgive me if I backed out now. And anyway, it did feel good to be blazing a tourist trail of my very own.

I immediately emailed Diego when I got back to the Airbnb. He politely confirmed that yes, the club did have canoes for hire. And it would only cost €40 to take a two-person boat out for a full day! The plan was coming together nicely.

We took the next day to psyche ourselves up and carbo-load for the three-kilometre paddle we were going to have to take across the lagoon just to reach the *start* of Venice and its canals. Inexperienced in such matters, neither of us had the first idea how much of an ask this actually was in a two-man kayak. But this whole adventure was about having faith in ourselves.

The one precaution we took was to leave in the early morning. This way, if it took us until lunch-time to paddle the first kilometre, there'd be time to get back before dark. We really didn't have the first clue about our performance levels.

Diego promised he would be there at the crack of dawn to issue us our boat and show us lifejacket stuff. He was and he did, although he inevitably had to pretty much dress me in my safety gear himself. (Yes, if my plane ever crashes and I have to put on one of those yellow things you just *believe* is under your seat because they tell you it's there, I'm certain that I'm more likely to drown trying to untangle befuddling buckles, toggles and pulleys than if I just start swimming.)

After that, he showed us a map of Venice that said that we weren't supposed to paddle in the Grand Canal itself. The main water thoroughfare on the fish-shaped island had a big red line around it. So there *were* a couple of rules - you just had to be a local canoeing fan to know them. And the Grand Canal thing was fine with us. We already knew that jockeying with all the brine-sloshing vaporettos that trundle up and down it would be suicide.

Diego put the canoe on a little trolley thing, gestured vaguely in the direction of the pier, and sent us on our way. We launched our little boat ourselves, gracelessly heaving it down the steps, plopping it in the calm waters of the lagoon, then gingerly lowering ourselves in. We managed not to capsize in the harbour, although in any case there was nobody about to watch us on that chilly, misty morning.

It felt odd just paddling away. We hadn't even been asked for a deposit. There was nothing to stop us taking the kayak to Albania and never returning. Nothing except the strength in our biceps, that is.

It was about faith in more ways than one. With the dense fog blanketing the Adriatic, we just had to believe Venice was out there. We could only navigate by following the causeway. The regular trains roaring along the causeway to our right were all there was to give us any assurance we weren't lost.

Clearly we were rubbish paddlers. Even before the water started to get a little choppy near Venice itself, nothing we did would stop the boat going left, in the general direction of Slovenia. Not even paddling exclusively with our left oars, it seemed, made any difference. It was really quite strange.

On the plus side, it was barely even breakfast time before we got halfway across the water. In the space of a mere half-hour the sun got up, the mist lifted the curtain on Venice and all our doubts vanished. As we twisted clumsily into the glinting Rio di San Girolamo, I welled with pride. We'd made it into the soporific Monday-morning waters of the Ghetto. Locals stopped unloading goods from their boats and stared. Then the first tourist shutter clicked. Oh, it made us feel smug all right.

What a wonderful, sun-bathed morning to be a traveller. What exhilarating freedom to glide those ancient waters, taking whatever back stream we wanted. A wonderland of weather-worn masonry, mysterious windows and colourful vessels unfurled alongside us. But the best thing, no question, is that we were masters of our own ship.

We drifted south, through the dank and secret arteries of Rialto. Best was when the sidewalks ran out and the waters snaked directly through the shadows between buildings. We snuck the wrong way up a one-way canal (Venetian waterways, like any Italian street, love a good one-way sign) to poke our noses into the Grand Canal. The traffic was scary as we expected, but we could still soak up the scene from the sidelines, clutching onto one of those barber-shop *briccola* mooring poles. We had no rope, after all, and could only guess what the parking rules might be.

Thus the relay-style refreshment stop that followed. I held onto a rusty ring on the steps beneath the Ponte San Provolo while Suz sourced a take-away plate of *chicchetti* from the little joint on the corner. Then we each ran for a welcome drink of water from the public fountain on nearby Campo San Zaccaria.

Venice does indeed offer free drinking water throughout the city, something of which I thoroughly approve. Particularly in a place that could make a killing selling the bottled stuff to bazillions of stupid tourists, among them so many British and German ones firmly convinced that all 'foreign' tap water is bound to poison them. The environmental toll this particular form of xenophobia takes in the shape of unnecessary plastic is actually quite beyond forgiveness.

Italy is a bit of a leader when it comes to the provision of public drinking fountains, although I suspect these are probably a relic of the Romans rather than the result of bold thinking by the mobs that generally run the land these days. Regardless, everywhere should follow their example. Drinking fountains are not merely reducers of plastic pollution and a boon to cash-strapped backpackers. They're an easy way to ensure that nobody, however poor, needs to go thirsty.

Humanity ought to have reached the point that anybody can access clean drinking water without needing a key to a front door. Because let's be honest, not everyone has one of those. It costs next to nothing to set up a drinking fountain...surely? For a government or a council planning their budget, it must be the equivalent of picking up a chocolate bar at the till. And if well-maintained drinking water stations for all isn't a good use of taxpayer pennies, then I really don't know what is. It'd be a pretty good spend of a company's CSR budget too, come to think of it.

While we're at it, how is it that in all but the most enlightened corners of the world, only people with 50 cents to spare have the right to access a toilet? Do the poor and homeless not have bladders? Another disgraceful shortcoming that should have been left in the Middle Ages. Okay, free toilets do attract those animals who do unspeakable things and cannot find the wherewithal to yank the flush chain, but that can't be a reason to do away with a basic right for all. By all means, let there be a pay toilet next door for those who can afford the inevitably more wholesome experience that comes with popping a coin in a slot.

Refreshed by our free Venetian drinking water, we tackled the open sea again. The *vaporetto* hub outside St Mark's made paddling a perilous game, especially as Suz had brought her iPhone with. We quickly saluted the majestic piazza, and St Theodore and his crocodile, then plunged under the Bridge of Sighs into the water alleys behind the Basilica. There, we earned a place in more Chinese holiday albums as we tried not to bash and scratch the laden gondolas coming the other way.

But although we must surely have earned a mention on the *gondolieri* WhatsApp group that day, road rage was scarce. Mostly they gave us a cheery *ciao* and smile. Only one got stuck into us, saying we simply 'weren't allowed'. Perhaps most know better than to get into an argument while they stand up on a narrow boat. One prod of my oar and he'd have been swimming.

This was the way to see Venice! I'm not sure there's ever been a time in my career as a traveller that I felt so pleased with myself. It hadn't been easy. This was nowhere to be found on Google. Nobody was handing out flyers. Kayaking in Venice probably wasn't encouraged, but it wasn't yet outlawed. And we'd made it happen! By Jove, there would have to be ice cream when we got back to shore.

We limited our explorations to the eastern and northern side of the Grand Canal, but doubtless didn't even see half the waterways before fatigue and a growing fear of sunstroke finally saw us trying to point our nose towards the open sea once more. Just after lunchtime we began heading in the right direction, at least insofar as it was possible in Venice, where you can't row in a straight line for very long at all. And that was fine. We'd had only the vaguest sense of direction all day. Losing ourselves in the water alleys, at walking pace or less, was exactly the point.

The city spat us out on the east side of the island, a little further round than where we'd entered in the morningtime. The open water was busy over here too, where speed limits fall away and all manner of boats whizz across in the direction of Murano and Burano, two other well-known islands on the archipelago.

We got our heads down and paddled through choppy wake after choppy wake. Once again, a lot of the movement was of a sideways nature. I'll never understand why we kept swinging left, but suffice to say we might have boated six kilometres rather than three by the time we got back to the mainland.

And did we take a smug photo of ourselves with Venice in the background? You bet we did!

Three Chimneys and a Sausage

There's nothing subtle about the landscape variations of Northern Italy. To stand in Venice, or Bologna or Milan is quite simply to stand in a vast plain. But look towards the north on a clear day, and you'll see the Alps or the Dolomites in the distance. These are serious mountains. Once you get into them, they don't mess about. In an hour's drive you can go from beach weather to ski weather.

It was time for us to do exactly that. While all I knew was that we were picking up a car at Marco Polo (of course!) Airport in Venice and driving up to the Dolomites, Suz had it all planned out: we were going to photograph some landscapes and stuff. I was delighted to have someone else doing the organising for a change. The last thing I want to do when travelling is bury my nose in a phone or a map, quite honestly.

I think it's nice letting things unfold. Being old enough to have crossed Siberia and Mongolia without TripAdvisor means I don't understand why everyone always likes to get their phones out just to find somewhere for lunch. I think it's okay to make a mistake or make a serendipitous discovery. But it can be fun watching them follow their little maps in different directions, like a bunch of fossickers chasing five-star gold.

"There's one 200 metres that way with 76 five-star reviews!" one of your party will announce.

"Wait, I've got one 150 metres *that* way with 53 five-star reviews!!" cries another, spinning around. "And it's vegan!"

"So the question is, are 23 additional reviews worth another 50 metres of walking time?" demands a third without a trace of irony. "What's the algorithm? Is there an app for that?"

The spontaneous joys and chance happenings of modern travel aside, it wasn't long before our little hire vehicle was looping down a winding road into the valley of Cortina d'Ampezzo. It's one of Italy's ski capitals, but today it was still engulfed in pre-season slumber. We stopped for a very quick look in an estate agent window. I wanted to get on the property ladder, let's not forget, and though I'd decided Britain was the safest course, it would be foolish to pass any half-decent place up if it had houses that were a tenth of the price. But it only took a brief squint at the display to learn that Italian ski areas were equally expensive places to buy houses. Who on earth had seven hundred and twenty-five thousand Euros, and where did they get them?

We were getting into Südtirol, which is the part of Italy where they actually speak German. Here, it was hard to imagine Venice being on the same planet, never mind a short drive away in the same country. There were no more scooters, zero boats and nothing looked old. The wooden houses were of Alpine style and the cows had bells around their necks. It would make much more sense to me if Italy stopped where the mountains begin. Because that's really where the Italians, well, stopped.

I always have a chuckle when I think about how some ancient migration of humanity from Africa to Europe must have played out. The people who would later be called Italians were the ones who looked at the mountains and said '*Mamma Mia!* Very high! Very cold! I'm staying here and drinking cappuccino! *Va bene!*'

I picture a few of the more energetic Italians deciding to push on and see what was up there. But once they got into the mountains, they started to realise that while the terrain was okay, what they really wanted to do was sing opera, eat cake and keep themselves to themselves. They turned right, and we now call these people Austrians.

In my imagination, another group managed to alienate itself from the party the moment the going got tough. They were constantly going off in huffs and wouldn't walk more than 35 hours a week. They seemed to find life very depressing, and loved writing about how bad everything was up in the mountains.

'Fine! Turn left and go down!' the others would have said. 'We'll be better off without you. You can strike to your heart's content down there.'

And so France was born.

Then there were the people who were in charge of finances for the mission. They looked after everybody's money, and grew to like doing that. When they got to the very middle of the mountains, they said, 'what a fine place to look after money!' and decided to stay put. They didn't stop anybody else from moving on, but were happy to let them leave some savings behind, just in case they might be passing through again. They learned three languages, so that people from anywhere could bring them money. These people became the Swiss.

But there was still one more group of travellers left. They were wearing t-shirts at the top of the highest mountain, and smiling about it. They weren't interested in banking or opera. They were an industrious lot, and they wanted to build factories. 'Look! Down zere to ze north! Ze land gets flat! Vi can build everysing there!'

And off they went. I like to think that's how Germany began.

I have these reveries every time I get to the fringes of the mountains that sit in the middle of Europe. Probably because the thought of travelling through them in pre-automotive times is about as scary as the peaks are beautiful.

The wild and special Dolomites were shattering my long-held assumption that all European mountains more or less looked the same. Some of the peaks seem to be made of just one rock, like menhirs misplaced by Obelix. They were jagged and angular, like a particularly wild day's stock prices outlined against the sky. If you've ever wondered what it must feel like for a fly to land on a particularly spiky tray of meringue, hike up towards the Tre Cime di Lavaredo from Lake Misurina and take in the panorama from the Rifugio Antonio Locatelli.

The Tre Cime are infinitely worth huffing and puffing your way up to what cannot be far away from the top of the world. The 'three chimneys' (it doesn't really work in English, does it?) are three gigantic slabs of rock, broadly resembling mutant asparagus tips. You don't have a hope of seeing them from roads way down below: these are mountains on top of mountains, leaning out over their own private valley. It feels like a secret place, even though it's not.

The Tre Cime actually have their own mountain hut, where you can do things like order hot soup and be slightly less freezing than you'd be outside. The Rifugio Locatelli commands a perfect view of three peaks from a suitably respectable distance, and we made it our home for three days of hiking, tracking skittish mountain goats (with some success, I might add), making giant cat-shaped artwork out of the rocks strewn on the valley floor, poking about in caves, shivering our way through snowy dawn and sunset photo shoots and sometimes just huddling in our sleeping bags.

"Hey, do you remember locking the car?" asked Suz during one of those sleeping-bag moments, without so much as a word of warning.

"I don't remember anything anymore," I replied. "I'm thirty-five."

It was true. How I'd crammed so much into my head for school exams was becoming an increasing source of mystery. There didn't seem to be room for anything much left in my head these days. Least of all short-term recollections.

"Well, if we forgot, there's not much we can do about it. We can't even see it from up here."

"Yeah, and if we did see robbers cleaning it out, I think they'd be long gone by the time we hiked down the mountain."

Suz laughed. "Yeah, how long did it take us? Three hours?"

"Something like that. We're at, what, three thousand metres? It's painted on the wall outside, but obviously I can't remember the exact number either."

"2450 metres above sea level to be precise," said Suz, flicking through her camera to find the picture she'd taken of the hut. "I'm sure we're just being paranoid about locking the car...right?"

"She'll be right," I said, trying to reassure my Antipodean companion with one of my favourite Aussie expressions, before ruining it all by adding. "And anyway, it's not like Italy has a lot of car theft or anything, right?"

"Or that we left our laptops in the car, eh?" said the Kiwi with a chuckle.

Just to be clear on this, we'd left our laptops in the car. And all of a sudden we both had reservations.

We hurried down to the valley a little faster than we otherwise might have the next morning, approaching our rented Kia with more than a touch of trepidation. But all was well: not only had we locked the bloody thing after all, but nobody had seen fit to smash a window either.

We decided to celebrate our successful hike and unmolested car with lunch in Austria. I thought it would be neat to drive over the Brenner Pass for a beer and a *bratwurst*, just because, and then turn back around into pasta-land. I'd done many a dramatic serpentine switchback up the Alps along the border between Italy and Switzerland - the Spluga, the Bernina, the Stelvio - but the Brenner still needed to be ticked from the list.

I'd heard a lot about the Brenner Pass, which always sounded so impressive in travel literature. Even a line as simple as '...*and then we drove our campervan south into Italy, over the Brenner Pass...*' evokes some kind of majestic experience in a way that other passes somehow don't.

It had to be down to the uncompromisingly Teutonic name for the thing, which conjured up fire, brimstone and engineering brilliance. The Brenner connected two countries and a brace of languages, but the name left no room for doubt as to which set of opera singers had constructed it. This was surely Austria proving they could be as industrious as the Germans, should they put their minds to it. Not that I knew much about Austria at all just yet.

A miracle of roadwork the Brenner Pass may be, but the experience left me cold. It's not a pass at all. It's just a big long stretch of highway on stilts, and at no point does the might suggested by its name actually hit you in reality. We had our *Würstl* in a small guest house at the foot of one of the stilts.

"It's not any more impressive from this angle either, is it?" I remarked glumly as I took a slug of beer. A beverage I don't even like, by the way. It just seems culturally irresponsible to eat a sausage in Austria without a beer and a dollop of mustard, which I don't like either.

"Nope. Let's eat our sausage and head to Bolzano!"

"Say that again!"

"Bowl-ZAAAH-noh?" she obliged haltingly, giving me another chance to laugh at her Kiwi-Aussie hybrid accent, this time with rising intonation thrown in.

Bolzano was another place I'd heard of, but this time not from travel books. I actually remembered its name from listening to *Sports Roundup* on the BBC World Service when I was a kid. Why? Because Bolzano had an annual athletics meeting - perhaps it still did - from which the reporters would always bang on about the long-jump and javelin records that were bound to be shattered in its unusually high altitude.

Two decades had passed since I'd last heard mention of Bolzano, during which time I assumed performance-enhancing drugs had become a far more relevant factor in record-breaking than anything else. Still, it was another name to which I wanted to put a face, as it were.

We parked in a charming multi-storey and spent a pleasant couple of hours walking around the city, which was in a festive mood that particular Saturday evening. On a stage in the main square a performance of distinctly Germanic traditional music was going on. The accordions and yodelling came as no surprise as all. We were still in Südtirol, after all.

I didn't see any pole-vaulters wandering the streets, but I did see some refugees huddled in a park on the banks of the river. Autumn 2015, of course, was the height of the migrant influx to Europe, with which I would shortly cross paths. I wondered how they'd gotten to a place as obscure as Bolzano. Maybe one of their number was a star athlete, just waiting to shatter a discus throw record and change his life forever. At any rate, they were all top walkers to have gotten this far.

As it so happened, we weren't exactly sure where we were going to sleep that night either. In 24 hours we were booked in to stay three nights with a CouchSurfing hostess in Portogruaro, all the way down on that warm coastal plain. For tonight, I was also quite keen to save on accommodation. If we drove a little further south, out of the chilly mountains, I would be more than willing to sleep in the car.

Sleeping in the hire car at least once on any given trip is something of a ritual for me. I've done it everywhere from residential streets in Perpignan to a parking lot at Imola race track to a farm gate near Tokyo Airport.

Granted, reclining the front seat of an 'economy' rental car may not always be the most comfortable option for nodding off. But if you're on a budget and you've got to choose between a hire car and a hotel bed, it's a no-brainer. You can sleep in a car, as I always say, but you can't drive a hotel.

Nowadays, the truth is that I really *can* afford a hotel bed. Even when I'm unemployed, as I technically was that night, I've got savings, although these are largely amassed, it must be said, from doing things like sleeping in cars. Perhaps the main reason I still liked to do it from time to time, apart from adding to my house deposit fund, was a simple refusal to get old. Give up the adrenaline rush that comes with beating the system, call time on youthful rebelliousness, and you admit that you're all grown up. And that's intolerable to me.

And yes, you can be sure that the system doesn't want you sleeping in cars. Not that I can fathom any reason why, apart from a general fetish for controlling tearaway elements of the population. In my experience this anti-car-sleeping lobby is a first-world thing. In a poor country, everybody understands the simple logic of a traveller sleeping in their vehicle. In rich countries, a person sleeping in a car is something for police with nothing better to do to pick on.

A sleeping person is *by definition* no threat to society. They are, after all, sound asleep. How could anybody be offended by it? What possible reason can there be for officialdom to feel the need to come along and rattle the cage? And yet they'll do exactly that. I'm not kidding when I tell you that a Dutch policeman once woke me up and said that what I was doing was *illegal*. He told me I should 'get a hotel next time'. I told him that I'd spent my last cash on hiring the car, so if he was so desperate for me to sleep indoors, he could pay for this 'hotel room' he was so keen for me to have. Or at least let me use his sleeper couch.

Okay, I didn't quite word it like that. But I hope you can see how silly it all is.

Over in Australia, where the rules on this are apparently similar, the ridiculousness climbs to impressive new levels. Here is a country where people drive vast distances along roads that have no corners to keep you awake. The authorities run costly campaigns about how you should take breaks, drink coffee and generally avoid causing mayhem by falling asleep at the wheel. Even without an ad campaign to help you, you surely know that the most responsible thing you can do when your eyelids droop on the highway is to pull over, and, if necessary, let that nap happen.

Are they going to lock you up for taking this life-saving course of action? You'd like to think not. Making it illegal to sleep borders on psychopathic, after all. And yet, at some hazy point, taking an accident-preventing snooze turns to 'overnighting in your car' and goes from being a solid-citizen move to a crime. Come on, what's the bloody *difference*? This is true stuff, I'm not making it up. And the only good it does is give people like me something laughable to write about.

Who decides if a bleary-eyed motorist sitting in a darkened lay-by in the barely-inhabited depths of Western Australia is a responsible citizen heeding the call of sleep or some scum avoiding paying for a campsite? When exactly does a power nap turn into casual, gratuitous sleeping? Is it allowed to be drowsy by day but not by night? Are there actually guidelines on this stuff in the police handbook?

Imagine two bored officers on patrol 120 kilometres north of Meekatharra, WA. Shortly before dawn, they pull up in a parking area behind a silent Holden. They see the driver is asleep and start the clock ticking. 'Mate, what's the stopwatch say now? Seventeen minutes! Right, the moment it hits 26 minutes, we bust him for sleeping rough. Whaddya reckon?'

'Not sure mate, sun comes up in three. Then it's daylight. Then he's not overnighting.'

'Bloody oath! If he'd been a few minutes earlier we'd have locked him up and thrown away the key!'

'Too right...'

Clearly some parts of the world have taken leave of their senses. But the good news is that it's pretty hard to actually get 'caught' committing this terrible felony. Holland was the only time I've had a policeman shine a torch in my face, exposing my dark secret. Choose a sensible spot, and you'll be fine.

And luckily, in Suz, I had one of very few travel companions I can think of who'd go along with a spot of car-sleeping. As one gets older, one notices fewer and fewer friends who will seriously consider this kind of adventure.

So we drove down to a dark place (at least by night) called Lago di Levico, found a shadowy piece of car park just around the corner from what sounded like a gigantic party going on next to a lake. We briefly thought about trying to join in on festivities at what we later discovered was an establishment called *Big Fish*, but were knackered beyond words. Which is exactly what you want to be if you're proposing to sleep reasonably well in the front seat of a small rental car. It's like trying to get shut-eye on a plane: if you have any traces of energy left in your system, you're probably in for a long night.

Next morning we woke up to a message from our would-be CouchSurfing host, whose parents had apparently gone cold on the idea of two strangers from Planet Internet descending on their home. The risk-aversion of age in action once more.

Disappointing though it was to lose out on the experience of Italian home life and three nights of free accommodation, it wasn't the end of the world. Sleeping in cars was out of the question now, what with my week-long holiday ending today. In the morning I would excitedly start life as a Skype-addicted, latte-sipping remote worker. I would need a chair, a desk and a solid connection to the world wide web. (Does anybody say that anymore? Even its lovechild, the good old www, seems to be slowly becoming redundant in everyday language.)

By now I'd booked myself lodgings in Ljubljana, so it was just a case of finding an alternative for three days in northern Italy. After that, Suz and I would go our separate ways, in search of places we hadn't been before. Having visited the Slovenian capital on a previous trip, she'd head off to Budapest, where I'd been just a few months earlier with Monique.

We didn't particularly need to be in Venice or its surrounds. For no better reason than the existence of a good deal on Booking.com, we settled on Treviso, a small but charming enough town between the mountains and the famed city on water.

Our digs, run by a Filipino lady, lay a few minutes out of the city centre. It overlooked a *piazza* and an ancient church. In any other country, the church would probably have made it into the *Lonely Planet*. But this being Italy, where there were even more interesting churches and squares just down the road, this clearly wasn't considered a special location. But the view from my desk had improved immeasurably since my last day at the office. Although granted, it didn't take much to outdo the sight of somebody's back, a printer and a coat-stand.

Speaking of work (a terrible subject, I know), it was also during my time in Treviso that I had a phone interview for a sports marketing job back in the UK. Much to my disappointment, it went well. A large part of me wanted to fail miserably at the job hunt, so that I could keep on remote-working wherever I liked. My savings weren't going to run out any time soon, after all.

Treviso also suffered from the glut of magnificence surrounding it, by which I mean it would be far more famous if it were in another country. It was a perfectly lovely little town, albeit one with a curious abundance of Benetton outlets. I quickly realised this was because the fashion company had been founded here. And given that I'd been madly in love with the Benetton Formula 1 team when I was a lad, Treviso was a happy place for me. It didn't hurt, either, that this was one of those curious pockets of Italy where rugby was a big deal. As a South African, I've always got a little more time for places that appreciate the game.

After three uneventful days in which email once again became a part of my life, Suz and I bid our farewells. I now knew for sure that she was a top-tier travel buddy. She'd been willing to paddle kayaks and sleep in cars, never assumed I could afford things without asking (travel pet hate number one, right there!) and most importantly participated in developing a multitude of in-jokes that (sadly) wouldn't make any sense in these pages. It was sad to part, especially as I didn't know when our paths might cross again. Sydney was more than a fair distance away.

On Wednesday, after my two-and-a-half hours of work were done in the morning, it was time to get out of Italy and head over to what sounded like the best country in Europe. Armed with the usual solid advice from *The Man in Seat 61*, that treasure trove of train travel information that was to be found on the www, I hopped on one of the many trains running along the Venice to Trieste line. From the grand old station in the seaside city that's changed hands so many times, I walked a few blocks to catch the odd little wooden funicular which for the price of two espressos will take you up the steep hill to Villa Opicina.

And when the little toy train dropped me off on the plateau above Trieste, I was almost in Slovenia. Trieste had looked interesting and I vowed to return, but right now I needed to catch the train that would get me to my next destination by nightfall. I just had to walk down the road to the sleepy station, where I jumped aboard a stumpy, graffiti-covered train to Ljubljana.

Winner Winner, Chicken Dinner

Slovenia didn't disappoint in any respect. It really did turn out to be Europe's best-kept secret. It might look like a chicken on the map, but spend a couple of weekends driving around and you'll find it's got far more going for it than an amusing shape. It's got soaring mountains, storybook meadows, bear-filled forests, shimmering lakes, fascinating caves and even a small stretch of coastline. And it's a far safer place than New Guinea, the planet's other bird-shaped country.

I'm not sure it's any exaggeration to say that all of Slovenia is pristine. I'm not sure they even know what rubbish is. Even in the centre of Ljubljana, the streets are spotless and the air is fresh. Although it's a small country with its fair share of people crammed in, it felt like a place where harmony with nature has truly been achieved. I was quite smitten.

Do you like the idea of opening a tap to find your glass filling up with wine? Go to Slovenia. And take lots of empty bottles, because this is the land of getting things from taps. I'm not sure how many free water fountains there are, but the supermarket wine dispensers and the wonderful milk machines that stand on street corners more than make up for them.

While I can take or leave wine, I've always been an enthusiastic milk drinker. So I nearly melted when I heard about these *mlekomats* that gave out what Slovenians called 'raw' milk. Apparently untreated in any respect, the stuff was very tasty. Which, having seen the countryside, didn't surprise me at all. I very much liked the idea that the milk machine in the centre of Ljubljana was directly connected, via a series of underground pipes, to some hard-working cow in the mountains.

Apart from that little bit of coast, where the Italian links are clear to see in the terracotta and *campaniles* that decorate the towns, Slovenia feels more like Austria or Bavaria than a piece of former Yugoslavia. Little onion-dome churches sit on hills, buses run on time, everything feels safe and people are reserved. Beer is the drink of choice, and everyone goes to the sauna naked.

In the summer of 1991, as other parts of Yugoslavia headed for bloody times, Slovenia secured its independence after just ten days of battle. Entirely fitting, to my mind. I imagine that the whole Yugoslav experience must have been an annoyance for the Slovenes, really. This northernmost of the republics must have felt like the studious elder brother, patiently trying to go about its Mittel European business in orderly fashion while hothead younger siblings squabbled endlessly about religion and what-have-you in the rooms downstairs.

Slovenia was my first introduction to proper seasons. How refreshing it was to enjoy a real autumn! The leaves were psychedelic orange, the nights were drawing in and the mornings were chilly, but when the sun was out you could walk about in shorts and perhaps a light jumper. It was fall as it should be, and I was surprised how happy a small thing like that made me.

England, you see, doesn't really *do* seasons. Winter rarely gets cold enough to snow, and summer isn't reliably hot for any length of time. There's certainly no spring or autumn. It's always sunny until ten in the morning, then nine times out of ten it clouds over till sunset. Most of the year sort of averages out to a damp grey, which is good neither for ice-skating and snowball fights, nor for swimming and picnics. That's why the English have to watch so much telly.

Ljubljana was really small. My budget lodgings were in the last street in the south of the city. If you went too far down the garden path, you'd end up on the orbital highway. And yet walking to the cute city centre, with its modest castle and its dragon statues, was nothing more than a pleasant stroll.

Although the area felt perfectly peaceful to me (granted, I am South African, so anywhere else feels safe) apparently it was considered by locals to be a relatively undesirable sort of suburb. "Bosnians," somebody whispered to me conspiratorially when I told them where I'd be getting off the bus. Slovenia, I gathered, was something of a promised land for work-seekers from those troubled siblings further south.

But it was surely thanks to people like Bosnians that Turkish-style coffee is a thing in Slovenia. It's the northernmost place in Europe that boiling up fine grounds in a special stovetop pot won't get you a funny look. Without Yugoslavia, I somehow doubt that the old lady renting my Airbnb would have left me a traditional *džezva* rather than a kettle. I quickly learned to enjoy the process of making a black, uncompromising, gritty Turkish coffee. It's a labour of love - powders, bubbling, stirring - that takes one back to the pleasures having a chemistry set.

And just like that perfectly autumnal autumn, this Balkan brew gave me a real sense of place. To this day, the smell of Turkish coffee takes me back to those bright Ljubljana mornings, when sunbeams streamed through the open door and onto my desk. To a time when I lived and worked (and did a second interview with the sports marketing agency over Skype) in Slovenia.

While my choice of country could not be faulted, Slovenia was a failure when it came to being cheap. Prices for everything else seemed pretty comparable to the rest of the Eurozone. (I wanted to tell them that they didn't have to try to be Germans in this regard.) The one exception was accommodation: I had a roof over my head for just a few Euros a night. And that, of course, is always the biggie.

While the country proved to be almost everything I wanted it to be, the big experiences that drew me here weren't quite what I expected them to be. First of all, I'd somehow got the date wrong on the dormouse thing. Or it had been cancelled due to the dormouse being ill. I forget the details now, but there was ultimately no dormouse tea party for me on that particular trip.

I did, however, get to see a real, live *medved*, or European Brown Bear. It wasn't too challenging, actually. I just got hold of the sleepy but helpful tourist office in a small town in the bear-ridden south, which put me in touch with a local hunter who would escort me to bear territory at dusk. The old boy didn't speak any English, but his socially awkward teenage son, who did, also joined the expedition. We jumped into their Jeep and thundered up into the tree-blanketed hillsides. Then we started walking.

First stop was what looked like a multi-coloured wooden caravan, full of little letterboxes. Decked out in sunshine yellow, brilliant blue and blinding red, it looked like something Dr Willy Wonka might have used as a mobile chocolate shop. But then I learned that it was actually a typical Slovenian beekeeping unit.

"These are all hives," said the son, walking around to the locked entrance. "And look, you can see that a bear has been here."

"Look where?"

"These scratches," he said expressionlessly, pointing at the long claw marks all around the wooden doorway. "He was trying to get in. To get the honey."

"Really? Bears *actually* go crazy for honey?"

"Yes, of course."

"Seriously?" I was floored. "That's brilliant! I always assumed that was just something AA Milne made up for Winnie the Pooh."

"Oh no," he said. "Bears, they really love honey. They're always trying to get in here."

Learning that all the cartoons were true pretty much made my day. I wasn't sure that actually seeing a bear would be as good as learning this fact.

And in truth, it wasn't. We climbed up into a small hide that stood on very big stilts and looked out over a decidedly artificial clearing in the forest. There was an automated machine that dispensed corn, which bears also love, apparently. There was concrete and wood and various other bits of man-made paraphernalia. Yes, a bear or two did come for a feed and a poke around, but the place felt rather like a zoo without fences.

Okay, such an arrangement did give me the best possible chance of a bear sighting. And when I'd paid good money and hired a car especially to get there, a bear sighting was a good thing. But ever since my youthful visits to Kruger National Park in South Africa, I've always felt that spotting animals in the wild should involve allowing Lady Luck to deal you that leopard kill. Sometimes you see nothing, but that's part of experiencing nature's fickleness. Therein lies the fun of *not* being at a zoo.

The best part, for me, was when the bears had left the clearing and we climbed out of the hide. We weren't exactly sure how far they had wandered off. Or at least I wasn't. So the moment my shoes touched the ground and I was down on their level, I felt that little bit more connected to the experience.

"He's over there," said the son, who'd obviously never lost track of our ursine friend. "Here, shine the torch into the trees. You'll see the eyes."

"You're sure? You want me to shine the torch into the bear's eyes?"

It didn't sound like a good idea to me. Wasn't that supposed to be a red flag to wild animals? I wouldn't like you if you shined a torch in *my* eyes. And right now, at a distance of perhaps thirty metres, I very much wanted this bear to like me. Even if there was a man with a gun in our party. What if he'd forgotten to load it?

"Yes, the bear doesn't care. You will see."

I swung the torch beam among the tree trunks. Then, two eerie specks of bright green. Looking right at me. A strange moment of communion between man and bear. I wondered what the animal was thinking.

We left him to his forest and walked on towards the Jeep. And I wondered just how many more bears we might be passing as we went.

I was surprised when the hunters suggested grabbing a bite to eat in the town. They'd not seemed like chatty types, and I'd rather assumed that they couldn't wait to be rid of yet another boring bear tourist. The suspicious part of me wondered if this was some kind of Chinese-style scam where I ended up paying the entire bill. But I went with it.

We landed up in a guest house, where I devoured something resembling a Viennese *Schnitzel*. The historic photos on the wall featured mostly local landscapes, and it was remarkable to see how different these hillsides had looked back in the black-and-white days. No bear could have hidden in the forest back then, because there wasn't any. We're always being told about deforestation and destruction, but these photos suggested people in the old days were much more cruel to trees. In Slovenia, as in so much of an increasingly urbanized Europe, nature is actually crowding in on us once again. It's terrific news for the wildlife trying to make a comeback.

Having planned to be out of Ljubljana for the whole weekend, I'd checked out of my lodgings there in order to save money. After all, I had a car to sleep in! But, as I've often found to be the case when I mention sleeping in cars, I didn't end up needing to do so.

"Do you have a hotel here?" asked the son.

"Er, no," I replied, cautiously optimistic as I always am when I have this particular conversation. "I'm planning to sleep in the car."

"I see," the son responded. His face gave nothing away.

He exchanged some words in Slovenian with his father. I hoped he wasn't a policeman in disguise. They probably didn't have much real crime around here. A car-sleeper would constitute major excitement on a Saturday night.

"You know, it's very comfortable," I added brightly, not wanting them to feel obliged to offer me a better alternative. "I've done it plenty of times. And I have my sleeping bag."

"My father says, you can sleep at our house," said the son.

I hoped it wasn't a euphemism for them making a bit of extra cash by renting me a room for the night. Things like that can get lost in translation, and the next thing you know you're being presented with an invoice on checkout. If that was the offer, I'd happily stick with the car.

But, since by this stage we'd all paid our own shares of the bill, I was feeling slightly less cynical. All the same, we weren't exactly chatting away like merry old things. I couldn't understand why they kept wanting to extend our time together. I didn't feel like I was bringing anything much to their evening.

"Well, I don't have money for tonight..." I said awkwardly. "The car is really fine."

They conferred in Slovenian once more.

"My father says, no problem," said the son, naturally without the smile one usually gets alongside that particular phrase.

I wasn't sure exactly what that meant either. It was possible, I supposed, that they really had been proposing selling me a room, and that now they felt bad about it. I'll never really know, but I did end up sleeping there, *sans* invoice at breakfast time.

They didn't make me drink Slovenian hard tack either. Actually they didn't make me drink anything at all. The only interesting thing that happened was that the son showed me the collection of reptiles he kept in his room. It was the first time I'd ever knowingly gone to sleep with a snake in the same house.

His room was massive. So was the entire house, actually. Slovenians, like most ex-Yugoslavian cultures, appeared to be great believers in the extended family living together, and their dwellings were designed accordingly. In Ljubljana as in the countryside, you'd find plenty of homes in which three generations lived - albeit often with their own floors or apartments.

I started to think these people were onto something. In England, the accepted practice for people my age was to fret about a house deposit and then, with luck, be a slave to a mortgage for 25 or 30 years, during which time you paid thousands of Pounds in interest. This is exactly where I was in life. Didn't it make a lot more sense simply to accept living in the same house your grandparents and parents did, and then let your kids live in it too? Of course it did: no-brainer!

I wondered where and when we in other parts of the world had lost sight of this obviously better way of doing things. It was relatively new, this idea that you could live without your folks breathing down your neck, and that you were somehow selfish or a momma's boy if you choose to do so. Maybe it was the fact that in more cramped places, you couldn't really *have* a house that big. Look at Holland. You were doing well if your 'house' wasn't glued onto that of a neighbour on both sides. Forget about swinging cats - you couldn't perform so much as a sun salute without bashing into the furniture. And if you were fortunate enough to have a garden, you could write off any aspirations of having a decent cricket match in it.

Then again, it might have been chicken and egg. Wasn't all this squeezing and squashing as much to do with every kid wanting their own place as anything else? As I walked about Slovenia and looked at these enormous houses, with their productive-looking vegetable patches and grandmothers hanging out washing, I began to understand some of what people meant when they talked about 'the destruction of the family unit'. The near-impossibility of home ownership in 'the west' was perhaps the price we were paying for our self-centred, individualist thinking.

Maybe it wasn't so bad, after all, if one person went to work, another did the washing and someone else looked after the vegetables or the kids. When parents in London told me it was cheaper to not work than to pay for 'daycare' for their offspring, I wondered if economics was trying to tell us something about the way we assumed we *ought* to be living.

And maybe my big plan to get my own place was just completely misguided. Perhaps what I should have been doing was moving in with my parents.

Because everything's so *right* there, Slovenia had exactly this way of making you ponder about what was wrong with the world. I mean, the country had completely failed to make a mess of its natural charms. If I had to drink unprocessed water from a substantial body of water anywhere in Europe, I think I would choose Lake Bohinj, fed as it is by startlingly blue streams gushing down from the Julian Alps. It's a magnificent place from any angle, whether you're at ground level looking at the mountain peaks shimmering their reflections in the lake, or taking in the vista from a giddy 1533 metres after riding the cable car up to the Vogel ski station.

It was to Bohinj that I took a train and bus for the Cow's Ball, another experience that turned out a little different from expected. It was somewhat more stage-managed than I'd imagined, and wasn't actually a case of all the cows flooding down into the valley at once. It was more about dressing up in traditional outfits that looked pretty Swiss to me, leading a few symbolic cows into a large field with a beer tent and various stalls selling local crafts, and then getting drunk in the sun.

Not that it was a bad day at all. The air was warm, the folk music was good and the cows were in good spirits. Plus I visited a marvellous waterfall. The Slovenian word for which - fun fact, I know - is *slap*. I hitch-hiked back to Ljubljana. Mainly just because I could.

But it was time to start thinking about Cyprus. Halfway through my stay in Slovenia, I'd found a cheap flight to Larnaca. Not from Ljubljana - that would have been far too simple - but from Belgrade.

Digital nomad that I was, crossing two borders to catch a flight didn't much bother me. It would be good to return to the heaving hodge-podge that was the Serbian capital once again. Having visited a decade or so earlier, I knew Belgrade would be a world apart from steady, quiet Ljubljana. And it was only an overnight train ride away.

Hot Horses, Cheap Digs and the Joys of Low-Cost Flying

Belgrade was not, it turned out, a simple train ride away after all. I'd bought a ticket suggesting it would be, but then the refugee crisis changed everything. Countries all over the region were closing borders. Regular routes, including my €15 train to Belgrade, were being suspended like wildfire.

From what I could gather, only a couple of hundred refugees were actually gathered in Slovenia. Most people who arrived here, it seemed, wanted to press on to Germany or Britain as quickly as possible. This didn't make immediate sense to me. Slovenia was surely a very nice place to claim asylum - I'd trade it for Britain in a heartbeat - but there you go. Nonetheless, Slovenia was playing its part in making things tough for anyone heading north.

The tightening of controls was also introducing curveballs for the forgotten few who were heading south. People like me, who were just trying to go about their backpacking trips without a fuss. The train was out for the foreseeable future. But I could still get a bus to Belgrade.

I wasn't particularly looking forward to the journey. Buses are down at the bottom of my list of preferred modes of transport, only a short nose ahead of flying. Trains are just better. I like just about everything about train travel - the big windows, the space, the reliable timetables and the possibility of actually lying down when you want to sleep.

But on this occasion the bus was the best option I had. Worse yet, the journey was to take place entirely during the hours of darkness, which meant that I wasn't going to be able to look at any of Croatia or Serbia. The only thing to do would be trying to force myself to sleep. And that almost never works.

I fortified myself with one last experience that had been on my list ever since arriving in Ljubljana: eating a horse. I don't mean I was really hungry and wanted to gobble down a fat pile of food. I mean *literally* eating a horse. For Slovenians, it was a thing. In Tivoli park in the middle of Ljubljana, there was a place that quite shamelessly sold horse-meat burgers. And with a name as marvellous as Hot Horse, I simply had to try it.

Interestingly, that burger was no better or worse than the typical half-pounder you'd get in a kebab shop on any high street in England. I will go so far as to say it tasted identical. Whether that offers any insights into the meat they were using in Britain, I couldn't possibly say.

Then it was time to head for the bus to Belgrade. I wearily walked down past the gigantic Union Brewery and found my coach, which was a pretty straightforward business at the quaint little transport hub that is Ljubljana Bus and Train Station.

I selected a seat in the back row - that prized one in the middle that lets you use the aisle legroom. Then, to my great surprise, I closed my eyes and slept pretty much the whole way to Belgrade. Perhaps it was something in the horse burger.

The only times I had to stir was when crossing borders. First the Croatian frontier at about midnight, and then, at a time Roald Dahl would surely have described as 'the witching hour', the gateway to Serbia.

Both of these involved getting off the bus and presenting one's papers to a suitably grumpy female officer. Both were seated in tiny booths set beneath marvellously socialist concrete canopies. It was actually quite an exciting novelty to pass through a real border in Europe, especially if one of them involved uniforms with Cyrillic letters on them - Serbia in this case. If I hadn't been wrenched out of my slumber to dopily complete the formalities, I would have found it rather invigorating.

It was finally daylight when we arrived in Belgrade. The first thing I saw when I got off the bus was a refugee camp that took up the entire square in front of the station.

Until that moment, one of human history's biggest migrations had for me just been something that happened on television and ruined my travel plans. Not any more. I do believe it was the first time I'd seen a UNHCR site with my own eyes.

It put my personal quest to get on the property ladder somewhat in perspective. But then, as most of us end up doing, I turned away and got on with the next thing I had to do in my own life.

This meant trudging up the hill towards the city, seeking my digs. As usual upon arrival in a new place, I stubbornly eschewed using public transport. Partly because I like to get my bearings on foot, partly because bus drivers never speak English and are always terribly grumpy with mutes trying to buy tickets without knowing exactly where they want to go, and partly because I always fear I'll make a snap decision about whether I should buy some kind of daily or weekly bus pass rather than a single. You need to feel the lay of the land before you can assess a serious investment like that.

My first few minutes slogging up the slope were enough to tell me that Belgrade was much as I remembered it from my last visit: a jumble. It remained an exaggerated caricature of a city thrown together with no plan and no architects. Nowhere could you hope to see such a scattergun collection of construction creations as in Belgrade. Imagine what would happen if you told a child to build a street full of medium-sized apartments and houses with all the lego pieces nobody else used, and you'll have some idea of how it looked.

The time-warp vibe hadn't gone anywhere either. TV aerials dating from long before satellite protruded from a jagged line-up of roofs. The oldest of old-school trolley buses still plied streets lined with kiosk after kiosk, mostly selling Serbian staples *burek* and *cevapcici*. Buildings limped on with bomb damage from those NATO air strikes back in the nineties. A gritty, crowded riverside city where nobody laughed at weirdness or dilapidation, Belgrade was like Europe's answer to Varanasi. Just like that gaudy city on the Ganges, Serbia's capital most assuredly did not look like anywhere else on the planet.

Given its medieval fort overlooking the confluence of the mighty Danube and the only slightly-less-mighty Sava, Belgrade could never have become anything but mighty. This was certainly the obvious place from which to run a country like Yugoslavia, made as it was out of several smaller nations that didn't always get on terribly well. And even though that union was long since dissolved, the former seat of power still exuded the same socialist-imperial might I'd also sensed on visits to Moscow. If I was in a schoolyard with Zagreb, Sarajevo, Skopje, Podgorica, Ljubljana and Belgrade, I know which one I wouldn't pick a fight with.

The authoritarian vibe may have had something to do with the use of the traditional Cyrillic script in official places. As I passed government buildings, statues and schools, I was reminded of the curious double-alphabet thing Serbia did. Anything governmental, social or commemorative was written in the faintly threatening alphabet the Serbs shared with the Russians, Bulgarians, Belarusians, Ukrainians and Macedonians. Meanwhile the young were gaily doing their everyday business in Roman letters. Which annoyed me, because I'd gone to the trouble of learning to read Cyrillic. I hate wasting my time.

I was sweaty and aching (backpacks never failed to bestow these twin delights upon my body, no matter how willing my mind was) by the time I reached my Airbnb accommodation. It cost all of seven Pounds a night to have my own apartment within a typical architecturally twisted family compound. It seemed Belgrade remained an oasis of genuine all-round cheapness. When the weekend came around, and I went out for a cycle with my friendly hostess Iva and her lovely friend Sonja, I bought drinks in a nice, Bohemian part of town. Three beers for three Pounds. Somebody tell the lads! Even I didn't mind buying rounds in Belgrade.

I was pleased that Serbia's crazy-low prices were still alive and well. If you were a remote-working freelancer, a cash-strapped student or even just wanted to experience one of the last places that still genuinely deserved to be called dirt-cheap, Serbia was a fine option: proudly non-European Union, non-Schengen, non-Euro...non-pretty-much-everything. If you were from just about any other economic jurisdiction in Europe, you could probably stuff a pillow-case with Serb Dinars and spend less of your home currency than you would on a new pillow.

Yet despite being the bargain that it was, I hardly knew anybody who'd been to Serbia at all. Maybe they thought there was still a war going on (there wasn't), or maybe, being a landlocked country, they didn't countenance it. But Belgrade *did* have a beach. A really long one, with plenty of cheap food and drink to hand. You only had to head to Ada Island - literally made for recreation on the Sava - to enjoy your holiday sand quota, with the bonus of fresh-water swimming. And summer is more reliably hot and windless here than at the seaside.

I really liked the city, mainly because it didn't look or feel like anywhere else. Not everyone spoke English. It felt like real travel, and I especially liked that big stuff had happened here relatively recently. I'm more of a 20th-century history kind of guy. I can diligently read plaque after plaque about things that happened in the 1500s, but absolutely nothing sticks. There's just no way I can relate to it. Give me, any day, a place that bears the marks of things that happened in my lifetime, or at least those of the older folk still living there. That said, if you *do* like 16th-century Ottoman history, Belgrade has plenty for you as well.

Moving further south, into Balkan heartland, meant Turkish coffee had a stronger foothold. Iva's mother, a wise and worldly woman if ever I met one, gave me a lesson in how to make it. Turned out I'd been doing it all wrong up in Ljubljana, where I'd mixed coffee and water, then boiled it up incredibly slowly. (Although I hadn't had much choice in that, because the hot plates in my room had barely merited the name.) What you're actually supposed to do is boil the water first, then add the coffee, boil it up again, take it off and stir it, then repeat and serve.

Then again, with the Balkans being what they were, I couldn't help feeling that the Bosnians or the Albanians would have me doing the coffee yet another way.

I enjoyed regular home-made coffees, shopped like a local and even got an empowering Serbian haircut, but all too soon it was time to move on. After just three days of getting reacquainted with Belgrade, riding bicycles amongst quirky buildings and occasional spurts of work, it was time for my crack-of-dawn flight to Larnaca.

I was going to have to break my own rules and take a taxi. The flight (6am, since you ask) was so early that the city bus wouldn't have a hope of getting me there in time. But I still hated booking a cab. Everything about them made me squirm.

As a general rule, taxis were an exorbitant rip-off. When I thought of how quickly those meters ticked merrily upwards in places like London, I wondered how the drivers weren't all millionaires. Because I sure never did see *my* bank account going up that fast when I sat at my office desk, doing a job that required more than just chatting about the weather and honking at cyclists. Maybe they really *were* all loaded, and the reason you never saw the same taxi driver twice was that they all retired to the country after one week's work. Perhaps it was the taxi drivers of the world who were the real illuminati. *Something* didn't add up.

People look at me funny when I get on my high horse about taking a taxi. But the thing with *people* is that they don't think. Offer a man forty Pounds for an hour's work, and he may take it with some enthusiasm. But will he be so keen to *save* twenty Pounds in exchange for spending half an hour longer on his journey home by using the bus, which amounts to the same mathematical value proposition and doesn't even involve working? No. He will jump in the first taxi he spots in the rank outside London Gatwick Airport.

Call me disparaging names if you like. But I like to think that it's because I give thought to such principles that I had a house deposit saved up. As well as enough pocket money to travel around Europe while I had very little coming in.

Costs aside, the very concept of a privately-hired car was just a bit elitist and uncomfortable to me. Moreover - you probably saw this one coming - jumping in a cab to follow a perfectly adequate bus down the road didn't give you a great carbon emissions rating. That said, though, it probably did trump doing the same thing with your own car.

More than anything, however, I avoided taxis because I had a pathological distrust of the people who drove them. It went hand-in-hand with similar suspicions about Delhi rickshaw men, Manila tricycle riders and, of course, Venetian gondoliers. I knew they weren't *all* pond scum - but such types had a long legacy of cheating hapless passengers. And mud, as they say, sticks.

A defining moment for me had come one chilly October evening in Tianjin, China, during my first international backpacking trip in 2002. That night, fresh off a train from Beijing and in need of somewhere to sleep before the ferry to Korea departed the next morning, I braved taking a taxi from the station to a hotel I had absolutely no chance of otherwise finding. This was long before Google Maps, but I had the address written down in Mandarin. And, thanks to my guidebook, I also had at least a rough idea of what sort of place it should be.

My man nodded gamely, gave me a toothy smile and proceeded to take me to an alternative hotel of his choice. Suspicious, but willing to see if it might be any cheaper, I did at least speak to reception before deciding how hard to punch the guy. It wasn't cheap at all, of course. And having my driver come into the building and hover behind me (presumably awaiting his cut) did not, to say the least, impress me very much. I paid him the bare minimum, and walked the rest of the way to my actual hotel.

Then there was the lengthy standoff in Qatar, with a taxi driver who claimed 'not to have change', until it dawned on him that I had nowhere pressing to be until my next flight took off in six hours, and that I wasn't going to move from his back seat until he figured out how to run a business properly. Then, miraculously, he found change.

Because of moments like these, and with apologies to any taxi drivers who might not be utterly dishonest rotters, I've made it my policy to take charge of my own travel destiny wherever possible.

At least my cab to Belgrade's Nikola Tesla Airport was cost-effective. Just like my flight to Larnaca. Actually, when I stopped and thought about this offering from Hungarian low-cost carrier Wizzair, I wondered if it was the most random route in the world.

Notwithstanding the fact that I was about to fly from Belgrade to Larnaca, how many people *actually* wanted to fly from Belgrade to Larnaca? Or, for that matter, from Larnaca to Belgrade? I just couldn't see any connection between Serbia and Cyprus. I was only there because this was the cheapest flight to Cyprus in the entire south-eastern half of Europe - and believe me I'd spread the net wide - and because I was an extraordinarily flexible traveller just then. To my mind, I ought to have been the only one on the flight. As always, though, it was jam-packed.

The moment I sat down on the plane and tried to go back to sleep, they were in my face over the PA. All airlines did this, but the budget ones were the worst. Always the same scripted platitudes dreamt up by some boring farts in the head office. Mindless words that *nobody* wanted to hear. I didn't want to be 'welcomed on board' or know that the purser's name was Toby. I simply wanted to shut my eyes without inane drivel hammering away at my eardrums.

And that was just the warm-up act. After being allowed a moment's peace during the take-off, the aircraft burst once more into a cacophony of lights and jingles as it morphed into a flying bazaar. Toby was at it once again, telling me about the mouthwatering hot ham and cheese croissants I could buy for breakfast. As was the fashion, he listed pretty much the entire menu, presumably in the hopes that you'd start drooling to the point that you'd hand over your grandmother for a lukewarm, rubbery slice of pizza.

Then they were onto the contents of the duty-free trolley, in which I'd never seen anybody show the slightest interest. After that came the clubs you could join, the charities you could donate to and a six-minute analysis of the in-flight magazine's advertorial offerings.

As if the endless monologue wasn't grating enough, they repeatedly used words such as 'purchase', 'wish' and 'beverage', none of which anybody ever 'employed' in real life. Oh, how I wished they would shut up.

As always, the delivery of all this drivel was astoundingly bad. Never could these cabin announcers get through their scripts without a lengthy hiccup at some point. Without fail, they always seemed to get confounded halfway through a sentence, as if momentarily thrown by the discovery of a page of Chinese characters in their sheaf of notes. And usually it was a sentence a five-year-old could finish. 'On page 73 of this month's jam-packed edition of our fascinating in-flight magazine, you can select from our tasty range of drinks and–'

And then they'd just...stop. For several seconds. Throats would clear and papers would rustle. Until finally the radio silence would end with a tentative '...snacks'.

Tough one to work out, to be fair. Especially when you read it out every day.

Obviously there was no such thing as a live reading test at air steward/ess school. If these people were to read the eight o'clock news, we'd still be stuck on the headlines at midnight.

I really do think airlines that know how to shut up and just fly the bloody plane have a lot to be said for them. The only communication that's going to make the slightest impact on me, apart from 'We're on fire!', is when they tell me if the food's free or not. There's literally *nothing* else I need to hear.

And if I could have been permitted a moment to actually think during the flight, I'd have had plenty to ponder. Primarily the question of where my life was headed. All I knew at that stage was this was to be the last chapter of my autumnal European wanderings. When our week in Cyprus was done, I would be flying back to London Heathrow with Christopher and Anthony. Because it looked like the time to try and be a grown-up had come: the sports marketing job wanted to see me in person for a third interview.

But, despite the insistent whittering of the Wizzair flight crew in my sleep-deprived ear, I did make it to Larnaca without drama.

And my first job there, it turned out, was to deal with the highly intoxicated Christopher who greeted me at arrivals.

Cantankerous Monks
and Bitter Boatmen

You've already met Christopher, the software-peddling colleague who first alerted me to my Peugeot's impending total brake failure. But there's more I can tell you about him.

Christopher was a bit of a grandfather ahead of his time. You only had to look at the waistcoats he wore to the office, or his habit of reading the Sunday newspaper on his own in pubs. But unlike Anthony and I, the two travel companions with whom he was to be stuck on Cyprus, he had his lad side. He was very good at smoking, drinking and staying up late. He liked a party, even if he didn't always get invited to that many.

At some point in the year, he'd earned himself the kind of nickname that was bound to stick. Being responsible for some of our company's sales operations in Spain, Christopher had been known to express frustration with our American HQ's translations of English sales materials into Spanish.

"What the hell, man?" he'd raved upon receipt of one such translation. "Their translators must all be Mexican. You don't say it like this in Spain...my clients are going to laugh out loud. This is Panchito Spanish!"

Unluckily for him, I'd been there to hear him use this wonderful new slur. After establishing that 'Panchito' was indeed a derogatory term the Spanish might use for any Latin American, I did the only sensible thing there was to do, and made sure it became Christopher's official nickname.

Today, Panchito flew into Larnaca a few hours ahead of my touchdown, late on the night before I'd embarked in Serbia. The plan was to meet at the airport when I arrived, and pick up our hire car. We'd need to spend one night in a hotel in Larnaca before Anthony's family flew back to England, at which point we could start occupying the freshly-vacated rooms at his house in small-town Cyprus for a week.

Well, Panchito was there to meet me, all right. Fuelled by the free drinks on the flight over from London, it turned out he hadn't left the airport all night.

"Hey man," I said. "I thought you were going to get a hotel or something?"

"Hey man," he said (this was an infectious Anthony-ism we'd adopted). "I was, but then I made friends with this Estonian guy."

"A random Estonian guy? What was his name?"

"I can't remember. But he was waiting for a flight all night and had nothing to do except drink. So I joined him."

Christopher obviously wasn't kidding about that. If we were still going to stick to the plan of picking up the hire car right away, then clearly I was going to be the one driving. Unkeen to hang around a Cypriot airport with an intoxicated Catalan, I handed over my licence and credit cards, warded off the usual dire warnings about the consequences of not taking all-inclusive insurance, signed in about seventeen places, grabbed a set of ignition keys and fired up the car.

The first place I took us was Kiti Beach, which I'd never heard of but was conveniently signposted from right outside the airport. It was already about 30 degrees (nothing autumnal about Cyprus this early in October) and at least one of us needed some fresh air. I'd done zero research on anything about Cyprus, but Kiti presented itself on a platter.

The splash-around proved restorative for both of us. We had a whole day to kill, so we took our time. The water was calm and flat. I was starting to realise, finally, that most of the Mediterranean was like this. The Med might be heaven for partying folk, but it has to be the worst possible sea for surfers. I can only think the narrow Straits of Gibraltar are to blame for making it like an overgrown millpond in so many places.

In time, Christopher started to feel a lot better. More so after we stopped for an early lunch in a nearby village. I don't recall what either of us ate, but it was *terrific*. And a first warning that Cyprus is nothing short of foodie heaven.

This was another revelation to me. I hadn't expected an awful lot on the food front. Unfairly, in retrospect, I'd assumed that Cyprus wouldn't offer anything much more than its fellow Mediterranean island Malta, of which my only culinary memory is of a bony, tasteless rabbit.

After the pleasant discovery that Cypriot lunches were going to be extremely good affairs, we drove into Larnaca. I instantly hated it.

There are very few places to which I take a violent dislike before even getting out of the car. But this, with its stupid tacky pubs showing football, and stupid tacky people sitting in them watching it, was one of them. A giant

McDonald's and Starbucks, all crowding onto the brown sand of what must be the island's least interesting beach, did nothing to redeem it.

In five minutes Larnaca was up there on my hate-list with Kuta in Bali, Surfer's Paradise in Australia and pretty much all of the Gulf States. Congratulations were in order. After all, it surely takes a special effort - an almost admirable dedication to destructive construction - to come up with the bland soullessness such destinations have made their trademark.

Neither of us had any desire for an adventure in Larnaca, so after an evening *moussaka* that sang (my goodness, who knew such wonderful things could be done with an aubergine?) we retired to the hotel and counted the hours until we could leave the city. I passed the time by watching England lose to Australia in the Rugby World Cup on my laptop, noticing every time I glanced up that none of the people in the lit-up, curtainless windows of the opposing apartment blocks appeared to be wearing any clothes.

Well, it *was* bloody hot. Practical people, the Cypriots.

Next day we hit the highway east, on which at least 99% of foreign visitors were heading for Agia Napa. It says something about my lack of party credentials that I hadn't even heard of the place until a couple of days into this trip. I always thought Ibiza was where people went for doing all that smoking, drinking and staying-up-past-bedtime madness, but it turned out that many of them go to Agia Napa too. It's a hugely popular spot for Russians, apparently.

We were part of the tiny fraction of visitors who were going to be taking the turnoff for one of the little villages in the parched interior. Liopetri, our home for the next week, was only twenty minutes from the glittering, azure coast but may as well have been in the desert. It's fair to say that this part of Cyprus isn't very strong on trees and greenery. Anthony's house turned out to be down a wide, dusty dead-end road on the edge of town.

It's probably time you met my friend Anthony. As was the case with Christopher, we were still colleagues, despite my having abandoned the job in Oxfordshire on a full-time basis. Remember, I was still remote-working for the company: even during our Cypriot jolly, I'd be continuing my two-and-a-half hours per day.

Anthony was a smart developer who lived primarily for Wimpy burgers, playing complex magic games and sleep. One of his most redeeming features was an outstanding level of inattention to his hair, which had a gigantic, curly life of its own. Like myself, fashion sense, drinking and general enthusiasm (burgers aside) were not among his strengths.

But Anthony always brought amusement to the table, with his raucous laugh never very far away. His favourite expression was 'I hate my life and want to die', yet he managed to use it with self-deprecating brilliance. He delivered another of his staples, 'I'm really, really tired', with a similarly deft touch of humour. Same went for the catchphrases 'you suck', 'this sucks', 'that sucks' or even sometimes 'they suck'.

All those standard Anthony phrases were usually preceded or followed by a brilliant anecdote from his amusingly clumsy and forgetful life. He revelled in his sorrows in a way that made you smile. Few could pull off wailing and vitriol the way he did.

Take the time when he recounted the story of finding he'd been tricked out of his wallet by a malicious trio of nine-year-old girls in a park in Madrid.

"Look, man," he'd wail as he retold the story of that fateful morning. "They asked to see my ID and I didn't feel like arguing. I was really, *really* tired, okay? I mean, whole thing sucked." And then he'd break into his curious cackle.

Then there was that other major Anthony-ism, which like all the others had a way of creeping into group vocabulary in a very short space of time. It was his trademark 'Hey, man!' greeting. You didn't have to be male for Anthony to receive you in this manner. He was very democratic that way.

The people who knew the three of us best had dubbed our little jaunt to Cyprus 'Lads on Tour'. Affectionately, I liked to think. But without a doubt it was more ironic than anything. Christopher's fondness for a tipple notwithstanding, we were not, as a group, the kind of chaps whose behavior in Mediterranean ports earns them a spot on late-night television shows. The chances of us tearing up the town weren't great.

We were an odd little club, really. On the face of it, we shouldn't have been mates at all. More than readily identifiable common ground, we were brought together mostly by our sense of humour and the fact that we didn't really fit into any particular subcultures.

Reading all this, you might be tempted to assume that being single was something we could all claim, but that only applied to two of us. Anthony had a long-standing (albeit long-distance) girlfriend. We didn't have fully-fledged geekness in common either (I couldn't code and liked sport), but some of us (Anthony) came closer than others. Not all of us were lazy, either: that was just an Anthony and me thing. We ribbed Christopher endlessly about his diligence in the workplace. Especially as it went against everyone's favourite Spanish stereotype.

But we had our strange little overlaps. Like Anthony and Christopher both wanting to become motorcyclists. They'd developed this urge back in the springtime, and spent most of the summer acquiring licenses, followed by the machines themselves. It amused me no end to think of these two as the world's least intimidating motorcycle gang. (Although they'd certainly had the other spectators choking on their tea when they'd come to watch me play cricket one Sunday afternoon, giving genteel Cumnor Cricket Club the fright of its life as they rasped their superbike engines up the driveway.)

But back to Anthony's house in Liopetri. The road had a ploughed field at the end of it. To me it looked far too hot and dry for any life to flourish, but those with a trained eye could apparently tell you that this was one of the 'red soil villages', known not only for the nation's (apparently) famous potatoes, but also figs and pomegranates.

And beyond that, it wasn't a terribly long way to the border with North Cyprus, or Turkey, or whatever you wanted to call it. Having made the pleasantly surprising discovery that it wasn't a big deal to get across the border anymore (I'd always pictured it like trying to stroll from Seoul to Pyongyang with a set of Christmas cards bearing Washington postmarks) we were all keen to do a little excursion to that mysterious land.

But that would come later in the week. Much of our time, especially at the beginning, was spent lolling aimlessly about on the front terrace making fun of each other, telling stupid stories and complaining about work stuff as only colleagues can. Christopher would drink copious amounts of whiskey, while Anthony and I would drink nothing much at all, preferring to plot where we'd eat that night's spectacular meal.

While both Anthony and I were far more passionate about food than drink, Christopher made us promise that we'd go out and party in Agia Napa at least twice in our seven nights. Our Cypriot host and I nodded vigorously, promising that the next evening we'd be less tired and more inclined to heave ourselves off the wicker patio furniture and pull on something that wasn't a pair of beach shorts.

Christopher was up against it, though, because Anthony and I are on the same page when it comes to late nights out. We're not against the idea of jumping around at two in the morning. We have no moral objection to it, and can even let our minds wander to a world in which we'd do such things. A world in which alcohol-fuelled 'second winds' would send us wild till dawn. Why, we'd even managed to see a post-party sunrise once or twice in our lives. But these had been rare occasions, and, quite honestly, probably occurred on the shortest possible summer nights. We were, quite simply, people who felt the pull of bed at night.

I'd love to be a night owl who doesn't need much sleep. For one thing, I'd have finished this book a lot quicker, without even needing to turn to amphetamines. Oh yes, I'd get a lot more done. Sadly, I'm cursed with not being much of a night person. And if you think there's a tradeoff, you're wrong, because I'm not much of a morning person either. Afternoons? I don't suggest you put me anywhere near a comfortable sofa or a sunbeam following lunch break.

I adore my sleep, especially when it's dark and nature says we must sleep. I'd done my time fighting my primal instincts and drooping eyelids. I'd been night manager in a hotel for six months. I'd driven trucks through the night in Australia for another three. I could fight the fight and I knew I could win it. I just didn't *want* to fight anymore. If I had the choice, then I wanted to crawl into bed.

I'd never, ever noticed anything akin to a 'second wind' effect. Alcohol has only ever made me more tired, if not a little depressed. If you're the sort of person who enjoys a few drinks at home (which I do quite like) and then calls a taxi to head for a noisy, smoky nightclub pounding with terrible sounds at one o'clock in the morning, then be my guest. But you're a very different animal from me, that's all I can say.

Christopher's attempts to stir up the laddish fire in our bellies aside, we gradually developed an appreciation of just how much influence Anthony's extended family had in this very small town. We visited his Aunt Maroula for lunch (a memorable banquet of lamb chops, halloumi, dolmades, bread and red wine) and visited his legendary grandad, who lived quite happily in a medieval cottage outside at the age of approximately 93. Grandad's actual year of birth was lost in the mists of time and thus subject to debate, apparently. But he was surely living proof that the Cypriot diet was as healthy as Dr Christiaan Barnard always claimed.

I'd be tempted to say grandad's cottage was in the 'garden', but that would be to imply flowers and vegetables rather than concrete and dust. Cyprus is the polar opposite to Slovenia when it comes to lush and colourful domestic exteriors. With no shades of green to save your eyes from the relentless sun and the omnipresent whitewash, sunglasses really are an essential companion.

Anthony was known to absolutely everyone in the village, it seemed, even though he'd never lived there and barely ever visited. It was quite enough that he was a member of his large family, whose name cleary dominated the local telephone directory.

One day, just after we were about to pull the car away from an expedition to the local shop, an elderly lady started loading up the boot of a car just in front of us.

"Careful not to run her over," I chortled. "It's probably one of Anthony's aunts."

There was a slight pause, before Anthony floored me with an almost deadpan reply. "You know, I think that actually *is* one of my aunts…"

I didn't make any more aunt jokes after that.

In the absence of WiFi at the house, my daily work was a little bit of a challenge. If Liopetri had been the kind of place with connected hipster coffee shops, I'd have gone to one of those to do my couple of hours every morning. But all Liopetri had to offer was a couple of general stores and one or two extremely basic bars. The kind at which old men sat on grimy plastic chairs, looking out over the baking, dusty crossroads.

There was also a post office, and it was here that I discovered a reliable WiFi connection. The post office, however, did not see fit to offer a table or a chair to sit at. I solved that one by pulling the car up at the pavement outside the entrance each morning, and doing my work in the front seat. Ridiculous but true.

Eventually we managed to stop being lazy and start seeing a bit of Cyprus. We swam at Agia Napa's Nissi Beach, the stunning turquoise waters of which must be the town's only redeeming feature if you're not looking for wild nightlife.

Agia Napa actually left Larnaca for dead when it came to tackiness. But I didn't hate it in the same way, if only because the tackiness was at least unique. Instead of the international chains and completely interchangeable establishments of Larnaca, here the streets were alive with distinctive themes. And I'd have believed you if you told me that their sole purpose was to elevate awfulness to the level of art.

Take, for example, the eye-opening *Jungle Mania* restaurant, which sits on the left side of the main drag into Agia Napa. The self-proclaimed home of 'the best food in town' was so extraordinarily over-the-top that I found it hard to believe we weren't in America. A big plastic hyena and a smiling rhino guarded the entrance to its interior, while one of the giant outdoor menus perched between the legs of a giraffe. Two elephants and two lions, split by a TV aerial, adorned the roof.

I can't tell you why the rhino was smiling and the other animals weren't.

In the dark heart of Agia Napa we fought off the advances of a Kiwi guy who (having obviously misread us quite spectacularly) thought we looked like candidates for 'party boat' tickets. It was the kind of cruise where timed drinking contests and compulsory hand-cuffings to members of the opposite sex were par for the course. Not even Christopher was interested.

What we *did* do was get on a sightseeing boat which would allow us to view the cave-riddled coastline north of Agia Napa, and eventually to get a glimpse of the abandoned city of Famagusta, which sits inside the buffer zone between Greek and Turkish Cyprus. It promised beer in moderation, swimming opportunities and a bit of an education.

And it delivered on all of this - with a healthy dose of sunstroke thrown in for Anthony, whose British side refused to countenance the protective cream we offered - before things got very weird indeed.

Just as people were getting comfortable on deck after another swimming break, pondering which side they wanted to tan next and whether they could be bothered to stand up when Famagusta came into view, our captain came over the airwaves with a rousing, scathing, vitriolic speech about the Turkish invasion of Cyprus in the 1970s.

Up until that point, the gruff, bearded skipper (who did a good impression of a superannuated Captain Haddock) had only come over the loudspeaker system to mutter harmlessly about the caves or settlements we were looking at, or to tell us we were encouraged to jump off the edge of the boat as many times as we could for the next thirty minutes. Then, if you'll excuse the maritime pun, he completely changed tack.

The moment he began speaking about Famagusta, it was as though he had been seized by the spirit. When it came to this little piece of history, our skipper was Angry with a capital A.

"Imagine if an invading army came to your town and raped your wives and daughters," he bellowed not long into the squirm-inducing tirade. "Leaving a trail of destruction and forcing you to leave your home with no warning. This was the behaviour of the brutal and savage Turks; how they slaughtered innocent Greek people."

Not exactly what holidaymakers sign up for, you understand.

Awkward looks began to be exchanged on the top deck as the ranting and raging went on. Several minutes of this frenzied, bloody history lesson went by, and then, as suddenly as it had begun, it stopped. We were back to our pleasure cruise, and the next announcement was an invitation to dine on the lower deck. But nobody had much of an appetite after our skipper's speech.

It is more than fair to say that the Turkish occupation is a highly emotive topic in Cyprus. But while I wouldn't say this anywhere near the raging mariner (who eventually took us back to Agia Napa in safety), I must admit I find it a little bit odd that the whole business is still considered an unresolved standoff.

It's now more than 40 years since Turkey took advantage of a political kerfuffle going on in Cyprus and invaded a portion of the island. Now I know that nobody likes being invaded, and I'll be the first to say that it's especially not-nice to boot people out of the part you've taken over on the basis of their ethnicity. But still, there's no escaping the fact that kerfuffles, invasions and the occasional booting-out are pretty much the basis of the entire world map we have now.

I don't need to go into this, do I? The whole history of Europe is one of invasions. This was a fact of life until just a couple of decades ago. If someone ran over your country, and you didn't like it, then you found some heroes and ran them out of town again. Those self-same Turks (then known as Ottomans), in fact, were key protagonists in many such confrontations across central and southern parts of the continent.

The coffee people drink, the borders they enjoy (or don't) and the way they worship today are all contingent on these battles going the way they did. Every nation could find a reason to gripe, to hate, to rage, if they look back into history. But, by and large, Europe gets on with it and looks forward.

With this in mind, and considering that the Greek Cypriots did not find heroes and kick the Turks out back in the seventies, can we not just accept that this is another of those thousands of things that happened in history? Continuing to pretend the north doesn't exist isn't really going to make for a constructive future.

Don't get me wrong: I am glad we have (almost) moved on from the barbarism of unprovoked invasions. And I don't mind the principle of the UN stopping such things from escalating and enforcing a global consensus of fairness. But I didn't see the men in blue sealing the Crimea from Vladimir Putin in 2014. Nor did they stand in the way of South Africa's little-remembered invasion of Lesotho back in 1998. So maybe let's wipe the slate clean - beginning with the widespread recognition of Turkish Cyprus - and start being consistent from now on.

A couple of days after our dramatic boat ride, we crossed the border into North Cyprus on foot. We used the designated point at Lefkosia and wandered through the very different surrounds of the Turkish side. After the big chains and banking offices of Lefkosia, the low-rise and sometimes derelict northern side of town had way more character to offer. It wasn't quite Seoul meets Pyongyang, but it certainly made for a visible change.

From there we hopped on a bus - paid for in Turkish Lira - to Famagusta. On this side of the fence it was known as Gazimağusa, and the truth was that only a portion of this 'ghost town' was actually empty. And even that part had UN vehicles running around its otherwise deserted streets, most of them probably acting out their ultimate video game fantasy.

We walked onto the surreal finger of active beach that's overlooked by the empty shells of what were once ten-storey apartment blocks, presumably full of residents back in the day. The sad-looking two-man pedalos were dolphin-shaped, although for some reason the dolphins sported long, feminine eyelashes. They could have fitted in just fine over in Agia Napa.

From this beach there was nothing really to stop you swimming around the fence and seeing how long you could get away with running amok in off-limits Famagusta. But not even I was tempted to be at the the centre of a diplomatic incident. I had an interview to be at next week.

Speaking of which, the idea of a creative property purchase came bounding back into mind when I spotted a couple of estate agent windows in Gazimağusa. North Cyprus, unsurprisingly, was dirt-cheap for apartments and houses. Considering the weather and holiday appeal was the same as it was on the other half of Cyprus, the potential for a return on investment was pretty high. You just had to see hope for a political resolution that would rocket prices overnight, or believe that sooner or later people will stop caring that Turkey isn't in the EU.

I loved the idea of scrapping all my plans to secure a mortgage and simply taking my deposit - not much more - and buying myself a sunny North Cypriot apartment outright. But shelling out for a property in the heart of a most unstable region, just 150 kilometres across the water from burning Syria, was a big thing on which to risk *all* of my money. I guess having the spare change to take punts on places like that is one reason the rich keep getting richer.

Much to Anthony's relief, we ran out of time to visit the Karpas Peninsula, which reached out into the Med like a snail's tentacle, on that particular day. Apparently the peninsula had wild donkeys, resulting in Christopher and I spending the whole holiday being vociferous about trying to get to 'the pointy bit'.

"Look, man," an unenthusiastic Anthony had been saying all week. "There's nothing in your pointy bit. We'll get there, and it'll suck..."

Now that we had got a feel for distances in North Cyprus, it was apparent that if we wanted to get to the end of the pointy bit and stare out at the sea like ancient Greek philosophers, or even just pet a wild donkey or two, we'd have to come back on another day. And get up inconceivably early to make it work. It was a long way by North Cypriot public transport, and our car hire company had made it very clear that its precious vehicles were not to go north of the green line.

"I'm devastated for you guys," he said, choking back the laughter as we got on the bus back to Lefkosia, "Sorry, man. Next time."

"You suck, man," said both Christopher and I in unison. "The pointy bit's awesome."

Anthony then fell fast asleep on the ride back to Lefkosia. We took pictures of him, of course. Doing that never gets old, does it?

It was that kind of trip. Anthony's girlfriend was quite right not to join us. We'd have driven any sensible person insane.

Instead of the pointy bit, we went to Kykkos Monastery, which was way over on the other side of Cyprus, in the high country where tall trees grow and skiing has been known to happen. The high point of that day - depending on your point of view - was my getting told off by a bearded monk after he caught me taking a picture of him bashing a gong for dinner or prayers or whatever.

"How can you take a picture of a monk, man?" said Anthony indignantly, shaking his head. "What were you thinking?"

"Hey, there wasn't a sign saying you couldn't take pictures of monks, was there? And besides, you have to sail close to the wind if you want shots *National Geographic* might want to publish, don't you know?"

"Yeah, but *everybody* knows you're not supposed to take a picture of a monk," said Christopher, clearly enjoying being on Anthony's side this time around.

"Maybe so," I resisted, "but I think that if monks are serious about living private and spiritual lives, maybe they should consider not inviting tourists into their monastery. That guy is a show monk!"

And I still think I have a point. If you want to be a proper monk, close the doors and I will respect your privacy. But don't set up a shop selling monastery honey and postcards, and then be surprised when camera-wielding freelance journalists get in the way of your ceremonial duties.

We also visited Aphrodite's Rock, halfway between Limassol and Paphos. I find this kind of experience more gripping than most of the ones you'll find in the guidebook. While I suppose (with reluctance) that the tales of Greek mythology aren't actually true, swimming about at the birthplace of a goddess feels infinitely more rewarding than eating a burger at *Jungle Mania*. When you tread water and watch timeless clashing of sea and rock at eye level, you feel tiny. It doesn't take much imagination to go back to the time when the ancients took in the self-same view, and legends were born.

There was only one more thing to do before we left Cyprus: go for that night out. We'd clearly failed to do two nights out, because we'd made it to the last night without managing a first one. And despite Anthony doing his best to claim tiredness and sunstroke were catching up with him, Christopher was not about to let us off the hook this time.

"You guys are *useless*. Come on, I'm not going back from Agia Napa and telling people I never went out!"

And so we went out. Since I'm not convinced drinking really achieves anything for me, I volunteered to be designated driver.

It was the first time we saw the party section of Agia Napa. And...oh, my. It was like twelve bigger, brasher *Jungle Manias* all rolled into one.

The night was relatively quiet, this being the end of the season and all that. Which meant space to breathe, places to talk and even room to dance. We met a couple of completely mad Russian girls - apparently not all the Russians in Cyprus were busy developing property in Paphos - one of whom habitually found ways of taking up the entire dancefloor by doing impressions of a stalking tiger.

There weren't, truth be told, a whole lot of stories to be told from the night. But Christopher seemed proud of us. We'd made it to 3am. We made it to late-night McDonald's burgers. And at least that meant we had a chance of catching some sleep on the flight back to London Heathrow.

New Job, New Home, Same Car

I've never been able to fathom how anyone can be nervous for a job interview.

Think about it: this is the only quiz you'll ever take where you're guaranteed to know all the answers. Seriously, all the questions are about *you*, aren't they? All you have to do is rock up and answer them. And you *know* the answers. A child of three could do this.

Moreover, human beings are really quite competent at talking about themselves. They positively thrive at it, in fact. A glance at the narcissism of social media is enough to confirm that we're better at it now than at any other time in history. Even offline, we talk about our lives and our work so much that we usually get to a point where we have to say, 'But enough about me. What have *you* been up to?'

So really, I cannot even begin to understand the angst that goes with a potential employer wanting to have a good old chinwag about your favourite topic. You don't even have to pretend to be interested in how the guy's new roof project is proceeding. You don't even have to ask how he's doing, come to think of it.

I see job interviews as a rare indulgence, usually with free coffee thrown in. I positively look forward to them. And unless you have something to hide, or don't truly believe you're good at what you do, I don't see why you shouldn't look forward to them too.

The only real danger is that you walk in wearing a shirt so terrible that they instantly dismiss the possibility of you working for them. Now *this* is something to worry about. Because unlike talking about the one subject you know better than any other, choosing an outfit takes actual skill.

Like I said before, picking an outfit for a job interview is more likely to be significant in a person's life than understanding the basics of geomorphology. But you can guess which one we spent hours on in high school, can't you? The education system's all wrong. How's it possible that I spent so many hours cramming on scree and terminal moraines - for which I have yet to find a use case - while nobody taught me essential colour coordination?

If school is meant to prepare you for making a living, then I know which one I'd be shifting up the priority list. Because while matching your belt and shoes might not *actually* be important, the working world will judge you on this stuff. And weirdly, it *expects* you to know about it, even though you almost certainly never claimed any competence in this area on your CV. Even though it shouldn't impact your ability to do the job awfully much.

I can think of plenty more life basics that would be far more useful for schools to teach than atom composition or algebra. Skills which go on being useful for *decades* beyond that final exam. What about up-to-date, in-depth and practical instruction in nutritious eating? What about actually teaching the latest recycling techniques, so one actually *knows* which plastic goes in which bin, and why? How about lessons in entrepreneurship? Or learning to spot fallacies and heuristics. Or time management. Or what actually makes the opposite sex tick. Or the fact that the letters 'YKK' indicate a good-quality zip. (I mean seriously, I had thirty-seven years of wasting my wages on products with crappy, sticking zips before I found that one out.)

And shouldn't all of us know how to grow and cook fresh food? This is a dying art, to the detriment of our health and the planet on a number of fronts. 'Home Economics' used to be a thing in schools, but I suppose it disappeared because only girls did it, and therefore it was considered sexist and outdated. Obviously nobody thought that making *everyone* do it might be the answer. After all, if we're not going to have that family unit that the Slovenians have, then we *all* need to find our way around a kitchen.

Just my two cents worth on how education could actually make life easier, lead to better decision-making and see to a more tolerable world. Should I start my own school, I wonder? I think it'd be a very good one.

It depends, I suppose, on whether you think school is just about passing an exam and getting a job, or getting into university. But I think that well into your teens, it should be a general foundation for living the best life you can. Algebra and rock formations have their place - but only when and if someone decides they want to pursue that field on a specialist basis. And that's what colleges are for.

But despite the holes in my education, the shirt I picked out for this interview obviously wasn't too much of an eyesore. Because I got the job. I'd start a couple of weeks later.

The position itself sounded like a scarily grown-up one. It was the first time I'd ever applied for something with the word 'manager' in the title. But I had to accept the whole responsibility thing, at least for a while. If you want to earn enough money to apply for a mortgage, then this is the kind of job you need.

There would be no more travelling for the next little while. Not until I had at least collected the three months of payslips I needed to get a mortgage, bought a house I could rent out for more money than I needed for the repayments, and retire to Barbados on the difference.

It's fair to say that I hadn't really sat down and done the maths on this. But getting a job was indubitably the first step. There was no need for a calculator on that one. I didn't have a hundred and fifty thousand Pounds, so I needed a bank manager to help me. And if I didn't have a 'steady' job, he'd tell me to get out of his office at once.

(Well, it wouldn't be an actual manager in an office, of course. This was the twenty-first century, after all, and actual human interactions were no longer something we can realistically expect. But after passwords and forms and various other hoops to jump through, the answer I would get was clear. It would just take longer than it would have done thirty years ago. Back then, two questions would have been enough for the bank guy to burst out laughing and tell me the score on my loan in no uncertain terms.)

Now that I had a bank-pleasing job, I needed to find somewhere to live for the short term. After all the drama of the last few months, and with my family unit a rather useless five hours away from the job, I was extremely keen to get my own place. I had, after all, made a vow to this effect.

Well, I didn't need to spend much time on the Internet to realise that some vows need to be shelved for a while. Living alone wasn't going to happen. The job was in Weybridge, one of the poshest parts of south-east England. This might look great on a company letterhead, but it's far from ideal for an employee hoping to live somewhere in the vicinity of work. If I wanted to live on my own, it would have to be a brutal commute away. And I was as uncomfortable with that idea as I was with sharing.

As it turned out, even living in a house-share would involve a bit of a hike. Weybridge didn't seem to *have* any house-shares. I assumed that was because it was full of rich people who didn't need to share with anybody except possibly their children. And even these would probably be spending most of the year at some stuck-up boarding school where people called one by one's surname.

So I grit my teeth and broke my vow. One last shared place was a means to an end, that's all. And if all went well, I'd be living in my own flat in six months.

So I narrowed down my online hunt to shared accommodation. After what had happened with Martin & Co in Oxford, I was at least determined not to get involved with an agency again. I didn't have friends or girlfriends to move in with in this part of the world, however, which meant I was going to have to rent from someone I didn't know. Perhaps even sign a contract.

The rentals landscape was different down here in Surrey. Here, a lot of renters seemed to be labelling themselves 'professional landlords.' People who owned multiple houses, rented out several rooms in each and even had a little company set up for this purpose. The implication was that they knew the rules, did things by the book and would be scrupulously fair to deal with.

Now, having got this far into my story, you can surely imagine I was not only extremely cautious on my viewings, but also a little tense when it came to landlords. Especially ones whom I perceived as enormous fatcats who'd lapped up a disproportionate share of the housing market and swanned about on their rental money all day. One false word from any of them, and it was going to be a swift 'no' to their room from me.

I quickly discovered that one such word was 'hassle'. It came into the conversation when one such 'professional landlady' was showing me around what looked like an affordable and reasonable place. Then she started telling me about the check-in and check-out fees.

"If you leave during the first six months, there'd be an extra 100 Pounds due in administration fees," she informed me. "That covers the hassle it causes us, you see."

Red flag.

"Oh you poor thing," I wanted to say to her. "But I perfectly well understand! I mean, even just for this house, you've already got thousands of Pounds of passive income to worry about every month. And if I only stayed three months, well, all you'd get is a measly two and a half Grand of money for doing nothing. What a headache to have to get out of bed and do a little paperwork! Simply the most dreadful *hassle*. Are you sure a hundred is enough?"

I didn't give the speech, of course. For a start, such words never occur to me in the heat of the moment. I just told her it wasn't what I was looking for, and then left.

And what was this business with check-in and check-out fees? I'd never seen such a thing before. Did this go with the territory of being 'professional'? It seemed odd to charge someone to sign up to be your monthly customer. It was like your local supermarket making you buy a ticket to walk in the door, wasn't it?

But it was entirely in keeping with the spirit of the times. We lived in an aggressive world, now, in which the race to provide good service and good products had been replaced by a frenzy of fee-gathering and process-smoothing. A world in which customers were now mere fools to be scammed, and had to hang their heads in shame for all the administration they were causing into the bargain. Everyone was charging us to become their clients - think about that for a second - and what's worse, it was usually hidden in fine print. Somehow we'd allowed this to become a socially accepted way for everyone from gyms to mobile phone companies to squeeze us for a little more. And now landlords were doing it too.

I calmed myself by murmuring another vow. (There's nothing quite like a good vow.) When I rent out my own place, I'll remember what it was like to be a tenant. I'm going to be the coolest, most relaxed landlord in the history of leasing.

The word 'hassle' didn't come up in the next place I viewed. The fees were less punitive, too, and the rent was cheaper. It was on a nice enough road in a nice enough place called Knaphill, on the outskirts of Woking. There would be off-street parking for my Peugeot. And you know what else? Google Maps told me it was conveniently close to Chobham Cricket Club.

"I'll take it," I said after a quick look around the place. This wasn't quite so pressured a rentals market as Oxford, but still, one can't take the time to make a considered decision when a half-decent room comes up. At least I'd had a lot of practice at this, and was starting to learn to trust my gut feeling. Plus, I liked the fact that I would be sharing with three guys. In my (admittedly limited) recent experience, that had worked an awful lot better than sharing with one girl.

In the end, I was going to be about a 45-minute cycle from work, which was completely typical of my UK commuting experiences. It turned out that I was also 45 minutes away from work by car. Ridiculous, yes, but it makes sense when I tell you that I could ride my bike along the Basingstoke Canal towpath, instead of crawling along the road in a long line of other single-occupant cars.

It was nothing compared to what some of my new colleagues put up with. Some were travelling up to two hours each way, usually thanks to the M25 orbital motorway, which luckily I would either cycle under or drive over. There was absolutely no future in living that way, if you asked me. But when you considered that British train tickets invariably (and incomprehensibly) costed a damn sight more than petrol for any given journey, I could understand why people did it.

Inevitably, my plan to sell off the car come the end of the cricket season was now on the back burner. It had made my life easy on no less than four move-ins and move-outs over the past six months. And if all went well, I'd need it for another move in the springtime. Plus, I wasn't sure I wanted to ride my bike that far in winter, or at least not every day. I would soon discover that Basingstoke Canal towpath, with its thick tree canopy, was possibly the darkest place in all the Kingdom on a November evening.

So I would keep the Peugeot for the foreseeable future. Especially since if the last half-year had taught me anything, it was that the future wasn't very foreseeable at all. My life had taken on a new and entirely unexpected shape in very little time, and all because that particular company in that particular place had happened to need someone like me at that particular time. Opportunity could just as easily have called in Brighton or Liverpool or Northampton.

But as fate would have it, I was now very suddenly a resident of greater Woking. And I had a bunch of hilarious new house-mates to meet.

Harries, Henries and Saints

When I discovered that I was to be sharing with a Harry, a Henry and a Giles, I had no idea what to think. My collection of house-mates sounded a bit like the name of a comic book series about a trio of naughty English schoolboys with catapults. Was this a promising sign? Or did it mean I was about to enter a world of trouble?

Harry turned out to be an irrepressibly cheerful and chatty golf professional - the teaching variety, not the kind that plays the European Tour. There was nothing not to like about the youngster. He hailed from a small town in Shropshire, and had a tendency to say 'mate' a lot.

"There's *nothing* where I come from, mate," he announced after returning from a few nights away and making my acquaintance. "Nothing! It's the smallest place ever. Have you met Henry yet? Do you want some chips?"

What a question! I always want chips. And Harry proved to be a great source of that kind of sustenance, because he lived exclusively on take away fish, chips and curry - the Shropshire education syllabus obviously hadn't included cooking either - and, to my regular benefit, was always ordering way too much for his dinner.

But no, I hadn't met Henry. He was in Thailand for three weeks.

"Mate, he's ridiculous," said Harry. "He's always coming home from nights out with some bird or other. Dirty bastard, I don't know how he does it! Mind you, I've seen some of them..."

He was making a face and shaking his head. "He's a roofer. Good laugh. Always up for a few beers."

As long as those beers weren't happening at the 'old man's club' down the road in St John's, at which Harry liked to pass the occasional evening. Because Henry, I soon discovered, wasn't at all impressed by this slow-going joint.

"Why d'you want to go and hang out with a bunch of old men?" he demanded of Harry upon returning from Thailand. "There's no women in that place!"

"But mate, they have an excellent snooker table and dartboard," Harry protested. "And mate, I have a girlfriend!"

It was true. Harry was in a long-term relationship that was now getting on for the ten-year mark. Henry, on the other hand, was constantly and earnestly trawling Tinder, Badoo and whatever other dating app was in vogue. This, along with playing poker, seemed to be his primary pastime. There was the occasional burst of work, but I quickly joined Harry in taking great delight pointing out how rare these seemed to be.

"Look, the weather's really bad the next two days," Henry would protest valiantly. "You can't roof in the rain, can you?"

"But even when you do have sunshine, you're never up before ten," I'd remind him. "And you're always home by four o'clock. It's not much of a working day, is it?"

"And where's this mystery van of yours?" Harry would chime in as we chortled away at Henry's expense. "I think you're a fake roofer, mate!"

"I have to park the van in St John's," Henry would explain for the umpteenth time. "You *know* there isn't space on the street here. And I've told you we work straight through lunch. Six hours on a roof is hard graft."

"Four hours, more like, considering travel time," I would cry. "And I don't believe that van exists. Let's see your roofing website! I'm going to Google it."

"No, don't!" Henry would snap, suddenly panicked about his Google AdWords bill. "Those clicks cost me money! I'll send you the link."

Henry shared my appreciation for looking after pennies. This was a guy I could relate to. I especially liked how he was perfectly happy for us to each go over to the bar and buy our own drinks if we had a night out. He took a similar mindset to his encounters with women.

"She didn't even offer to pay for a drink," he would often complain upon return from one of his many first dates. "I suppose it's *okay* on a first date...for the guy to pay...but she didn't even offer!"

But while Henry's dating strategies amused me on a regular basis, what really encouraged me was that a fellow skinflint was already a property owner. He had a flat in Woking, which he was currently renting out. Now he was in the process of buying another place for his portfolio. I liked to think that his having got this far at a similar age to mine had everything to do with his careful spending habits.

For me, it was handy to have somebody around who knew how house-buying worked, and who could (or so we were told) inspect a roof for deficiencies into the bargain. I peppered him with questions about everything from mortgage applications to interest rates, even learning at least to see the argument for the intuitively revulsive idea of taking an interest-only mortgage.

So Henry and Harry were pleasant surprises. Harry, unfortunately, was only going to be around for a month or so. At that point, another unknown party would move in. This was a shame, because apart from giving me food, Harry didn't use dishes, didn't make a noise and didn't care about anything much. How could his replacement possibly be any better?

Giles, the third housemate, was a different sort of a person. He lived almost entirely for the purpose of worshipping Southampton Football Club. He hadn't missed attending a game - home or away, be it in England or Europe - for six whole years. It was, needless to say, quite an extreme commitment. After rent, football tickets and football travel, there was simply nothing left of his salary each month.

I'd heard that people like this existed, but I'd never actually met one before. The funny thing was, Giles wasn't even from Southampton. It's just that this was the club his father had supported ("my dad brought me up proper, he did") throughout his life. And this is almost invariably how it works with football in England. Giles was born into a 'Saints' family, and there was nothing more to it than that.

I was extremely relieved that despite being a season-ticket holder who travelled on raucous buses to games with his fellow 'away fans', Giles wasn't much of a hooligan. He'd go to the matches and then come straight back home, retiring to his room in his red 'Saints' hoodie to watch highlights of all the other games he'd missed. And in the brief window of summer that doesn't offer any football, he would go to Lord's to watch cricket.

I had to admire his dedication. Apart from work and football, Giles didn't seem to need anything else in his life. He was at his happiest in front of the telly with a large bowl of pasta, tuna and grated cheddar, especially if he could join us in throwing a couple of barbs at Henry's roofing ethics whilst in the kitchen.

Henry and I, meanwhile, became obsessed with the idea of getting Giles to come out with us. We were both convinced he'd be a bit of a legend after he had a couple of lagers in him. We badgered him on Facebook and we badgered him in the lounge. I even tried serenading him from the landing as he lay on his bed and watched football one Saturday evening. But it was to no avail. Giles liked to taunt us with the occasional 'maybe', but in the end he would never show up.

Harry moved out at Christmas time. But not before he won a gigantic slab of turkey meat in a raffle at the golf club. It was already cooked, and sitting in a huge baking tin waiting to be gobbled. He invited all of us to help with this enormous challenge, but for some reason I was the only one who actually did.

"Aren't you going to eat any of your own turkey?" I asked Harry each day, wondering if I could possibly get through all of it unaided before it went off.

"Nah, mate, go for it," he'd say. "I've got curry here."

There's no part of my mind that understands buying food when there's something free - particularly something as unusual and interesting as a turkey - in the fridge. But I've noticed a lot of people do this. If you're struggling to save a house deposit of your own, ask yourself if this is a tendency you exhibit.

Not even Henry or Giles would help me out with that damn turkey. In a house where there was never much competition for use of the kitchen, cutting it into slices and warming them up was all just a bit too much like cooking effort. Regardless, I couldn't just stand by and watch perfectly good food go to waste.

I did defeat that bird in the end. It was arguably my biggest achievement of that English winter. But once I was done with it, I didn't need to see a turkey sandwich for a very long time.

When Harry moved out, he was replaced by a German called Sebastian. A perfectly nice and unobjectionable guy, albeit one that had a girlfriend constantly glued to him in quite sickening fashion every weekend. Considering that the incumbent trio had signed up for a no-couples house (because coming home to the kind of cuddling-under-the-blanket sessions that make you want to vomit isn't something any single person really enjoys), and that she didn't actually pay rent at our place, it was definitely a change for the worse after Harry.

And, in another contrast to our departed housemate, these two cooked like crazy. Whenever the girlfriend was visiting, they would embark on humongous Jamie Oliver projects, complete with carefully-prepared bowls of ingredients, clouds of flour and an unacceptably excessive use of hummus. And with two of them bashing about in a (even more sickeningly) slick demonstration of harmonious co-cooking, it suddenly made the kitchen unusable to the rest of us for long periods of time.

What really made your stomach turn was the way they shared every little job in the kitchen. Could one of them sit and have a glass of wine while the other cooked? No chance. I swear they had his and hers potato peelers, and would lovingly gaze into each other's eyes as they skinned the spuds with outrageous contentedness. With their beatific half-smiles, they could have starred in a magazine spread about kitchen installations. I never saw them fight once.

I don't mind couples being happy together. But this kind of sickly serenity needs to be practised behind closed doors. Had I come home and found them going at it like animals on the kitchen counter, I would have found it far less objectionable than these grossly indecent displays of innocent affection.

Not only is it a bit rubbish to be edged out of your own kitchen by this kind of thing, it's also no fun watching two people do a relationship so *wrong*. Sebastian didn't have any other friends, nor did he do anything much apart from wait for each weekend, when she would travel to visit him at our house. I feel sure she lived a similar life, watching TV every night while she pined for Friday. I hated seeing these two so wilfully put every egg in the same basket, so certain that all each of them would ever need was the other. You wanted to knock their heads together.

Still, their naive contentedness was a mere trifle compared to what I'd endured in past house-shares. Neither of them once tried to tell me where to put my soap, nor to switch off the power to each appliance at the wall. They watched stupid movies on the television, sure, but it wasn't a big enough deal for the rest of us to make a thing about it. At the end of the day, I wasn't annoyed enough to want to be 'that guy' who tried to ban your girlfriend from coming over. Because I know I'd hate that guy.

Work was easy, as it always is. I don't mean to say that there's anything simple about getting out of bed early and actually *going* to work, especially if there's cricket to be watched or there's some creative project you'd rather be working on. For me, having had a taste of flexi-time remote work, there was a certain challenge in returning to the discipline of appearing in a certain place at a certain time.

But once you're there in the office, it's just a question of doing the job you've signed up for. This was particularly easy for me, working as I was in an agency. The job involved constantly listing one's achievements and justifying one's plans to clients with memories like elephants, so slacking was never an option. But when the day's work was done, I would almost invariably go home and switch off.

(I can never understand why so many people insist on bringing the dramas and stresses of the work day home to share with everyone else. I'll put it in three words: no one cares. Most people don't even care about their own work - never mind how condescending your boss was in the meeting today. Save the work talk for your colleagues.)

I had never worked anywhere quite so English as this agency: the office demographics made going to work like a trip back in time. As the white South African in the room, I *was* the diversity. And being a sports marketing agency, you can imagine there was something of a male bias too. Monday mornings were mental, with banter about the weekend's football bouncing around the room like a hot potato. I couldn't make head or tail of it, and just got funny looks if I tried to turn the conversation to cricket. Great lads, though: we found plenty in common in the end.

By the time March rolled around, and I had those magic three full payslips in the bank, I certainly couldn't claim to be unhappy with life. Work was full of challenge and the odd spurt of travel, while home was generally cosy, comfortable and friendly. There was no reason to believe I might need to flee my latest house at short notice, either. And it was already time for the new cricket season - with no car shopping required!

Things were so good that I was tempted to just *live* for a little while. Kind of like I'd done the previous summer in Oxford. But I couldn't lose focus now. My grand vision of becoming a grown-up with a permanent home, never again to face dictatorial soap storage protocols, confront the horrors of referencing or *hassle* landlords with my monthly cash was there for a reason. The moment had come to start looking for houses.

Commence Operation Mortgage

Before I could get excited about actually looking at houses, I had to go through the exhausting business of getting a mortgage approved for real. I'd explored all the online calculators and visited all the comparison sites, and none of them suggested I would have a problem. But I was nervous. Because it was usually only at the point of execution that my unique set of circumstances made computers melt down.

If I'd had so much trouble with getting references for a rental, I couldn't begin to imagine how much of a head-scratcher I was going to present to a would-be mortgage provider. Showing yourself to be creditworthy to buy property seemed to be the ultimate exercise in social conformism. I knew that it was all about having a job, a verifiable address and a recognized bank account with a salary flowing in every month.

You didn't have to be a cave-dwelling hermit to run into problems getting a loan. Even those with the temerity to be self-employed, as Henry testified, are considered dangerous propositions in mortgage-land.

So I was scared something would go wrong. But at first glance, there was no need to be. I'd gotten a job with the express purpose of being able to say, 'Look, Mr Bank, I've jumped through your hoops!' I'd signed a lease and passed my probation at work. I now had my three months of payslips, and was basically a Certifiable Upstanding Citizen. I should look forward to a warm reception at my lender of choice. I was a solid sort of person who would never default. I was Their Kinda Guy.

(Just to be clear, I am absolutely the kind of guy who would never default. But the modern world wasn't going to let such immutable hardwirings get in the way of a computer error message. And that was the part that worried me.)

Of course, their method of establishing what Kinda Guy I was could only be described as pointless nonsense. Daniel Kahneman would have a field day with the three-month thing. I mean, in all seriousness, what did these banks think they were doing drawing up repayment deals spanning *thirty years* on the basis of seeing evidence of three months' income at a certain level? Because there was pretty much only one certainty regarding a three-decade view of your future, and that was that you'd only be in your current job for a fraction of it.

It was ludicrous that this trio of payslips counted for anything at all. Why couldn't we just admit that current employment status had virtually no bearing on any worthwhile calculation? It might have been so in my parents' generation, when people stayed at companies for five decades and were then presented with a set of beer mugs and a pension. But the world didn't work like that any more. Companies hired and fired each time a contract or two was won or lost. Workers, led astray by the relatively recent rhetoric that we ought to be 'happy in our jobs', were constantly disappearing in the hopes of a change for the better. So instead of mulishly obsessing over steady employment with a company, a bank would be far better off to look at one's long-term performance in the domains of savings, debt and history of *some* regular income.

The system was entirely silly, but still, I couldn't change it. And I had to believe it was going to work fine for me if I just hung in there and made sure I ticked those boxes. Those in the know told me that the moment the relevant computers were happy and your property deal was done, you could then go off and be a cave hermit or hike the Altiplano - as long as you paid up every month.

Since I totally abhorred the idea of paying the bank money-for-nothing that was apparently called 'interest', my plan was to put down as much cash as possible and keep the loan amount to a minimum. Cash that I was jolly glad to have right now - payback for all those turkey sandwiches and airport bus rides was finally here! But of course, we no longer lived in a world where the bank would just believe me when I said I had thirty thousand Pounds ready to pay down. I needed a *piece of paper* to prove that this was so.

In fact, the bank wouldn't count anything that wasn't liquid, such as stocks and shares. Not even if I provided a beautiful printout of my assets.

Now, this particular insistence was a lot more understandable than the three-months thing. I'll grant you that. But still, my shares were in *Google*, for the sake of goodness! In the old days, a bank manager with a brain might have looked at those and said, 'Invested in the world's most powerful company? Well, tickle me pink, I don't see those crashing overnight! I think we can let you hang onto those till the last minute, son!'

Not so in 2016. Computers had come along to replace common sense, and when these saw the word 'shares', they simply said 'no'. So I had to sell my fast-appreciating Google stock (and more besides) just so I could show a bank statement with the proceeds listed. This was box-ticking at its most annoying. It cost me real money.

After all, I was nowhere close to actually needing to hand over the cash itself. Not given how long a house purchase is supposed to take in England. There was every chance the whole project would run askew for some reason, and I might never have needed those Pounds at all. Still, they had to have a paper that said I would have the money *if and when* the big day came.

All just ass-covering that wasted my time, robbed my money and gave me admin I wasn't all that keen on tackling during my lunch breaks, when eating tuna-and-sweetcorn sandwiches should really have been priority. If banks were really serious about an accurate mortgage offer, they'd have made me put every penny on that bank statement in some sort of holdings account for as long as any purchase offer was valid. Because as it was, there was nothing to stop me going out and spending it all on sweets once I'd given them this sodding piece of paper, was there? Dunderheads.

Why didn't I go storming off to a less fussy financial institution, you may well ask? Because I knew each and every one of them was guaranteed to make me jump through the same stupid hoops. This madness was all regulatory tripe that had to be done. Identikit processes in an identikit world. It made me want to bang my head against the wall.

Still, if these incredibly dull regulations, which had basically reduced bank managers to keyboard jockeys, were a reaction to preventing the 'easy credit' that had caused certain recent financial meltdowns, then fair play. The rules were achieving what they set out to achieve. Absolutely nothing about this credit process could be described as easy. It seemed clear that 'easy credit' would never be allowed to happen again.

I won't go into the various other silly delays involved in my getting a mortgage offer. Let's just say that it was early summer by the time I had something official in my hand and was able to start looking at houses. A whole spring I'd never get back.

But, finally, the exciting part was here: viewing bricks and mortar. Or at least, it *should* have been exciting. But it was mostly painful. I did have a full-time job, after all, and one which kept me very busy. Taking phone calls from agents during work hours was almost never practical. And evening conversations wouldn't work: I was knackered and they were closed. There were also no viewings on Sundays, which cut fully half of the available weekend time out of the equation.

If you want to sell houses (or cars or biscuits or model train sets, for that matter), then I have a novel idea: be open when the rest of the world *isn't* at work. Most of the English-speaking world has never really managed to wake up to the opportunity here. I admire the logic of the French in this regard. Their bakers and butchers will close on a Monday, a Thursday or some other random day when their customers are likely to be stuck in the office. And that makes perfect sense to me.

The estate agent business in South Africa used to have a brilliantly efficient solution, which didn't even need the Internet to run like clockwork. When I was growing up, Sunday was universally known as 'show house' day. A bunch of signs at major intersections would point you in the direction of for-sale properties in the area. All you had to do was follow the signs. Anyone could rock up at any house, and have a nose around.

As a kid I loved doing exactly that. All those strange and wonderful houses! While one's parents earnestly debated the state of the gutters and poolside tiling, you could smell the curious odours that pervaded other people's coat closets and pet their cats.

I think they've had to abandon that open-door policy in South Africa now, what with the growing popularity of waving guns in people's faces and taking all their stuff. It's a shame human beings have turned into such savages in such a short space of time.

But why they didn't do 'show houses' in considerably less savage England was an excellent question. There, the protocol was to set up an appointment for every viewing. This meant endless phone calls between prospective viewer and current owner, always via the agent, to settle on a suitable time. If you were trying to line up multiple appointments in one area for a particular day, you can imagine the juggling that had to go on. Considering that these juggling calls had to be surreptitiously taken in the office hallways, usually without a spare hand to write anything down while you discussed places you'd never heard of, I found it all quite exhausting.

In order to get even a few house viewings done in a given area, I needed to plan a day off work and start making the calls a week in advance of that. This is why it was well into the summer before I really started getting a feel for the market.

In view of the rather limited loan for which I qualified, the 'given areas' would be a bit limited. I would either have to live in a tiny box in a grim suburb, or a slightly larger box considerably further out from work than I currently lived. Considering the British willingness to spend thousands of hours a year whiling away huge chunks of their lives on packed commuter trains, I was still far too close to London to expect to get a bargain.

"You should look at Southampton," said Henry, who was about to finalise the purchase of a buy-to-rent flat in the port city on the south coast of England. "It's still really reasonable down there."

"It's not like Portsmouth, is it?" I asked suspiciously. I'd been to Southampton's neighbour before, and found the navy town a quite loathsome place.

"No, Southampton's sort of the nice bit of Portsmouth, if you know what I mean. And there are fast trains to London, if you want to rent the place out."

"People commute from *Southampton?*" I asked incredulously. "I mean, isn't that just somewhere Giles goes to watch football?"

Henry nodded to the first question, and shook his head to the second.

"I guess some commuters *will* actually consider living there, won't they?" I mused out loud. "Just have to wait until everywhere between here and there gets too expensive to live. It's bound to happen. Southampton will just be a suburb of London one day."

Henry nodded again. "And then you can watch the prices go up..."

So one of my days off saw me take a drive down to Southampton. That's when it struck me just how easy it was to spot an estate agent, even if you were meeting them on a busy street and didn't have the first clue what they might look like. Especially the men. They always had ridiculous amounts of gel in their hair, incredibly shiny shoes and a clipboard under their arms. They'd invariably be wearing a suit and a fake smile, too.

I suppose that donning the same formal work gear a city banker would wear is supposed to make you look professional. But on a twenty-year-old working in a three-man office selling houses in suburban Southampton, I just thought it looked laughable. Our fathers might have expected to dress that way for their first job out of college, but in the 21st century a suit had come to mean you're doing something *really* important and very clever. Or that you were attending a ball.

These estate agents were not, I think it's fair to say, doing anything particularly clever. There's a certain type of person one finds working in a small-town British estate agency. I may stand corrected on this, but I'm told it's one of the few desk jobs for which you don't actually need a qualification.

The performances of Southampton's finest property sales talent did little to dispel my preconception that all they'd needed to gain employment in this line of work was a good suit or a decent make-up kit. I mean, these people weren't even very good at answering the most basic and essential questions about running costs for the property they were selling.

"Good afternoon! Reginald, is it?" a typical conversation might go.

"It's Richard, actually. Hi."

"Oh, sorry, Sir."

I don't much like being called 'Sir' either: I'm not your headmaster. When will these British estate agents realise that behaving like a normal person might be an approach worth trying?

"No problem, I've already been called Roger and Rodney today. Is that your leaflet about the house?"

"Oh yes. Indeed it is, here you go, Sir. You'll find all the info you need on there."

"Does it have the Council Tax rate I would expect to be paying every year?"

"Um, let me see. No, sorry...I don't think that's on there. But you can Google it very easily. I think you just type in 'Band D Southampton'. Or is it a Band C? I'll have to check with my colleague and get back to you on that."

"Gee, thanks," I would be tempted to say. "I know the annual local authority charges must be an unusual question for a buyer to ask about a property. Sorry to have caught you off guard."

I returned from Southampton clutching a series of brochures, almost all of them missing key information about council tax and ground rent. The trip each way took an hour and twenty minutes in the Peugeot, which was continuing to save my life. Finding my way around unknown bits of Hampshire like Southampton, Alton, Aldershot and Frimley by means of capricious and confusing bus routes would probably mean three viewings per day instead of six.

Anyway, so Henry was right. Southampton *was* cheap. I could get a proper house there for my money, instead of a mere flat just about anywhere nearer. But it was not realistically commutable to my current job. Did that even matter?

"You should look nearer Weybridge," insisted my father, who was unsurprisingly against any moves to Barbadian hammocks or caves. "That's where your job is. And you can't drive that far to work every day."

"Yes, I know," I replied. "But it would probably only be for a few months. Then I'll get retrenched, or rent the house out and live somewhere cheaper, or find a job in Southampton."

"I think you need to settle down for a while."

"But it's not 1970 any more!" I bellowed. "You don't join a company, buy a reasonably-priced house down the road and start a family any more. Nowadays you join a company, commute fifty miles to somewhere you can afford to live, and then wait for some curve ball to come along and change everything anyway. Buying a house is a long-term commitment. A job isn't. Not any more. I should buy where it's a sensible deal, not base everything on where I happen to be working right now."

I liked my logic, although I did fear death by commuting if I ended up staying in my current job longer than I thought. Eventually, though, my dad and I talked myself out of buying as far away as Southampton. Especially since I had found a place in Aldershot, which was way, way closer to where I needed to be.

Aldershot was an interesting case. One of the most important British Army locations, it was a little over an hour from London if you got the right train, which made it a very rentable sort of place. However, it was an island of squalor in a sea of Hampshire poshness. It was as bad as Portsmouth. Being a military town just doesn't seem to do a place any favours.

As a result of being seen as a bit of a slum, the prices in Aldershot weren't half bad. If you were willing to assume that the town's location would ultimately make it fall prey to gentrification, it could be a smart place to buy.

Plus, there was also a certain poetry in the fact that Aldershot was the town in which my mother had grown up after the Second World War. *Plus ça change*, and all that. Moreover, I even had a colleague who lived there. So I knew you could make an Aldershot commute work.

The flat I had discovered seemed an absolute bargain. High up in a tall and ugly building that used to be an office block, it was unusually spacious (a huge plus) and commanded an actual view to the hills beyond the town. If you looked directly down, of course, you would see a dank and miserable street consisting of shops selling gold, special SIM cards for Polish people who hadn't discovered WhatsApp calling, and Nepalese takeaways.

But as long as I didn't spend much time looking down, everything would be okay. And escape was easy, because the flat was five minutes' walk from a station that had those fast trains to London. And anyway, I didn't mind Nepalese food.

I felt the apartment was a place I could live in, at least while I got a feel for the running costs and planned how feasible renting it out and moving to Sri Lanka might actually be. Henry came to see it, and couldn't find any obvious physical flaws. And even my old man approved of the purchase.

So, after a final scout that revealed a more than acceptable cricket club in the vicinity, I did far and away the most grown-up thing I'd ever done. I made an offer on the flat.

And, even more terrifyingly, the owners accepted it.

Time Stands Still

I might have made an offer to purchase a flat, but I was nowhere near done. Anyone who knows anything about buying a house in England also knows that an offer - and even having that offer accepted - is only the beginning of a minefield that can very well blow up in your face.

Once an offer is accepted in England, the lawyers, surveyors and electric inspectors spend six weeks or more doing all sorts of clever and specialized things. These include charging you 'administration fees' to conjure up the same papers for which every hopeful owner in the history of the property has also paid fees. Papers which probably take about six seconds to access.

During these weeks both the buyer and seller wait around, unable to make anything other than hypothetical plans around such trifling matters as moving in, moving out or their next property purchase. Their lives go on hold until the legal green light is given.

Another quirk of the system in England is that both the buyer and the seller can simply pull out of the deal until the paperwork is wrapped up and money changes hands. Making or accepting an offer isn't binding in the slightest. Puzzling, isn't it?

But the best part of this whole business, without question, is its contribution to English vocabulary. The following terminology is virtually unknown outside England, except perhaps to stand-up comedians. Are you ready? Then I'll hit you with it.

If the seller changes their mind or gets a better offer, then you as the buyer have been formally *gazumped*. If your buyer, on the other hand, decides a hovel in Norwood Junction is a better idea after all, then you're the victim of a *gazundering*.

These are real words. And it's perfectly reasonable, I think, to turn dinner table conversation to house-buying in England just so you can use them.

While these words kept me smiling while my offer was going through the motions, the legalities seemed to be taking an inordinately long time - even in comparison to the worst-case horror stories I'd heard. While hanging around and waiting for a phone call telling me I had been *gazumped*, all I could do was enjoy the summer. Fortunately there was much pleasure to be had.

I cycled to work more often than not. After spring came, suddenly the towpath was full of animal life. The swans had cygnets, which if you were lucky could be spotted riding on their parents' backs. Then the little grey birds got less little by the day and less grey by the day. And by the second half of the summer they were barely cygnets at all. There were geese, too, nasty Canadian ones who weren't afraid of bicycles and simply wouldn't budge from the middle of the path.

I counted myself lucky not to get attacked by one of these hissing, squawking, gnashing animals. One evening, returning from work and having just passed a pub called The Pelican, I happened upon a swan and a goose who appeared to be having a difference of opinion that threatened to bubble over.

I hung back at a safe distance, waiting for things to kick off. I wondered if I should reach for my phone in anticipation of a viral contribution to YouTube. But the birds broke it off before it got really hot, stalking off in opposite directions, swaggering proudly as only large waterfowl can.

With the arrival of summer, suddenly there were humans all over the canal too. It was daylight practically all the time, so out came the joggers. And great hordes of schoolkids, too. One thing these disparate folk always had in common was that they were *invariably* in my way. Blissfully unaware, they'd always have a heart attack when I went past them.

But what do you expect, if you're going to run along bang in the middle of a rather narrow path while you block out the world with your headphones? (If you're one of those people, this is *not* a rhetorical question. I really want you to tell me how you see events unfolding in such a way that you don't get a painful shock when a bike overtakes you. Email me.) Or if you're so busy telling your classmates about the latest bus shelter you defaced that you wouldn't hear a bomb drop?

While schoolkids, with their shrieking inability to walk in a straight line, are somewhat irritating at the best of times, it's the runners that I really didn't get. Going to school and being a teenager is kind of a compulsory thing in life, but you have to make an active choice to pull on a pair of shoes, run down a road, and then run back up it again.

I'm not hating on the idea of exercise here. Absolutely not. I just don't understand why so many people choose such a mind-numbing way to get it. Don't they know there are balls to be chased? Footballs, cricket balls, tennis balls, rugby balls? Chase a shuttlecock if that's your thing, but please tell me you can think of something better than running down a road.

Playing a sport is not only much more fun, but it has a marvellous way of giving you something else to think about besides breathlessness and burning legs. The getting-fit part becomes a by-product that takes care of itself.

But not so for the runner, surely? What else can they have on their minds but clock-watching and counting...down...the...kilometres...one...by...one? It's not as though there's any essential skills challenge to consume your focus. Last time I checked, putting one foot in front of the other without falling over was something most of us mastered before we learned to speak.

As for doing it on a treadmill in a gym, without even so much as a cygnet to look at, don't even get me started. When I walk past those giant windows stuffed with exhibits wearing completely serious expressions, who've paid good money to go into a building and do something that's been free to do outdoors for literally millennia, I feel sure humanity has lost its collective mind. These people will never have house deposits, I'm perfectly sure of that.

Then again, I probably have no right to talk about mindless repetition, considering that one of the high points of my summer was doing a 12-hour non-stop batting practice session at Chobham Cricket Club.

But at least I was doing that to develop an actual skill that needs actual practice. Admittedly I also did it to get a day out of the office, thanks to my company introducing a scheme under which we could get an extra day's leave to take part in a charitable activity. And so it was that the Against Malaria Foundation reaped several hundred Pounds worth of benefit from my overwhelming passion for doing anything other than work, as well as actually getting good at hitting cricket balls.

The summer wore on. The runners kept galloping up and down the towpath. One sunny morning we awoke to hear that Britain had voted to leave the European Union, and wondered if we were still dreaming. The property lawyers slaved over hot contracts. And on the longest day, I went out in a field with my didgeridu. It was a sunny Midsummer's Eve made utterly perfect by the fact that England were playing Slovenia in the European Championship football in France. (If you ever want to know what post-dystopian England will look like, wander the land's deserted streets while England have a match in a big tournament.)

I learned good ways to annoy Henry, such as pointing out that all his shirts were grey, or joining him on one of his regular poker tournaments and being the one to come away with money. I watched Pawel, my Polish neighbour, go about his business - building houses or drinking vodka, depending on the hour - with vivacious enthusiasm. I got to know the local greengrocer in Horsell, and was pleased to discover that they would still trust customers with an IOU. They bought a lifetime's loyalty that day.

While I lived it up, Giles got a chest infection. Without warning he stayed in his room for a week, not even emerging for a bowl of cheese and tuna pasta. Since his door was always closed and we didn't actually know whether he was home or not, we started speculating wildly about his whereabouts. Had he been mistakenly locked up as a football hooligan? It was much more fun than knocking on the door, I guess.

But the most serious consequence for Giles wasn't so much being quarantined or thrown into hospital. It was that he had to miss a Southampton match. I'd like to tell you I was nice and sympathetic about this. But instead I laughed and said, "Haha, now you'll have to start all over again! Six years to go!"

I'm sure he'd have killed me outright if he could have gotten up.

Then, in August, came an unexpected twist. My company lost a couple of contracts and I, along with some other colleagues, was given two months' notice. I'd been in the job for less than a year.

I most definitely wasn't as distraught by this as some might be. As a general rule, in fact, I quite enjoy losing jobs. It forces you to try things that would otherwise seem like madcap schemes. The last time retrenchment had occurred, in South Africa, it had given me the impetus to fulfil my childhood dream of playing golf almost every day. That's when I'd learned that I was actually able to survive, and sustain my golfing into the bargain, by writing freelance magazine articles. But I doubt I'd ever have been brave enough to voluntarily quit that job - or any job - in order to do that.

With this latest twist on my career, I might be able to follow a new madcap scheme. I could do all kinds of things with nothing to lose. Hell, I might even be able to write books about buying cars and losing jobs!

But this particular bombshell was trickier than it might usually have been. Even if it did prove rather beautifully that I was right to think basing a house purchase around job location was short-sighted, and that the bank's computers weren't as clever as they thought, it introduced a new annoyance to the whole house purchase thing.

Not with respect to my loan: the bank had their precious three payslips now, so I had a mortgage offer valid for six months. Ridiculously, you might well say, my impending loss of employment didn't need to affect the house-buying thing whatsoever.

No, the main irritation - as usual - was not being able to make any plans. And believe it or not, I *did* like the idea of making plans - it's just that I never had all the information I needed to do so. Even if it was something as simple as what constituted desirable toaster specifications, there was always that little piece of the puzzle missing. And in the big jigsaw that was my life, those pieces were quite large and important ones.

How can you apply for another job if the question of your domicile is still in some lawyer's in-tray? Or, if you're thinking of being a full-time author instead of applying for anything at all, how can you do so when you don't know if the far-more-viable living in your own place thing is actually happening? How can you keep paying rent when your salary is about to dry up? How can you give notice on your house-share when you don't know if or when your purported flat will be ready for move-in? How can you do anything but curse and wait?

Once again I had to thank my lucky stars (or my own inertia and self-delusion, perhaps) that I still had the Peugeot by my side. Apart from certain favoured sets of underwear, the car was about the only remaining thread from Oxfordshire the previous summer. For that I was grateful. Whatever my next move, and no matter how much I wanted to plan it properly, it looked destined to be last-minute and involve moving stuff in a hurry. That's when you *really* want to have a car.

While losing my job wasn't a reason to abandon the Aldershot dream, I did start paying closer attention to the thick sheafs of paper that the lawyers kept sending me. They looked incredibly boring, and I assumed that their presence in my home was merely a legal formality. The lawyers would tell me if anything *odd* was happening, wouldn't they?

But I forced myself to read through everything, making notes and queries as I went. I was, after all, about to spend pretty much every penny of my life's savings on this. And while the English process may drag on for a stupidly long time, at least one of the main purposes of its existence is making sure you're not about to buy a house that's going to fall down. I thought I might as well take advantage of that.

As August drew to an end, it became clear that all was not well. From what I could gather from the complicated papers and records, I was buying into some seriously dodgy territory. I wasn't so much worried that a burst pipe had flooded my flat and a couple of others just a couple of years previously, leading to an outright evacuation of the building, as the fact that the management company was incompetent and sly enough to have earned actual media coverage for its underhandedness.

It's okay, in principle, to have to pay monthly fees to the building's owners for the overall maintenance and upkeep. But when said owners are collecting over fifty thousand Pounds a year, yet have no reserve fund for extraordinary costs, one smells a rat. I would have to religiously pay these supposed professionals every month, yet there was no guarantee they weren't going to slam all the tenants with an unsolicited 10K bill the moment the elevator needed replacing.

The elevator didn't even go all the way up to my floor, for pity's sake.

By now a collection of unpleasant recent letter correspondence between the current owners and the management company had joined my growing pile of house paperwork. I only had to read a couple of these missives to learn that the current owners hated the management company's guts. The bad blood boiled down to a fight about compensation following the flooding business. Dated not all that many months previously, you could sense the poor owner's desperation to cut ties as soon as they possibly could. Hospital pass, anyone?

Even the lawyers were telling me to think very, very carefully. Given that they would lose money if I pulled out of the deal, I took this as an *extremely* serious sign.

Did I want to give up and do a spot of gazundering? Of course I didn't. I'd spent the better part of year getting a job, three payslips, hunting houses and then sitting through all the legalities. And now, it wasn't just a case of binning the Aldershot flat and moving on to the next one. Things like earning money with which to eat were once again a priority. My mortgage offer was on borrowed time, too. Without a job I was no longer a Certifiable Upstanding Citizen, and I wouldn't be able to get another loan without a new job and more payslips.

If I pulled out of this deal, that would be it on the house-buying for the time being. The whole grand plan would have failed. I *really* didn't want to give gazundering a thought.

Just in case it came to that worst case scenario, though, I started making job applications in exciting places like Berlin, Vienna and Amsterdam, where there seemed to be plenty of positions for first-language English speakers on offer. If this apartment was going to turn out to be a dud, then I was pretty keen on getting out of the United Kingdom. The shock Brexit vote, in fact, was a strong and sudden incentive to use that British passport to work in Europe while I still could.

Even without the Brexit push, though, I wasn't much in the mood for picking myself up and trying again. I'd spent a year trying to be a grown-up and it was starting to look like it might not have worked. If that was the case, then it was a sign that England sucked and grown-ups sucked. Banks sucked and the system sucked. To compound matters, another cricket season was all but over. I really ought to be a cave hermit. Or at least go and learn to speak Dutch properly.

Reclining Armchair Season

Sometimes, in life, the stars actually *do* align.

I was certainly a challenging case for the celestial bodies. I'd been given notice on my job, and by the start of September I'd also decided to tell my landlady I would be leaving the room I was renting in Knaphill. Thanks to my mulish refusal to waste rent whilst I held the peculiar status of about-to-be-unemployed potentially-imminent-homeowner-who-might-break-off-the-deal, things were now even more complicated by the fact that my rental would end a week before my job did.

I could have specified a more convenient exit date, so this wasn't a great example of making life easy for myself. But with my salary about to go, saving a week's rent was first priority. I now needed somewhere to await developments without having to commit to anything like a rental period - and I needed it fast.

And if there was one cliche I clearly still believed in, it was the notion that fortune favours the brave.

Or maybe it's that fortune favours the idiotic. Whatever, salvation arrived in spectacular form. Just when I desperately needed a free and flexible roof over my head while things panned out, I received an offer to take care of a two-storey, two-bedroom house in Surrey. A house fully equipped with sports channels and a reclining armchair. Mine for a massive five-week period whilst its owners went to Colorado.

To put that in perspective, I almost never got offered house-sitting gigs, probably because people who know me well know that I'm capable of breaking just about anything. Especially Venetian blinds, which I swear were created with the sole purpose of befuddling me with their pulleys, ropes, flick-switches and twist-knobs. The systems vary subtly in different homes and countries, so there's always something new to learn. I end up cautiously pulling and prodding until something happens. Usually that something is the whole damn thing slamming down on me, plunging the room into a darkness and me into a miserable, often fruitless, battle to haul it back up again.

With this in mind, a five-week stint with no real commitment was nothing short of a sensational development. The owners were good friends of mine who saw having someone to water the plants more as a bonus than a necessity. I didn't have to be there the whole time, and I was assured that if I got a job (or a home) somewhere else, I could just lock up and go.

Better yet, the house didn't even have any blinds. It just had curtains - and I fancied my chances against those. (Although I did tend to break the ones with drawstrings. They didn't like being pulled. But why *wouldn't* you just pull them? Like revolving doors, drawstrings on curtains are classic human over-complication.)

Moreover, if my life was still becalmed when they got back, I could stay with them as long as I needed to. Under the circumstances, it was about the most terrific news I could have hoped for.

With the nights beginning to draw in, the mighty release of unemployment imminent and all those sports channels at the end of a remote that would be under my exclusive control, it's fair to say that I wasn't in a major hurry to leave before the five weeks were up. Being jobless, after all, brings a rare opportunity to unwind completely. Unsullied by that nagging feeling that your precious week's vacation is flying by far too quickly, it's a far preferable brand of relaxation. One that's good to savour for a while.

The house was in Merstham, the name given to this particular part of Surrey's endless sprawl of commuter towns. Merstham sat right on the M25 orbital highway and ran pretty much directly into the next towns on either side. Like a slew of places thirty-odd miles from Buckingham Palace, St Paul's Cathedral *et cetera*, it used to be a small country village in which you might feasibly have set an Enid Blyton book. Now, it's been gobbled up by the morbidly obese city that is London, and offers up the delights of trains whizzing in all directions and even a rough council estate of its very own. This lay just a couple of blocks away from the house, and provided heavily-fortified shops, unlimited sports betting opportunities and the occasional spot of knife crime.

There were also millions of cars in Merstham. Being far enough out of central London that people didn't have the option of an underground network, and yet still with a terrifying population density, there was probably more traffic than there was in the city. And since an overground train to anywhere cost (as usual) about triple what petrol would, my Peugeot and I had little choice but to join the fray.

English suburban roads in places like Merstham were built in quieter times. Driving a car around them nowadays is quite unlike driving a car anywhere else. The unique challenge comes from the fact that on all but the most important roads, people are able to park their vehicles on both sides of a road that only has one lane in each direction. This gives rise to a situation in which there's a narrow chute down the middle, through which only one car can pass at a time.

This in turn means that most of driving in Britain involves assessing whether the chute is clear. If it is, you barrel through it, and anybody trying to enter it from the other side has to pull in behind the last parked car and wait till you're through.

If two cars arrive at their respective ends of the chute at the same time, out comes the stubborn Anglo-Saxon politeness that would have a German or an Italian shaking their heads. One car flashes headlights to tell the other car to go first. But the other car flashes headlights at the same time. Each is saying 'Please, I positively insist,' not wanting this stranger to consider them rude or selfish. The German or the Italian would plunge through the minute they got an invitation, but in Britain nobody moves: it's like a weird manners standoff.

But just when you think everyone in the country has gone polite to the point of insanity, the cars behind each of the duellists will start up a bad-tempered honking that reveals just how fake all of this is. At which point the protagonists will both suddenly go, their desire not to upset the people behind now firmly outweighing their wish to show civility to the motorist at the far end of the chute. Grabbing at their handbrakes and clutches in a mad, consideration-for-others-fuelled scurry, both lurch forward into the channel, only to realize they're now face to face. One of them will have to reverse out of it once more. As if on autopilot, each will dutifully do exactly that. And so it begins again.

Meanwhile, in the soundproof interiors of their Vauxhall Astras, they're all muttering 'wanker' under their breaths.

And they'll say the same thing, oddly enough, whether the guy at the other end is trying to be excessively polite or, like a German, charging through at the first opportunity.

The worst thing about British roads, though, is the ubiquitous 'white van', which is quite the most appalling vehicle you could ever hope to meet. I suppose it's possible that the same make and model of windowless light commercial vehicle is also a feature of roads in other countries, yet I'm not sure a Frenchman would get your drift if you tried to turn the conversation to a *van blanc*. He'd more than likely reach for the wine cabinet.

But in Britain, everyone knows what you mean when you say 'white van'. They're typically driven, very badly, by self-employed types such as painters, plumbers and chimney sweeps. (I don't know if there are any more chimney sweeps, but I'll bet a white van would be ideal for those long brooms if there are.) I've just discovered that these machines even have their own Wikipedia page.

My problem isn't with the way white vans are driven, nor even the people driving them - plumbers are essential to civilized existence, after all - so much as the fact that their tall, broad and thoroughly opaque design hogs your entire field of vision. Motoring along behind one is surprisingly disconcerting, and makes you realise just how much you rely on looking through the windscreens of the vehicle ahead. If there's a Ford Fiesta between you and that stray sheep that wanders onto the road, chances are you'll also see the animal coming. But if you're stuck behind a wall of white coachwork, you wouldn't know if King Kong was standing in the fast lane. And when the bricklayer up ahead has to jump on the brakes ahead of you, you'll be last to get the memo. I don't like it.

I presume the invention of these vans made thieves realise how much they rely on looking through windows too. If I had to guess, the main reason white vans don't have windows is so that carpenters can leave their drill sets in the car overnight without creating an obvious temptation. Still, there's something forbidding about these machines and I wish they'd be banned.

With driving around Merstham and its surrounds such a jerky, stop-start experience, I avoided getting in the car if I possibly could. Of course, I needed to drive to work for the first few days - again, train fares were orders of magnitude dearer than fuel - but after that there wasn't much temptation to go anywhere at all.

After all, I didn't know a soul in the area, the weather was turning rotten and England were playing Bangladesh in some fascinating televised cricket. Applying for jobs was something one could do from an armchair, and waiting for news on my property was, well, just waiting. The nearest big places were Gatwick Airport and Croydon, both of which strongly lacked pull factors at any time of year. There were whole days on which I didn't leave the house.

When I did venture out, it was usually to travel. I popped over to Dublin for a bachelor's weekend. Two weeks later, now thoroughly unemployed and still in limbo, I headed to Hereford for the corresponding wedding. And, perhaps most interestingly of all, I went for a one-night trip to Vienna. Because

I'd had a nibble on one of the lines I'd thrown out for a job in continental Europe.

I hadn't exactly been pushing the boat out on the job applications. Not just because I had savings and (currently) free lodgings, but because my supposed house purchase meant I didn't know *where* I ought to be looking, or not looking. So unless I spied something in one of those particularly appealing European cities - somewhere cool enough to make me abandon my supposed flat or at least commit to the scary option of renting it out from the get-go - I wasn't going to bother.

There was another reason for my poor applications tally. After building up a great deal of experience in the world of job-hunting, I had by now developed strict policies about the processes I was willing to pursue or not pursue. If it was going to take me all night to apply for one measly job, then that job was probably out. Searching for work was a question of expected value, and the potential reward for me to spend three hours jumping through hoops with heaven knew how many other candidates, with heaven knew how small a chance, would have to be a truly knockout opportunity.

Barring the job of a lifetime, I was no longer going to apply via any system that required the automated extraction of my resume. This was the increasingly popular methodology under which companies got candidates to throw their carefully-crafted CV's out of the window and put the same information into boxes that suited their computer systems. 'Don't worry, it won't take long,' their websites crooned, 'Just upload your resume and our software will automatically populate our application form.'

The trouble was, it never, *ever* worked. You ended up with a form that listed Wynberg Boys' Primary School as your first employer, boldly stated that you performed such managerial-level roles as 'married' between the years of 2011 and 2013, and confidently named your birthplace as 'basic Spanish.'

It's funny to think about this now, but when it's late on a school night and some faceless company insists on ripping up and re-doing that perfectly good CV you slaved for hours to create, just so a computer can determine your destiny, then I challenge you to find a smile. I wasn't going to play chicken with those companies anymore. If they were too lazy to read a good CV and didn't respect the time I'd put into making one, then I probably didn't want to work for them anyway.

At the opposite end of the spectrum was the most delightful thing to hit the job market in years, namely the 'Apply With Your Profile' button on

LinkedIn. This was a most elegant and simple way to apply for a lot of jobs in a short space of time. I genuinely loved it. One click - you could add a targeted note if you wanted - and your future employer would be alerted to check out your profile. You were done in seconds, and if you had a good profile with good references, examples of work and perhaps a video, then it told more about you than a CV would anyway. As I write this system is still going strong, and I think it should absolutely be the future.

But it was a more traditional approach that had now earned me a plane ticket to Austria and back. The company advertising for an English-language writer in Vienna wasn't big enough to have a malfunctional CV processing system, so all I had to do was write them an email with my resume attached. Old school.

My application met with considerable and sustained interest. After a Skype interview, which mercifully didn't break up and die like most of my Skype calls usually did, I wrote a trial piece on the subject of artificial intelligence. And following what seemed to have been a positive reading, I was now being flown to the Austrian capital to meet the crew.

(Speaking of Skype, can anybody who might be reading this in Seattle have a quick look out of the window and find out if they *do* actually have any geeks in the vicinity of Microsoft HQ? If the supposed abundance of highly-paid nerds can't deal with making video calls work properly after all this time, I motion that they're overrated, play way too much table tennis and deserve the sack. Or is fixing Skype beneath these super-coders; the tech-world equivalent of cleaning the toilets? Does Microsoft perhaps need to hire Guatemalans to do this work as well as mopping the lavatory floors?)

At this stage, the writer job in Vienna was the only application that had really come back with interest. But the work was neither here nor there. I could do any job. My thoughts were entirely about the destination. The real question was whether I wanted to live in Austria rather than Holland or Germany, or anywhere else that might have an English-speaking job for me. If this meeting went well and I got an offer, should I take it?

I supposed this overnight stay would be a good opportunity to check out the city's vibe and see if I might feel at home there. In my twisted mind, Vienna already had a distinctly seductive edge over Berlin or Amsterdam. Why? Because I hadn't been there before and knew nothing about it. Of course that shouldn't have any bearing on a decision about a move that might last a lifetime - Vienna could always be done on a weekend break - but sometimes this is how I work things out.

And surely one could read something into the fact that schnitzel had always been my favourite meal? Imagine living in a city that had schnitzels (and an abundance of decadent cakes, from what I was reading) lounging about waiting to be eaten!

As I stepped onto the plane at Gatwick Airport, I was already feeling rather tempted by Vienna.

Beer and Coffee?
In the Same Room?

I emerged from the front doors of Wien Mitte station, crossed the forecourt and beheld the city that might just become home. Over the pedestrianized street loomed a vast grey wall of building covered with logos reading *Thalia*, *DM* and *Village Cinema*. This boring shrine to consumerism was all I could see in front of me. In many respects it was like driving behind a white van.

I was fresh off the airport train and didn't want to be looking at a place like this. The October air was crisp. I took a big gulp of it before turning around and following the orange signs towards the *U-Bahn*. I needed to head a few stops on the orange underground line in the direction of Ottakring, alighting at Zieglergasse. From there it would be a short walk towards the hotel that my prospective employers had booked for me.

The train had a rickety, rattly vibe to it. The Vienna metro was definitely a bit retro. If you wanted the doors to open, you had to grasp firmly on the handle, a great ratchet of a thing that looked as though it had been taken right off a mincing machine, and give it a proper shove. There was no way to do it that didn't look passive-aggressive.

Not that there was anything wrong with the train. It got me to where I was going, and arrived when the display said it would. I admired those LCD-style platform displays. From far away you thought you were looking at whole letters, but when you got up close you realised they were made up of tiny little triangles. The *Wiener Linien* could make up any combination of letters and numbers by lighting up the appropriate triangles. It was perfectly adequate, just as long as you didn't want Comic Sans script.

It was getting on for nine in the evening, and there were only two things I wanted: a walk and a schnitzel. But first I had to get to my hotel. This proved simple enough, since I'd printed out a map from the Internet.

Call me a dinosaur, but I always prefer having a map. Partly because it means I can actually get a feel for direction instead of moronically following a blue arrow on my phone, partly because a map's batteries never run out and partly (well, mostly) because using navigation in other countries means paying extra data charges. Where the lazy succumb and pay whatever their mobile company slams them with at the end of the month, I arrange printouts whenever I can.

Beating the mobile giants in this way is surprisingly satisfying, but beyond that I *really* don't want to be a phone moron. When I travel, I want the bigger picture. I want to know where north is and see how far from the Danube we might happen to be. Just following your phone seems like cheating to me. If the journey is the destination, then navigation is the journey. Still with me?

The Hotel am Brillantengrund was full of character, with skinny little rooms, sausage pillows and an interior courtyard that felt almost tropical with its abundance of plant life. The only thing that confounded me about the place was one particular sign in the bathroom.

Set on a black background, it portrayed a white, vaguely anthropomorphic stick figure indulging in what looked to be emptying his bladder - three drops were clearly illustrated, suspended in mid-air but seemingly on target. I thought what the stick figure was doing seemed fair enough, but the sign didn't agree. A big red stripe swept right across this fairly innocuous bathroom scene.

I didn't understand the exact nature of the injunction. Was urination forbidden? Or just male urination? Merely doing it standing up? I was puzzled and fascinated in equal measure: was my hotel really trying to dictate the rules around relieving oneself? If so, how were they going to police it? Was there a GoPro under the toilet seat, squinting its beady eye up at how you were planning to take care of business?

I wasn't about to call reception to find out. And I really needed the loo. I probably did something illegal at that point, but I'll never really know.

What I did ask them down at reception was what sort of food they might have on offer. My mouth was watering for that schnitzel by now.

"Filipino," said the guy on reception with a smile.

I reeled. 'Filipino' was just about the last answer you'd expect to such a question late on a Wednesday night in October in Vienna. He might as well have said they were dishing up Tajikistani cuisine.

"Seriously?" I asked.

He nodded. Clearly he wasn't kidding. Clearly these Viennese were incurable hipsters, if they passed their evenings wolfing down Manila-style rice. Damn them! Where was my schnitzel?

"Okay, forgive me if I won't be joining," I said to him. "Do you have any ideas for where I can get some Austrian food? I'm only in town for one night, and I'm not going to judge Vienna on the quality of its *adobo*."

He smiled and pointed me in the direction of a *Gasthaus* where he assured me I would be able to get a schnitzel. This involved trotting back down towards Mariahilfer Straße, where I'd only just jumped out of the subway. This was another pedestrianized street - if you were willing to discount the bicycles, taxis, sweeping machines, delivery trucks and even buses that seemed to have an exemption. I like the idea of a street just for walkers, but it kind of defeats the purpose when you still have to watch out for the occasional heavy vehicle threatening you and your Christmas shopping.

It did look an awful lot like Mariahilfer Straße was the sort of place people would come shopping in droves. It wasn't particularly pretty, and it had all the international chains I'd have found over in Croydon. The kebab and pizza joints were comparable too, although in Austria they spelled it *Kebap*.

But as soon as I saw a *Würstelstand*, I knew I wasn't in England. It took a while to stumble on one, actually, by which time I was getting pretty hungry and struggling to find the schnitzel restaurant. So I settled for a *Würstel* instead.

Such fare was, after all, an equally appropriate culinary introduction to a city whose name is strongly linked with sausages. Although the Viennese apparently refer to those particular sausages as Frankfurters.

I wasn't sure exactly what the etiquette was here. I saw people getting sausages cut up on paper plates with a white roll on the side. Others received sausages cut up on paper plates *without* a roll on the side. Yet other clients got whole sausages on paper plates with a dollop of mustard. What did I want? And how would I get it with my non-existent German?

In the end I went for the 'hot dog' option on the display above the kiosk window, mainly because this sounded like something I couldn't mispronounce. My sausage was presented to me in a hollowed-out baguette. I hadn't seen anybody else devouring one of those, and it didn't look terribly traditional. I dare say the others milling about the stand thought me a frightful philistine.

But it tasted good, that was the main thing. My choice of sausage, more by luck than judgement, was a fine one. I went for *Käsekrainer*, because I happened to know that *Käse* meant cheese, and that cheese could never be a bad thing in a sausage. They probably don't do bad sausage at all in these parts, but my *Käsekrainer* was particularly delicious. Even if the melted cheese inside did leave a few burns when it flung its boiling-hotness into the depths of my mouth as I took the first bite. Rookie error, I guess.

My evening feed now dealt with, I pondered whether I should head for the centre and the 'sights', or simply wander wherever the road took me. The map made the centre look awfully appealing: it was dotted with 'gardens' bearing imperial-sounding names like *Volksgarten* and *Burggarten*.

'Garden' sounds infinitely more civilized than 'park', I always think. The sort of place one might go and read a newspaper, as opposed to the sort of place where gangs of youths kick footballs around and the next generation of yobbos rattle about on swings.

Appealing as the centre sounded, I thought the better of it. Parks (and gardens) aren't very good at night, after all. And did I want to base a possible life decision on gawking at the city's top attractions? Far better to stroll some ordinary streets - the kind of streets I might end up living on - and see what they felt like.

I had next to zero knowledge about Vienna, apart from what I'd seen on the map and a vague awareness of dancing horses and certain foods. I think that goes for most people, come to think of it. You're sure it's probably charming, but how many people do you know who've actually *been* there?

Strictly speaking, it wasn't quite my first time within city limits. I'd skirted them on two separate occasions back in 2003, when I was in my first heady weeks as a motor-racing journalist and was twice sent to cover events in the southern Austrian state of Styria. This had involved flying to Vienna, caressing the edge of town in a hire car and then jumping on the highway heading south.

Actually those distant trips meant there was one further thing I knew about Vienna. Which was that the city was close to a lot of other places. When I'd left the airport, the first thing I'd noticed was that most of the signs were for cities in other countries, rather than destinations in Austria. Barely were you out of the multistory and you could get in a lane for Bratislava or Budapest. Or even for Prague, if a bit of Czech took your fancy. The signs for Viennese suburbs, written in cursive, came across as something of an afterthought. Perhaps the Austrians considered themselves terribly worldly and European, and didn't think much of people merely heading to somewhere in Vienna.

'You're going to *Simmering*, Klaus? Seriously? What do you want in a working-class hole like that? Are you one of these people who've never travelled? Come one, man, we're in Europe now! You can't fester in *Vienna* all weekend...join us for wine-tasting in the Hungarian hills!'

Maybe a sense of wanderlust really did develop in post Cold War Austria. Jutting into the Eastern Bloc as this half of the country did - it was pretty much punching a hole in the Iron Curtain, actually - the Viennese were a stone's throw from a lot of exotic places that presumably weren't all that easy to visit pre-1990. Bratislava, for example, is only 60km away from Vienna.

All of this closeness was a major attraction, because going to other countries is something I like being able to do. I'd been sneaking closer looks at European maps, and getting a sense of just what a traveller's dream Vienna was. Not only was Slovakia right there, but so too were Hungary and the Czech Republic. My old friend Slovenia wasn't a million miles to the south, either.

When I'd arrived at Wien Mitte Station, in fact, I'd seen a place called Česke Velenice listed as one of the destinations on the departures screen. I felt pretty sure that this didn't sound like an Austrian town. Despite living in four different countries, I'd never been in an essentially suburban station where you'd see a foreign city as a destination. (Which will probably be much more believable if I tell you that those four countries were Australia, South Africa, Britain and the USA) It was both fantastic and enchanting. This kind of thing was definitely going to count in Vienna's favour.

Tonight, though, I was going to try hard not to waste time looking up how easy it would be to whizz across a border just for kicks. This was about getting to know Vienna, which by the way is just about the most easterly place in which you can expect to be greeted in German.

From the *Würstelstand* I strolled down Mariahilfer Straße, folded up my map and thrust it deliberately into my pocket. It was a perfect night for walking - cool and quiet - and strolling wherever I wanted is what I would do. Up until a reasonable hour, at any rate. I did have a big meeting the next day, after all.

The first wonder I encountered was an establishment called Cafe Ritter. It was getting on for ten in the evening, and there, through the tall, broad windows, I could see waiters in suits carrying shiny silver trays of food and drink to what looked like a contented clientele. Some people were evidently still in the mood for a coffee, while others were receiving frothing, golden beers. All this was quite shocking to me.

The concept of coffee and beer co-existing simply doesn't compute if you've spent too long in Britain. The British are incapable of having a quiet beer in the same room as someone sipping a tea and petting their poodle, and this is especially true after sunset. The beer drinkers will always get rowdy and unpleasant. That's why they got separated out, and establishments that sell beer in Britain are generally dark, sticky and wouldn't have a clue what to do with a coffee order.

It's just like the football fans, you see. Supporters of opposing sides have to be fenced apart from each other. And it's for their own good. Let them mix, and they're bound to tear each other's eyeballs out at some stage. Britain's traditional approach to mixing hot-drink people and beer people is just good pragmatism.

And yet here I was, observing quiet glasses of *Stiegl* being consumed in perfect harmony with cappuccino-swiggers and late-night newspaper-readers. The beer drinkers looked to be chatting quietly, not causing a disturbance to anyone. How was this possible? Why were people drinking coffee so late? Who reads a newspaper with schnitzel, on their own, at this sort of an hour? Or takes their dog out to a cafe, for that matter? And why wasn't the kitchen long since closed, come to think of it?

I didn't step inside, merely gawked through the window a little longer, trying to imagine how long such chandeliers would survive in the same room as a bunch of true beer louts. The waiters in bow ties were simply surreal. Between them, the numerous canine guests, the evident willingness to serve a proper meal even after 10pm and the generally nostalgic air of the place, I rather liked the look of it all. If Viennese cafes were to be like this, then they would have to be another tick in the city's favour.

I started walking downhill, away from the big shopping drag. Up on the right loomed another astonishing sight. How can I describe it? The building was like a particularly unsightly flour mill, with a skinny verandah running around the top. This verandah flowered into a broad circle at each corner, so that when you looked up at the thing, it looked a bit like Mickey Mouse had left his ears up there. The whole leviathan structure was made entirely of unadorned concrete. Mickey's ears made no difference: it was appalling. It would have been ugly on a Bulgarian industrial estate, never mind the middle of Vienna.

Locals know that this unique addition to the neighbourhood is one of five *Flaktürme* that were thrown up by the Nazis when they occupied the city in the thirties and forties. But my Viennese history was hazy, and the words *Zerschmettert in Stücke (Im Frieden Der Nacht)*, printed big and bold and *sans serif* on the concrete above the verandah, did little to answer any questions. Not even when I got to the other side and saw the English translation, which read *Smashed to Pieces (In the Still of Night)*.

The only thing I could tell for certain was that the building now served as an aquarium and, on the outside, a practise wall for nutcase climbers. Which is all rather fitting, I suppose. It was built by nutcases to begin with, after all. And filling it up with water seemed a profoundly sensible thing to do with such a monstrosity.

I mooched onwards at a glacial pace, a *flaneur* tonight if ever there was one. I've learned that you can only walk this slowly if you're on your own. Other people don't like it, even when they're on holiday. I guess they've just gotten used to power-walking, and can't process not being in a hurry. (I hate power-walkers and don't begin to understand them, by the way. They should stop it at once.)

But if you can bring yourself to float through the streets, I recommend ultra-slow as the ideal speed for the city traveller. You see more unfolding around you, you soak it up better and you'll spot more interesting photographs to take. And if you like to meet locals, your body language says that you're open. It says you're not rushing off somewhere.

Granted, in stranger-averse Europe projecting this slow-going interest in everything around you doesn't make much difference in terms of encounters. But somewhere like Asia or Africa, where people think nothing of walking up to someone they don't know, that 'open' vibe always has the potential to make you new friends. Especially if the colour of your skin makes it clear you're not from around there.

Exception: places where people might like to rob, mug, pickpocket, hassle or bug you. In places like this - I'm looking at you, Barcelona, and you too, Johannesburg - it's good to keep up the brisk pace of the person who knows where he's going. Especially if the colour of your skin makes it clear you're not from around there.

A word of caution. Maybe it's just me, but walking slowly tires you out much more than walking quickly. Nothing leaves my legs more leaden than the sluggish, stop-start kind of stroll you take around a museum or an art gallery. I'll hike up a mountain and down before lunch and still make it around the shops in the evening, but put me in the Tate Modern and I can barely stand up for the rest of the day.

Knowing I could sleep like a corpse in a couple of hours, I kept on going slow. I noticed the little numbers on each street sign changing from seven to six. I gathered that Vienna, like Paris, Prague, Budapest and I'm not sure how many others, had a system of numbered city districts. I wondered if their use was as widespread in spoken language as it is among the French. It would be a great shame, I thought, if people in Vienna didn't actually use the fun suburb names I'd seen on the map: places like Hundsturm, Favoriten, Alsergrund, Simmering, Strozzigrund. None of these struck me as the kind of suburb names you'd find in, say, Frankfurt. Strozzigrund sounded like the name of a travelling circus. Simmering is something that winter beef stews do. Hundsturm sounded a bit like something postmen have nightmares about. These names *had* to be a joke. Or at the very least, I hoped to find jesters in funny hats hopping about in all of them.

But the streets here were quiet: no lively jesters, nor anybody else. I could hear my heavy footsteps on the paving as I looked up at the stylish buildings around me. I don't know much about architecture (did the Disney references give it away?), but the three- and four-storey houses around here reminded me of Paris. And if people were living in them, they were getting on with it very quietly. The air of peace was quite striking for a capital city. A peculiar cloud of contentedness seemed to hang over the place.

Vienna didn't disappoint on delivering reality to match those vague cliches I had in my head. Twice I walked past open windows, out of which floated the melodious sounds of somebody practicing the piano. That seemed to fit my incredibly vague knowledge of classical music: weren't Mozart and his chums always busy impressing courts in Vienna? I was sure of it! And then there were the chandeliers: every other lit-up window seemed to offer up at least a modestly indulgent lighting installation. Such excess, such dedication to musical leisure! It was all so far removed from IKEA lampshades and televisions flickering *Bake Off*, which is what I would surely have seen if I were peering through windows in London right now.

After a stop to buy some sweets (I was instantly hooked on Haribo's *Milchbären*) and a drink I can't recall, my zig-zag down the hill ended at a relatively busy road called the Linke Wienzeile. After crossing that, I found myself on a bridge overlooking a canal and an *U-Bahn* line that ran in parallel, several metres below street level. The canal looked pretty industrial, and capable of dealing with a minor tsunami, but right now it had only the most pathetic trickle of water in it. It was a sorry sight, really, and I concluded that this certainly couldn't be the Danube, nor anything to do with it.

I watched a couple of trains go humming along beneath me. The city seemed to be working well. I crossed the bridge and walked on.

Immediately things became a little busier and visibly less Austrian. I was moving away from the centre on Reinprechtsdorfer Straße, plunging into the heart of a district apparently called Margareten. This was where life got a little more gritty. Shops offering a variety of cellular communication services grew more frequent. Groups of men chatted over tea or hookah pipes, and whatever they were talking wasn't German.

It was quite the sudden change, but please don't imagine I'd stumbled into a miniature Antananarivo or Jakarta. It was a turnaround only on a Viennese scale. Just a little less quiet. Everything's relative.

I walked on, keeping it simple by going dead straight. I wondered if this was the kind of area where I'd afford to live, *if* I got an offer and *if* I accepted that offer. I scanned shop windows and street noticeboards to get some clues, but learned only that there were fewer chandeliers on display here. And that parallel parking (my *bête noire*) was the only kind of parking they seemed to do in Vienna. Oh, and that it was a postman's dream: the Austrians appeared to be *very* good at street signs and house numbering.

Reinprechtsdorfer Straße ploughed on for a long time, but eventually spilled out into a public transport hub called Matzleinsdorfer Platz. Not only charmless, with its brutally practical bus stops underneath the vast railway bridge, but even a trifle seedy in its evening abandonment. Things were getting worse.

Had I found the scariest part of Vienna? There was every chance. When I walked without a map in this way, I often succumbed to some magnetic force that drew me towards bad neighbourhoods. It was a real knack. You simply can't teach it.

The most memorable example had been in the nest of thieves that is Barcelona. I was mooching in the direction of Montjuic Park, but from the bottom end of Las Ramblas. Letting fate guide me, I ended up at some sort of dodgy back entrance near the docks. Locals shake their heads and bury their faces in their hands when I tell them where I went that evening. Then they nod their heads with a weary sigh when I tell them I got a rock thrown at the back of my head by a wiry youth.

Funnily enough, I never much liked Barcelona after that. And not just because of what happened to me. I heard screams in the night outside our window, which I later discovered was our fellow guests being relieved of their baggage.

If I was Spain I'd be only too happy to let the Catalans go. As long as they take their horrid city with them.

Right now, many years later in Vienna, I took my arrival at Matzleinsdorfer Platz as a sign to turn around. It was getting late, and anyway, reaching *really* big roads and giant bridges is usually a sign that pleasant walking conditions are about to deteriorate. They always do when you get far enough away from the city centre to start encountering hardware megastores with their own parking lots.

I walked back to my hotel in getting-to-bed mode rather than discovery mode. Probably intimidated by a quick-step that might have bordered on power-walking, nobody approached me. (Although clearly I wasn't accessorized as a true power-walker would be. I wasn't checking my phone, nor clutching a Starbucks cup or a shiny briefcase or businesslike handbag. I'd have been found out instantly in Canary Wharf.)

I found the Hotel am Brillantengrund with no trouble, made another possibly illegal use of the lavatory, and fell into bed.

The next day I walked down Mariahilfer Straße towards the city, which is what most sensible people do instead of striding to Matzleinsdorfer Platz in the middle of the night. Today I had good reason to follow the pack: the office was right in the middle of all the action.

I found it in a road just off Vienna's famous, timeless Ringstraße, with its classic trams, stately trees, well-behaved traffic, imperial opera houses and libraries and its curious sense that nothing could possibly be wrong with the world. The company occupied one floor of a building that was called a *Palais* and boasted a number classical statues taking care of the roof ramparts. It had one of those ancients lifts that you only find in continental Europe, in which the machinery's frightening wheezes and clunks convince you that you've just embarked on the lift's fateful last voyage, destined to airless maroonment midway between two floors.

Luckily there was still life in the machine, and I made it to the third floor. I met who I needed to meet, had lunch with my prospective team, had a final chat about money and ascertained that a job offer was on the table. I was honest about the situation with my house purchase, and prayed a little more time to decide.

There was much to ponder as I got back on the plane.

Decisions, Decisions...

It looked like the time to take decisive action had come. Vienna had definitely spoken to me, so now I had to stop lounging around watching *Ross Kemp* (you really had to admire the man's ability to find the very darkest corners of every country and make you want to avoid going there at all costs) and waiting for phone calls from lawyers and agents.

This house-buying lark was holding me back, and needed to be resolved in one way or another. Either I was going to be a boring adult and buy a flat, or I was going to seize the chance to go skipping off to Austria before they gave the job to someone else.

Or could I do both? Sure, in theory. I could complete the sale, quickly find a renter and let the apartment pay for itself while I went and lived in Europe for as long I wanted - perhaps forever. And one day, if the building didn't fall down, the apartment would give me free money. It seemed a nice compromise, and one that would allow me to live in Vienna rather than somewhat less desirable Aldershot. But that whole idea rested upon, well, completing the bleeding sale.

I'd now been waiting *months* for the so-called management company to send through the complete accounting paperwork for the building for the previous three years. Not only was this supposed to reveal any dodgy practices the management has been engaging in, but it was a legal requirement too. And the longer they failed to provide the financial statements, the more convinced I was that the people running the building were up to something.

I got onto the seller's lawyers, who predictably babbled on about not being allowed to talk to me. But I didn't hang up the phone without telling them they might want to do a little chasing if they wanted their client's sale to proceed. With Austria now a real alternative, I was starting to feel like I could take this or leave it.

I communicated to all concerned that I'd pull out in a couple of days if this went on. Suddenly chasing was going on everywhere I looked. My lawyers chasing the seller's lawyers. My lawyers chasing the management company. *Me* chasing the management company. So many people hounding three twitchy little pieces of paper. What kind of suspicious surgery were these clowns performing on their accounts?

I had a long and very grown-up chat with my lawyer, who seemed to have developed something of a human side after a couple of days chasing my case. She explained, quite gravely, why the absence of a reserve fund for building work was a long way from being a great thing. And how it meant I'd need to have somewhere around £10,000 in my pocket at all times, just in case. I strongly agreed that this was a negative. She advised me to think long and hard about proceeding.

It shook me that a representative of the legal profession was concerned enough about certain aspects of this property sale that she was willing to talk herself out of the fees she'd get if the deal actually went ahead. You'd have to take that kind of behaviour from a lawyer rather seriously, wouldn't you?

I didn't think I could stomach the idea of paying monthly fees for the building's upkeep *and* having to keep several holidays' worth of cash in my piggy bank for the rest of my days. One or the other, but not both. Especially not the latter. If I kept the flat all my life, I was basically being asked to take thousands of Pounds to my deathbed. I'd be constantly angry about that.

My lawyer followed up with a letter that basically egged me on further to pull out, and keep my fee money in my pocket. *It is a concern that the service charge accounts are not readily available,* read one line. 'Concern' was a word that really struck me. It's one that crops up shortly before violence explodes in so many movies, as in 'My three huge henchmen and I just dropped by to express that we have certain *concerns* about your incursions into our territory, Mr Sanchez.' In the context of my life's biggest financial decision, it had no less of a brooding threat about it.

Since the place I was house-sitting also happened to be in the process of getting sold, it just so happened that I needed to open the door for a surveyor and valuations expert to come and take a look one afternoon. It was part of the legal process for *that* house, which was of course going far more smoothly than mine was.

Once he'd finished looking around, I decided to pick his brains. I explained some of the ongoing *concerns* about the Aldershot deal.

"One thing I've learned," he said chirpily. "Is that management companies are either brilliant or terrible - nothing in between. And from what you're telling me, this isn't one of the brilliant ones."

"Yeah, I think they're up to something," I said glumly. "How do they keep finding ways to spend the exact amount they collect in service charges each year?"

"It's a good question and you're right to ask it. Maybe it's all above board. But ask yourself, is it worth the risk?"

This guy was good. Sometimes you need to hear the perspective from a complete neutral. Someone with no interest invested in the situation.

"Probably not," I shrugged. "I just got a job offer in Vienna. If this is a dodgy deal, I can just walk away to Austria. It'd just be a shame, after so many months of waiting around."

But deep down I knew that the waiting around shouldn't be a factor in making a decision. Or at least not in such a massive one. Time invested is a sunk cost. Choosing a path should only be about the available information in front of you. And ironically, that information suggested that *not* buying a property was actually the most grown-up thing I could do in the face of so many legitimate doubts. Not being the greater fool never sounds very heroic, but if the facts suggest 'no' is the right answer, then it's a fair option to take.

"Vienna, eh?" The surveyor's voice shook me out of my philosophizing. "Speak German, do you?"

"Nah, it's an English-language writing job. But learning German's definitely the plan. I've never tried immersion before. I know it's a tough language though. And I've got a feeling that the German they speak down there might be a bit different. I think going to Vienna to learn German might be a bit like going to Glasgow to learn English."

The surveyor laughed. "Don't worry, they'll always understand your textbook German, at least. And it gets easier! My wife's German, and once you get the hang of it it's actually quite logical. *Very* logical. When you figure out how words are put together, you can even start making up your own."

Dammit. Here I was getting more reasons to go to Austria, and more reasons not to buy the flat. I really wanted to give the flat every chance, but I'd been doing that since July. It was now late October. I needed to give an answer on the job and my five weeks of house-sitting were almost up. I couldn't shake the feeling that Vienna, with its waiters in bow-ties, was more alluring a mystery to me than Berlin. And that it would be warmer for longer in summer than Amsterdam or Helsinki, which is where the next opportunities might come along if I turned down this one in order to hold out on the apartment.

I made one last call, trying to save my property ownership dream. It was to an independent advisor for a frank chat about the situation. Apparently paid to help people like me talk things through in plain English, I found him

169

sympathetic. But his take on things was much the same: this purchase might bite you later.

Sometimes it's nice when everyone gives you the same answer. I think I'd reached my decision. There was only one reasonable thing to do, and that was to pull out. To gazunder.

I gave it one more day for those missing accounts to turn up. When they inevitably didn't, I phoned my lawyer and said I was washing my hands of the whole business. She said I was probably doing the right thing.

I also had to phone the estate agent, whom I had really struggled to shut up when he was trying to sell me the house and extract an offer. This time all I got from him was, "Okay, got another buyer lined up. Bye."

And as quickly as that, it was over. The whole darn year-long house-buying project. The move away from the lodging travails of Oxfordshire to the promised land of Surrey and a new job. The 'stop-gap' house share. The chats with Henry, the calculations, the forms, the pro-versus-con lists. All those months of waiting and all those thick wads of contract, swallowed up in a single ten-second phone call. All for nothing.

And that was just the *time* I'd lost. I'd gotten poorer through all of this. I'd handed over hundreds of Pounds for a surveyor to check out the flat, plus a few more for the lawyer's basic fee. I'd been needlessly forced to sell Google stock of four-figure value. I'd used whole tanks of petrol driving about viewing houses. And I'd also bought Henry a breakfast fry-up after coming to examine the Aldershot flat with me.

It was rather a sobering moment.

Not for one moment am I saying I had a bad year. In the end, it had been quite a pleasant one. When I wasn't playing grown-up and hunting houses, my work had given me the chance to interview the likes of Rory McIlroy, run photo shoots and get force-fed tequila by celebrities I won't name. I'd had handsome laughs and interesting nights out with my work colleagues. I'd travelled to Jersey and Ireland, Abu Dhabi and Spain. I'd enjoyed my birthday weekend at the London Sevens rugby. I'd played a ton more cricket, surviving that 12-hour practice session rather better than I thought I would. I'd even found time for a few good dates. But I was always in a holding pattern; never quite settled. Waiting for payslips, waiting for forms, waiting for lawyers. It was the year of waiting, waiting and more waiting.

The way it eventually panned out was another reminder that everything you try to plan can change, and probably will. The year of buying a house and perhaps having to live in an undesirable part of England had become the year of not buying a house and rather going to the capital of Austria. But of course, it had taken all of that year for this to become apparent. A fine advertisement for living the moments.

I *was* going to Vienna, wasn't I? With no house-buying frolics to keep me in the UK and Brexit hovering as a very distinct push factor, I was clearly Europe-bound one way or another. There was the option of staying in Merstham (or with my parents) and waiting for another European job to come along. But I wasn't sure that would happen any time soon. Advertisements reading 'English-speaking writer wanted' were a rare thing, and particularly so if the job was in mainland Europe. And the next one would probably be in Berlin or Amsterdam. And those places seemed like tame options now.

And when I started to think about practicalities, so too did flying to Austria.

I needed to leave the house in Merstham and it looked like my destination would be Vienna.

I had my car sitting in the driveway. The Peugeot also needed to go somewhere.

I'd probably want to take quite a lot of stuff to Vienna, where I hoped I might stay for a long time. It occurred to me that cars are good at taking quite a lot of stuff.

Flying's *not* good at taking a lot of stuff. (Flying's good at taking your scissors, your water and your favourite body spray out of your possession.)

Wait a second...

...I could *drive* to Vienna!

Road trip? Yes. Definitely. Oh my goodness, I simply *had* to take the Austrian offer.

I'd love to say 'I pulled out my map of Europe, unfolded it and smoothed it out over the kitchen table' at this point. It has so much more of a ring to it, don't you think? But the grim truth is that I called up Google Maps and zoomed out to an appropriate scale. (I challenge all the greatest minds in Silicon Valley to find a way to make that sound anywhere near as exciting.)

I pored over the laptop screen. Having zoomed in on Vienna, just to see how close it was to all those other countries, I zoomed all the way out, to see just how far away it was from southern England. I wondered what the most interesting route would be. In which sleepy Alpine village would I stop for some crisp air, a good night's rest and breakfast involving cheese? How many miles were we talking? And would the Peugeot make it without exploding?

(In my second-to-last job in Witney, one of my most earnest colleagues regularly recounted how he'd once had the same make and model of car, and that it had been running just fine until it exploded on the highway. I thanked him wholeheartedly each time he sowed this little seed of doubt in my mind.)

I asked Google some of these questions. The distance between Merstham and Vienna was apparently 914 miles. It was a 15-hour drive if you took the quickest route. That way involved no Alps at all - and nor did the second- or third-quickest routes. We were talking Dover-Calais-Brussels-Cologne-Frankfurt, then a run south-east all the way into Austria, and from there directly east across the country into Vienna.

As European road trips go, this wasn't the most appealing route. I'd driven across Belgium a dozen times already, and didn't expect a lot more excitement from the German *Autobahns*, except perhaps in speed limit terms. I was tempted to investigate a more southerly, more scenic route involving Switzerland, if time would permit.

When I really started to think about it, I wasn't sure it made sense to drive to Vienna with all my stuff right away. Maybe it was better to find a place to live first - one with parking, ideally - and *then* drive the car from Britain.

But whenever it would happen, what better way would there be to get a real sense of place for the city to which I was now certainly moving? None that I could think of. Getting somewhere slowly, across the land or sea, is the only way to really enjoy that moment of arrival nowadays. Air travel robs us of the sensations and the excitement you get from crossing borders and changing languages. And it steals that delicious tension between accomplishment and anticipation, as you watch the miles on the signposts run down.

There's something particularly compelling about a British car leaving Britain and going to Europe. It's got everything to do with the fact that Britain's an island. Even though there are now chunnels and ferries to cross the water, English cars still don't get out much. Not in the worldy way European ones cruise about from country to country. To see a picture of an English-registered car sitting in the middle of, say, Berlin, and be told it was driven there from home, is just kinda funny. The more angular and more clapped-out the car, the more it looks like its only natural home would be a Tesco parking lot in Grimsby, the funnier it gets.

It might be a thing you only get with regular exposure to British humour, but somehow a humble English car amuses as a metaphor for the confused Englishman in a bowler hat who has taken a wrong turn and ended up amongst frightening foreign people who speak a strange language, instead of at the local post office. That's why an old, ugly car is always funniest: the proverbial English inattention to matters of style is starker against a European backdrop. It underlines just how wrong a turn had been made.

My car certainly fell into the angular and clapped-out category. It had never lived anywhere outside of the gentle home counties of England, dutifully collecting its MOT roadworthy test each year, ferrying cricket equipment about and trying not to get in anybody's way. And now, just as its thoughts may have been turning to a comfortable retirement, I was going to haul it right out of its comfort zone, bowler hat and all. Let it drive on the right hand side of the road for a change. And why stop at Vienna? Had anyone ever driven a Peugeot 306 from London to Kiev? I liked the idea and fancied the challenge.

As always happens in the few minutes after experiencing a wild travel impulse, irritating doubts and sensible considerations came bubbling to the surface. Assuming the car made it to Vienna, would there be any downside to having it there? As long as I was absolutely clear that I had a parking space, I didn't think so. With all those other countries in driving distance, and so many obscure Moravian (not to mention Bohemian) villages to visit, suddenly continuing to own a car seemed a very nice advantage. Maybe I'd find a cricket team too, and still need the Peugeot for its original purpose.

I guess that's what happens when you jump onto the slippery slope of vehicle ownership. There's always a reason to keep it just a little longer. In my case, I think a large part of it was just wanting to ride the wave of having bought something that hadn't broken down or presented me with some catastrophic compatibility issue I could never have considered. ('Oh no, Sir, this Peugeot only runs on Japanese Donkey's Blood. Don't you know *anything* about cars?')

I fleetingly wondered if the Austrians would give me any grief about registering my car, being right-hand drive and English and all that. Common sense suggested that the world had real problems to solve, and that within the European Union they could just let me get on with driving a perfectly functional car. But I'd learned not to expect common sense when dealing with the world.

Google proved woeful on throwing up much information about this. The Internet in general is truly terrible when it comes to matters of regulation. The official government websites, even if you can somehow zoom in on the right five subsections, usually leave you with burning questions and nobody to whom you can pose them. Sometimes there's a random blogger who's posted an FAQ on things like registering British cars in Austria, but these are always dated 2013 and you've got no idea if the rules might have changed since then. And anyway, no blogger can confidently state any of the facts on such matters. There's only one opinion that counts: that of the humourless official behind some counter who is going to shake their head and say, 'No, we have a rule that English 1600cc Peugeots that run on Japanese donkey's blood cannot be registered in Austria unless you have the engine system converted to run on *Lebanese* donkey blood. And then fill out form 45B67/T/65C, for which you need a sepia-tinted mugshot with orange borders. And then pay us a €700 inspection charge.' But people who work behind counters don't blog very much. You have to walk up to their counters to know where you actually stand.

Since these counters were on the other side of the continent and trying to phone them in German wouldn't get me very far at all, I resolved to worry about it later. If the worst came to the worst, and the Austrians wouldn't allow my car for some reason, then I could take it to the Ukraine and set it on fire. Or try to deliberately crash it on a track day at the Brno Autodrome. Or simply leave the keys in the ignition in a small Hungarian border town.

All things considered, I thought, the best course of action would be to enjoy my road trip and being able to drive my own possessions across to Austria, but treat any subsequent car-related activities as a bonus. I thought this a healthy attitude: I'd had a year and a half of use from the Peugeot, which already wasn't a bad return considering what I'd paid for it. And that's before you factored in what it was saving me in moving costs or extra luggage. Airlines see cricket bags as a major cash cow, you know.

Most of my thoughts, as you can see, were entirely consumed by my road trip. Not trifling matters such as whether it was the right job for me, whether I fitted into the company culture or prospects for career advancement. All that was a bit like shopping: something to dither over. I much preferred to let a travel impulse make the decision for me.

But I did find time to write an email formally accepting the job, and arrange a start date for just after my stay in Merstham ended. Then I booked another flight to Vienna. And this time it was for real.

Rudolf the Eternal Student

The year of buying a house - which had turned into the year of *not* buying a house - was officially done. The next year would be the year of...well, nothing special. Definitely no more pretending to be a grown-up. And no jumping through hoops to show what an upstanding citizen I was.

Instead, I was going to focus on enjoying life in Vienna: making new friends, learning German and generally being amazed with all the new things surrounding me.

I arrived back in the city on a Friday evening, with my job set to start on the Monday. This time I stepped out of the metro system at Kettenbrückengasse. Quite close, it turned out, to the spot where I'd marvelled at the *U-Bahn* running next to the canal on my previous recce. The semi-outdoor and semi-underground station itself, themed white and green, was far too pretty to be a metro stop. With their awnings and cream floor tiles, its platforms were more like stately verandahs.

I was here because I'd booked an Airbnb around the corner for my first couple of nights. Goal number one for the weekend was to find somewhere to live. I couldn't quite believe I was moving to *another* new city again. That life had turned upside down in the blink of an eye once more. None of it seemed real just yet.

What information I could find regarding the rental market wasn't all that encouraging. Vienna apartments were cheap, apparently. But securing a spot in one wasn't easy. I hoped and prayed that Vienna apartments would at least be cheap enough for me to be able to live on my own. Because don't you worry, I hadn't forgotten the unpleasant sharing situation that had set me on this path in the first place. If there was one housing mission whose flame still burned, it was the dream of solo living. And apart from it being *better* to live alone, having this as an affordable option might make getting somewhere to live a bit easier. I wouldn't have to prove my inherent coolness to a committee of house-mates, like I'd had to do in Oxford.

By chance, my Airbnb was a short stroll up the same hill down which I'd unwittingly gone a couple of weeks earlier. The fact that I seemed to be going over old ground already was perhaps an early hint that Vienna wasn't very *big*.

First job was to dump my bags. Then I would see whom I could call about viewings. There was no time to be lost in the race to secure a permanent roof over my head.

Only it didn't quite work out like that. Because my Airbnb accommodation proved to be very distracting.

My host had a quintessentially Austrian-sounding name (let's call him Rudolf here), so it felt a fitting one to ring when I reached the address and surveyed the buzzers. Once I was beeped in, the heavy wooden door slammed shut behind me. Ominous reverberations followed its dull thud.

I found myself in a dark, deserted hallway that seemed positively poised to echo the next sound I made. I looked everywhere for another of those superannuated elevators. Normally I avoided these if I could, but tonight my bags weighed a ton. But there was no lift in sight. The spiral marble staircase it would have to be, then.

It was all feeling quite authentically Mittel European so far, I had to admit.

I climbed three storeys with my murderous suitcase in tow. Not knowing how long it would be until I found a place, and hence just when I could bring the bulk of my clothes with me by Peugeot, had forced my hand into packing rather a lot of them. I hate heavy luggage like I hate taxi drivers, but it seemed to be lumbering me rather often these days regardless. I trudged wearily upwards. The sound of each step bounced around the windowless, carpet-free stairwell. I must have sounded like a one-legged horse trying to pull a snowplough up the stairs.

When I reached the third floor, the door to my temporary new home was already open. Rudolf, who proved to be an elderly chap who looked like he'd drunk rather too much in his life, was waiting for me in the entrance hall. Even as I was shown through to my room, it quickly became clear that I was going to be living in an eccentric little house - even by budget Airbnb standards. This wasn't just some guy with a spare room. It was an entire house-share with a couple of spare rooms. This wasn't an arrangement I'd come across before.

My room was accessible only via the kitchen. Rudolf gave me a tour around it with a straight face. For him it seemed unremarkable that the duvet cover on the bed must have been taken straight out of some ten-year-old's bedroom some time in the nineties. It was adorned with an image of an (apparently) famous Austrian cartoon mouse whose name, surprisingly if unimaginatively, was *Die Maus*. Anyway, *Die Maus* was kicking a football on my mattress with considerable glee.

My room also contained a chest of drawers. You couldn't actually use them, mind you, since they'd been creatively shoved in an alcove on the far side of the bed. On the wall-mounted shelf across the room, meanwhile, I found what must have been the world's smallest ironing board: only a single safari sock would find itself enough room on this contraption.

A vast photographic print of a 1980s street scene from somewhere in Ireland, dominated by unglamorous people unloading Nissan Micras, as well as a fat guy staring longingly through the window of Foley's Guest House Restaurant, was sticky-taped to the wall.

On the floor I found the kind of radio and compact disc player I used to know very well. I pressed the lid to open it, almost certain I was going to find some random CD inside. I wasn't at all disappointed to discover Anton Bruckner's 4th Symphony sitting in the tray. How very Austrian. How utterly Airbnb - or at least when you make a habit of operating within the left hand extremity of the website's price range filter.

I didn't actually *mind* anything about my room. I liked that it had character, and describe it all here purely for literary purposes. Hotel rooms don't provide nearly so much entertainment and interest. They cost a lot more, too.

My window looked out over a light-deprived hexagonal courtyard. Way down at the bottom, under the glare of about two dozen windows and six jagged storeys, someone seemed to be making a valiant attempt at a vegetable patch. They probably didn't struggle to gather water down there, I thought to myself. Sunlight, on the other hand, surely had to be a scarce resource.

After taking all of this in, I joined Rudolf and former house-share resident (also a Richard - this was seemingly an acceptable name in Austria too) in the kitchen, where they were speaking in what sounded like strong regional accents. They switched to English quickly enough, which is when I learned that they were reminiscing about bills from 2002. Two thousand and *two*? What madness had I wandered into?

But 2002 was nothing. It turned out that this place had been a house-share of sorts for *thirty-two years*. And Rudolf himself, the main renter, was the central thread in the apartment's story. Apparently this had been his student digs, and he'd basically never left. Now, I would guess, he was in his sixties.

At times they would lapse back to German. I'd now tentatively started learning the basics, but it was too difficult to follow much. Unable to process the thick Linz dialect filling the airwaves above my pint glass, I looked around the kitchen for amusement. Collages of mostly ancient photographs featuring former renters and a much younger Rudolf lined the walls around the picnic table wedged into one end of the room. The kitchen was tidy, but everything looked old. A basket of assorted bread rolls lay on top of the fridge. I wondered how long they had been there.

Jars containing tiny amounts of pasta, lentils and other assorted dry goods were stuck by their lids to the underside of the shelf above the sink. If you unscrewed them by twisting the jar itself, I presumed you could get at the content. Whether you'd want to, in this particular case, was another question. Alcohol bottles - Christmas *Glühwein*, Felser Rum and something Hungarian called Tokaji - lurked dustily on the top shelves. I didn't feel much like trusting any of them.

The rubbish bin - after 32 years, remember - was a plastic bag bearing the seal of Hofer (that's the Austrian version of Aldi) supermarket hanging on a hook. And I soon discovered that the tap with the red dot on it ran cold, while the tap with the blue dot on it ran warm. Of course they did.

Apart from his weird living arrangement, Rudolf was an interesting and extremely well-travelled guy. In a mix of German and English, he plied me with tales of his various sea expeditions long after the other Richard had left. He also plied me with some cocktail of pear or apple called *Most*, served in strange little overgrown shot glasses whose cleanliness I chose not to inspect too closely. Above the food cupboard on the far wall, a bust of a man who looked like he might have followed a bright star to Bethlehem watched over us. No doubt another of Rudolf's bizarre travel mementos.

Such souvenirs were everywhere you looked, as I discovered on the first occasion I headed down the hallway en route to the WC. Such as the splendidly random 'Tactical Pilotage Chart' of a small slice of Black Sea coastline, dated October 1980. It hung on the wall and showed its yellowed age with no shame.

Was I already encountering the splendid Viennese quirkiness I'd been reading about? Who knew, maybe lots of people in this city remained in their student lodgings for the rest of their lives and had sea charts on their walls. Maybe such behaviour wasn't so weird after all.

This time, though, the toilet room didn't have any instructions on how to use the facilities politely. Instead it had two warped shelves piled with books nobody had touched for decades. Even higher up in this ludicrously tall, tiny room, another shelf. On it, four small suitcases were stashed. The one in bumblebee yellow would have looked perfect in Tintin's hand as he boarded a steamer on one of his 1920's adventures. You couldn't possibly reach any of this ancient baggage without a ladder.

And then I saw, resting against the room's curved fifth wall, a ladder. Perhaps the suitcases were in more regular use than I'd thought.

One poster on the door shouted about *Auf der Suche nach dem echten Wiener - an audiobook by Martin Just*. Another featured a bedraggled protestor, floating in water beside four yellow drums and bearing a banner about saving the last jungles. Behind the toilet itself was an elongated window as tall as two cricket bats and about as wide as that ironing board in my room. (Perfect for defending your apartment with a bow and arrow, I supposed, if it weren't for the fact that it overlooked the *inner* courtyard.) You could spend hours being fascinated in that WC.

The washroom, meanwhile, lay across the hallway. Its basin was so broad and wide you could almost have had a bath in it. Each of the other five house-share residents had a labelled place for their accoutrements on the nearby shelf. But in contrast to the Teutonic order of the labelling system, Rudolf's shelf was exactly the kind of dusty and remarkable mess you would expect from a bachelor in his sixties. I counted nine toothbrushes, mostly quite beyond any hygienically acceptable use. Amongst these were scattered refresher towel sachets from restaurants around the world, hotel soaps still in their wrappers and even a free sample of mouthwash.

Rudolf, it seemed, was a serial collector - but no great shakes at actually using anything. Not only was his bathroom shelf the place sanitary products went to die, but I never saw him eat so much as a morsel from the kitchen in my four-day stay. Maybe that's why he never had to brush his teeth.

You could lock yourself in the washroom by means of a funny little hook that you could twist just enough to catch the door frame. But then it would dawn on you that one of the 'walls' in this room - which also contained the shower - was actually a curtain. I peered behind it on my first visit, and was taken aback to see, in my direct line of vision, an unshaven, tousle-haired man reading an iPad in a bed. It later became apparent that the only entrance to his room was via this, the house share's only shower room. Somehow I wasn't completely shocked.

Would I want to *live* here? After 15 years in house shares, I could categorically say that I would not. But would I take it over a five-star hotel for a week-long city break? Categorically yes. Airbnb - particularly cheaper ones like this - frequently offered more 'experience' for a fraction of the price. If you'd rather have zero interaction, an identikit room you'd find anywhere on the planet and spend three figures per night, then the Marriott would always be your friend. For a short-term visit, a place like Rudolf's was my bag.

That said, I think Rudolf had quickly reminded me of what happens if you spend your entire life as a house-sharing student. I was absolutely all for nostalgic mementoes and a friendly jumble, but also all for a little privacy and a clean toothbrush.

So I spent the first night getting distracted by the chain-smoking, red-faced Rudolf, drinking funky pear juice and looking at some chilling memorabilia from the *Anschluss* era. Passed down from Rudolf's parents, these included passports and the special licence the Nazis made you get if, like his old man, you claimed to be an artist.

Art clearly meant a lot to Rudolf. Just down by the station he ran a 'gallery', which I would soon see with my own eyes. It was barely any wider than its door, only a few metres deep and mostly didn't have any art. Or customers. (Unless you count dust as an art form, that is.) But he religiously opened up from four until seven every weekday evening, and all day on a Saturday. As far as I could tell, his 'gallery' was just a very unusual man cave.

Rudolf's life was really the thing that belonged in a gallery. It was nice to marvel over, but I didn't particularly want it for myself. I was more resolute than ever about finding myself my own place. Best-case scenario? I'd wrap it up the very next day.

House Number Umpteen

That Saturday, I threw all my energy into viewing potential flats. And I do mean *all* of it.

I could be quite dog-and-bonish about this sort of thing. Pouring money into Airbnb accommodation, where I would never be able to entirely unpack and settle (nor trust any of the drinking vessels), didn't have much to be said for it. Nor did I want to be doing viewings once work started, if I could help it. I'd experienced that during my first week's employment after I turned up in Sydney for a working holiday a few years earlier, and found it to be a colossal pain. You couldn't really manage more than one or two viewings in an evening, what with not having much of a feel for how long it took to get from one place to another. Also, people who were free to indulge in daytime viewings would snatch rentals up before you could even get to the property, and oftentimes you could expect a late-afternoon call telling you not to bother coming.

From what I'd learned thus far, the imposition of a *Provision*, usually from lettings agents - my favourite people, you'll recall - was a popular racket in Austria. A *Provision* is the same kind of 'administration fee' about which I've already subjected you to a rant. But the Viennese ones made British ones look like Monopoly money. You might easily think I'm joking when I tell you that some Vienna agents were asking for one or two or three *thousand* Euros, absolutely non-refundable, for carrying out the tricky, highly specialised task of issuing a standard rental contract to any one of the hundreds of people waiting in line to rent the place.

This was a crying outrage. No way was I going to let such 'professionals' blatantly rob me in broad daylight. So I joined every *Provisionsfrei* Facebook group I could find, looking for a 'private' rental from anybody who didn't appear to be a maniac who would sneak in and change the locks the first time you left the house, or blame you for heater fluid running out of their manky old radiators (My heartfelt thanks once again, Mr Johnson). The risk - if risk there really was - of going private seemed a lot lower here when you weighed it against the fees you were saving.

I managed to confirm three apartment viewings on that first Saturday. It was as fine a way as any to get my bearings in the city. The first was in

Ottakring, at the very far end of the U3 line. This, like Simmering, was supposed to be a down-to-earth suburb from where your solid, salt-of-the-earth working *Wiener* hailed. It's where they made the yellow cans of Ottakringer beer that haunted the city's every bus stop.

Ottakringer was the true Viennese beer, known in local slang as a *Sechszehnerblech*, or literally '16 metal'. As in the tin that comes from the 16th district. Go up to a *Würstelstand* and order an *Eitriger und a 16er Blech* (*Eitriger* being the local word for Käsekrainer, with rather disgusting connotations I won't explore here), and you're apparently a true Viennese.

Frankly I didn't think much of Ottakring. It was grim and depressing. It wasn't ugly or dangerous, somehow just a bit grey. And this first viewing was with a grumpy estate agent called Doris. (You'd be surprised how many Dorises there are in Austria.) Perhaps her ill-temperedness stemmed from the fact that there was no *Provision* on this apartment, and she wasn't going to get a handsome four-figure tip for standing in a kitchen, buzzing some people in and showing you a room containing a bath before announcing 'bathroom'. There wasn't anything *wrong* with the place, but it didn't speak to me either. Flats rarely do when they're empty, I've come to realise. When a place feels 'homely', I suspect, it has everything to do with the furnishings. Take out the sofas and wall tapestries, the magazine racks and rugs, and you're left with a soulless shell. I tried to imagine it filled with IKEA's latest wonders, but it was a struggle. I just didn't connect with it. Probably just because of the beady-eyed Doris glowering in the corner.

The next flat belonged to a friend of a friend. Much more my kind of deal. Friends of friends are, by a long way, much more trustworthy than agents. They can find bits of old furniture they don't need and throw them into the flat for you without a fuss. They'll give you keys before you sign contracts. They probably won't keep your deposit on the basis that a fly once settled on the mantelpiece, and you didn't have its footprints professionally cleaned. It had to have potential.

This one was all the way over on the other side of town - not very far, then - and saw me cross the mighty Danube for the first time. I spied the water from the U1 metro line, which jumped above ground not far north of the gigantic Prater park and crossed the water by means of a bridge. At which point you could see the first half of the big, wide river very well indeed. Then the train stopped at the Donauinsel station, which sat above the long, skinny island of the same name that split the river in two, and you could peek out of the holes they'd thoughtfully left in the wall behind the platform. After that your red-line train would cross the second half of the river and reach the high-rises east of the river - among other things, the United Nations had its European base here.

Vienna seemed to have an ambivalent relationship with its river. Unlike all the other great Danubian cities, it didn't course through the centre of town. There were none of Budapest's pretty citadels, Bratislava's watchful castles, or Belgrade's medieval forts. These dramatic structures don't really work unless you've got a hillside next to the river, and Vienna, to be fair, had never really had all that many contours to work with.

Back in the olden days, the Danube was an ill-disciplined sort of river, prone to flooding over a wide area and leaving whole Viennese families with wet socks. (This still happened upstream, apparently, in country towns like Krems an der Donau) I supposed that was the reason why the city's historic centre was built some distance west of the Danube itself, with only the fast-flowing *Donaukanal* to remind everyone that there was big water out there somewhere.

With Vienna's river flow now having been engineered to within an inch of its life, due to the Donauinsel (entirely artificial and 21 kilometres long) and other arrestingly Teutonic water management projects, the city's newer districts had now been able to creep right up to the Danube's banks. But you could hardly call them pretty. As far as I knew, Vienna didn't even offer a sunset dinner cruise on the Danube. And that, in a European capital, should tell you something about the viewing on offer.

Yet while half the city could go about its business for weeks on end without seeing the Danube at all, the river still played its part. When the sun came out in summer, it seemed the Viennese would treat it as a seaside of sorts, and be found sprawled out in various states of undress (and I do mean the full spectrum here) all along the Donauinsel. But given that swimming in the Danube's strong current is never to be considered wise unless you want a free ride to the Black Sea, you'd apparently find even more of them over on the banks of the Alte Donau, a dammed (or at least even more highly-controlled) horseshoe of river that provided safe swimming for literally thousands of bathers.

Even if you weren't the swimming type of Viennese, though, you'd probably still have an opinion about what lies east of the river. Everything over on that side was decidedly un-medieval, and it was there that you'd find one of the city's very few clusters of skyscrapers. Plenty of snooty first-district types, I was already learning, would tell you that nothing east of the Danube counted as Vienna at all.

Given that the first thing you hit after the U1 line returned to dry land is the United Nations building, it was possible to sympathise with that point of view. The UN employed thousands of people there, all of them apparently on enormous, tax-free wages. Most scandalously, though, they had access to a hidden members-only international supermarket, where the chosen few could buy liquor and sweets and packets of crisps from every corner of the planet. Most of us would never see this supermarket: people spoke of it in the hushed tones you reserve for something that might prove to be hearsay.

The supermarket explains why one of the first things you had to do if you moved to Vienna was to befriend someone who worked at the UN. If you were nice to them, they'd be glad to smuggle out those tarantula pies and hippo-flavoured crisps that made you pine for home. Flaunting fizzy drink cans from America and chocolates from Argentina was one of the few ways you could really show off in a city that has a socialist soul stretching all the way back to the interwar 'Red Vienna' period. Perhaps leave them on conspicuous display when you had visitors, and you could say 'I have a friend working at the UN' in a conspiratorial whisper, before taking another conspicuous sip of Irish whiskey.

The UN-station was where I got off to see this particular apartment, which lay in the rather charming suburb of Kaisermühlen. It sat on the tip of another island, flanked on one side by the Danube and on the other by the Alte Donau. To get there you had to turn your back on the skyscrapers and head south into a low-rise part of town that looked like it had long kept itself to itself. It had the low traffic circulation and unhurried vibe so typical of areas that are dead ends. And despite being east of the Danube, not all of the buildings were modern and ugly. Kaisermühlen (22nd District, if you're wondering) looked like it had both history and a sense of community. Plus, you were in walking distance of plentiful swimming opportunities. I liked this part of town straight away.

The flat itself was quite a long way down, towards the dead-end bit where the island tapered off and the Alte Donau joined the main river. A brisk walk or a short bus ride from the metro, it felt like a gem of a location: convenient and central, yet somehow blessed with a chilled island vibe. An oasis in the city, if you will. And my feelings warmed to the place even more

185

when I spotted a very traditional-looking *Gasthaus*, a specialist schnitzel take-away and a classy ice-cream parlour in the apartment's immediate neighbourhood.

Any fears that the whole schnitzel thing had been made up by tourist brochures were already proving unfounded. In fact, I'm not sure any city could have lived up to a food stereotype quite so well as Vienna. While America does not, sadly, offer up fat people eating burgers on every park bench, and nor does Scotland provide the sight of amorous couples sharing alternating bites of take-out haggis, and I didn't see a single Icelander eating rancid shark when I went to Reykjavik, Vienna was heaving with schnitzel joints. It was a pleasant surprise to discover that the local speciality was for sale absolutely everywhere, sitting proudly alongside burgers and pizzas in shops that were frequently dubbed *Schnitzelhaus*. You could even get a schnitzel delivered to your home, just like a pizza.

Kaisermühlen looked perfect. My kind of suburb. So of course the apartment wasn't perfect at all. Life would be far too simple if perfect things aligned that well all the time.

This was a typical Viennese *garçonnière* (Austrians, like the Dutch, apparently think using the occasional French word will make them appear cool), which is the standard one-room flat in which a great many *Wiener* live. Typically boasting a surface area of 45 to 55 metres squared, including a small separate bathroom, there's nothing at all wrong with them if you're content with sleeping in the same room in which you cook. Lots of people live in these for decades, and turn out just fine.

I was no longer keen on this kind of dwelling. I'd done it once before, in Cape Town, and spent the better part of two years feeling like a caged animal. There wasn't anything wrong with that place either - the four walls were just too close. If something bad happened in one room, you couldn't go stalking off to another to gather your thoughts. Because there *wasn't* another room. It was claustrophobic enough living in one of these alone. I couldn't imagine what it would be like for a squabbling couple to share a bedsit.

Even a small balcony can make such a flat considerably more tolerable, but the place in the island suburb didn't offer one. It was on the ground floor and the windows looked onto the car park. That depressing view counted against it.

But more than anything, I just didn't want to exist in a tiny studio. It's a really hard thing when you grew up in suburban Africa, under broad skies and a garden big enough for a cat to get lost for several days. So that flat, much as I liked the area, wasn't going to work for me.

So why wasn't I just looking at bigger apartments, then? The same reason I'd convinced myself to live in that studio in Cape Town: bigger apartments were too expensive for one person. It was way better than England, where even a studio would be too expensive for one. At least here there was *some* alternative to having house-mates.

These *garçonnières* were all quite reasonably-priced, by the looks of it. If I was willing to live in an overgrown prison cell, then I could have one tiny place where I could be as selfish as I liked. I just really, really didn't want to live in a place where you'd have to share your bedroom with the aroma of Wednesday evening's tuna salad. I wanted somewhere big enough to do a push up without my elbows crashing into a vacuum cleaner or a chair leg. After a succession of lodgings that failed miserably as home gymnasiums, this was a minimum requirement.

(Not that I could actually complete more than about three push-ups. I just considered it a rather useful measure of what constitutes a reasonable living space.)

Why *do* we all insist on living on top of each other? Think about it: we've come to consider it *normal* to fly for hours across empty fields where thousands of people could do star jumps and press-ups and even freestyle somersaulting routines, and then plunge into cities where the houses are piled up in stacks called apartment blocks, in which people are forced to choose between an extra foot of mattress and having a bedside table.

I'm quite sure visitors from another planet probably wouldn't see this as normal at all. They'd think us bat-shit crazy.

I get that this is an economic thing, tied up in complicated questions of land ownership and property prices and job availability, and that we're stuck in a system that takes advantage of our need for some kind of lodging vaguely near some kind of employment. None of us, I hope, are individually nuts enough to want to live in shoeboxes without so much as a patch of grass to call your own, and so cramped that if you have a child then you have to balance things out by throwing out a casserole dish. It's just the system as a whole that has a screw loose. Whether you think that's by design or not, I suppose, is down to your fondness for a conspiracy theory.

If you looked at the bigger environmental picture, it was probably good if cities stayed as compact (read 'vertical') as possible. Stacked living made things less fun for urban dwellers, but left us with more countryside - which was a good thing full of marvellous possibilities. All we needed now was to give people the *choice*, instead of forcing them to work in towns and live in dog kennels.

I still yearned for an opportunity to beat the system, and live in the country, where the same money I'd need for a studio flat would get me acres of land. Alas, I hadn't yet found that stable remote-working opportunity I needed to commit to rural living. But I couldn't help thinking that this far into the age of the Internet, there really ought to have been more such options.

I would keep looking for that golden way, always. But right now, still bound by the city, I at least hoped I could find some sort of compromise.

The third and final apartment I viewed provided just that.

This appointment followed an advertisement posted on Facebook by a private landlady. The rent, at €800, was right at the scratchy edge of my price range, and perhaps even beyond it. But after the morbid, ugly twists and turns that had characterized my various lodgings challenges over the preceding 18 months, I was feeling unusually motivated to treat myself.

The rent may have been a good couple of hundred higher than the *garçonnière* alternative, but then the space on offer was somewhere around double. At first glance it seemed a good case of whatever the opposite of diminishing returns was.

As I made another cross-city journey to the end of the U4 line at Heiligenstadt, and then got on a bus for eleven minutes, and then got off it and walked up a very steep hill, I wondered if the reason the value looked good was that the apartment was on the edge of the city. I could see it wouldn't be the easiest to reach in a hurry.

I stood outside for half an hour, fruitlessly ringing the doorbell for number nine. My prospective landlady, who apparently owned two apartments in the building, was waiting in number eleven rather than number nine.

Brilliant. How was I to find that out, when I hadn't gotten as far as organizing a SIM card for my phone yet? (I'm always amazed at how blasé people are about the use of a good old-fashioned doorbell these days. 'Just call me', they always say, as if batteries never go dead on freezing doorsteps, or they never accidentally leave their phone on silent, or you love running up roaming charges for no good reason. Doorbells still have their place, everybody, and will do for a long time to come!)

We found each other eventually, and she offered me a businesslike handshake. She was Russian, it turned out, so I wasn't very much surprised. Russian women seem to love a good handshake. Not for them this decadent, patriarchal European cheek-kissing culture.

Which does make things an awful lot simpler when travelling, I suppose. Etiquette can vary by region in these matters. On a trip to Belgium, I'd learned - first hand - that men in the Ardennes greet each other with a single nuzzle, on the left cheek only. After all those years of practice at attending to both sides, the goalposts had suddenly shifted again. Still, Europe would be a far poorer place if these little quirks and twists died out. (Not that I wish to quirk or twist any Belgian men, I must stress).

When we got inside number nine, I almost felt moved to song. It was massive. It was a proper flat, with a ginormous (think small yoga class) living room, a modern kitchen big enough to hang out in, a toilet room, a bathroom with bath and shower, and a bedroom that was actually on a different level. *Upstairs*! Never in my wildest dreams had I thought I might afford a solo place with actual stairs.

And when you looked out of the windows, the benefits of hiking up that calf-busting hill became all too clear. The house was surrounded on three sides by forest, with a bedroom balcony looking back onto the cool, calming trees. And when you looked out of the three big, slanting living room windows you were rewarded with an immensely, indescribably vast view of the Danube, the edge of Vienna and miles of surrounding countryside.

I thought of my house-hunt in Sydney again, where my plan to treat myself to a place with a view of the Harbour Bridge and the Opera House had been scuppered by the rent being not just a little bit pricier than I'd usually go for, but actual millionaire territory. After I ended up living with Suz instead, I'd had to settle for six months of gazing at the framed photo of the harbour in the living room.

Well, this was going to be reward for Sydney. No more settling. Five years after failing to find that room with a view, my time had come. This was going to be a yes.

I didn't care how far out of town it was, or how much it cost, nor even that it currently had no useful furniture inside. I was *going* to make it work. I scanned the place for catches and snags in as adult a fashion as I could muster, but, like with my Peugeot, I knew I was going to take it barring an actual corpse in the closet.

Anyway, I couldn't find a snag worthy of mention. Apart from the suspicious fact that it all seemed too good to be true. But was this, at last, reward for some of the stress and unpleasantness I'd had to deal with where previous lodgings were concerned? Had the pendulum finally swung in my favour? Had fate at last dealt me an above-average hand?

Or maybe it was just something to do with the local economy. After so many years holed up in places where you couldn't swing a cat (I do hope nobody has ever tried to put that expression to the test), I was bowled over to have moved to a city where I could afford an actual apartment, with multiple rooms and more storage space than I could possible use. I'm sure it would have been well beyond my means in the city centre, but here it was within my grasp.

I was on the edge of town in the most literal sense: as you stepped off the bus you saw the sign indicating the end of the federal capital's own state and the start of Lower Austria, the state which surrounds it. My road, this isolated little dead end that reached up into the forest on the side of the incredibly steep Leopoldsberg hill, was the last on this side of town to have a Vienna postcode. But, quite critically, being on the edge of a small city is very different from being on the edge of a big one.

The bus from my stop to Heiligenstadt would take no more than eleven minutes, and from Heiligenstadt - the end of the tube line, remember - it would take a mere twelve minutes to get to Karlsplatz, right in the centre of the city. There, I would alight for work and walk a few minutes to the office. It was hardly going to be a killer commute.

In my head, I compared these numbers to London. Living twelve minutes by tube and eleven minutes by bus from your work, you probably wouldn't even have left Zone One. Which meant you couldn't live there at all, unless you earned a banker's salary. If you went far enough away to be able to take up affordable lodgings in, say, Zone Three or Four, you were getting into the realm of hour-long commutes. And this would be without getting a view or a forest or twice as much space or any of the benefits of vaguely countrified living.

I didn't care what any Vienna snobs might say about me living 'miles away', my knowledge of the non-choices people faced in super-sized London told me this was a very good deal. Vienna was small enough that living half an hour from work brought tangible gains in terms of value. You could live on the edge of town and do a reasonable commute, or, if you preferred, you could choose to live somewhere small and walk to work. In a smaller city like this, it seemed you could at least have a choice. Instead of being herded into a tiny room in Selhurst with barely a say in the matter.

Was I going to get punished by public transport costs, as I most certainly would in Britain? There, you'd have to spend at least half an hour with a calculator to work out if that 'cheap' suburb in Zone Four would really be such a great deal after you'd paid a year's exorbitant train fares. But in semi-socialist Vienna, even a half-wit like me could do the math without a calculator. An annual transport pass costed €365, which, if you've not had your morning coffee yet, is a mighty reasonable one Euro per day. There weren't any stupid, confusing zones to think about either - it didn't matter where in the city you lived. This was public transport as it should be. By golly, this was turning out to be a fine city!

What about supplies and provisions, living in this no-man's land that was barely still Vienna but not quite Klosterneuburg, the next town up the west bank of the Danube? No worries there either, thanks to the Spar that had thoughtfully been put up just yards from the otherwise isolated bus stop at the bottom of my hill. Even if I couldn't keep the car in Austria, then, I had a shop within walking distance.

Speaking of the Peugeot, there was yet another perk to living right on the edge of town. You could park where you pleased in my narrow little street. Not only had I found myself a flat in double-quick time, but my road trip was now well and truly on.

191

A Marathon in the Dark

The first thing I had to do after signing the lease and giving my Russian landlady a significant portion of my life savings to cover deposits, was to get some basic furniture in the house. Most of the elements could wait, but something soft to sleep on was paramount.

By now it was Monday, and I'd started work. I would move out of Rudolf's place and sleep at my cavernous new abode that very evening. I'd convinced my new landlady to drive me, my heavy suitcase and the key out to the flat rather than meet me and my heavy suitcase *at* the flat. I figured she'd be driving anyway, and fortunately she agreed it couldn't hurt to bring me along, rather than leaving me to haul shoulder-breaking baggage on the metro and bus. That was one godsend.

The other was that I had something on which I could temporarily sleep. One of the tenants in Rudolf's digs had lent me one of those thin mattresses people put on sun loungers. It was a long way short of ideal, but it was definitely preferable to the parquet floor. I felt sure *that* wouldn't be very forgiving at all.

With Vienna's shops all closed on Sundays, and work getting in the way of my life as usual on the Monday, proper mattress shopping hadn't been possible yet. Besides, I wanted to measure just how much space I had, and do a little looking around.

I had no experience of buying mattresses or any other furniture - something I was quite proud to say in my mid-thirties - but at first glance things you might want to sleep on were bloody expensive. Way more than they cost to make in Xiamen City, I'd have wagered.

The sun-lounger mattress and the thin blanket I'd snatched from a department store on my lunch break made for a sorry sight when I got to my new home and laid them out in the bedroom. But the good news was that I conclusively had space for a sizeable double mattress.

That's right, a proper double. Not for me this odd European habit of putting two skinny mattresses next to each other, throwing on two separate duvets in vaguely overlapping fashion, and then pretending it's a double bed. If you're going to share, which one day I might have wanted to do, then why invite mid-bed crevasses and air leaks into the equation? And even if you're *not* going to share...oh, I despair.

Continentals are completely mad when it comes to beds. They make half-arsed doubles, as if they don't really want to commit to getting too close to one another. But if you think that would make them enthusiastic specialists at setting up twin rooms, think again. Book a twin for a business trip in a European hotel, and nine times out of ten you'll end up sharing one of these not-quite-doubles with your colleague of the same sex. It's like the worst of both worlds.

It crossed my mind to wait until my car was in Austria, in order to be able to pick up a mattress and bring it home. But even if my Peugeot was already parked outside in the freezing street right now, it wouldn't be big enough to cope with such behemoths as double mattresses. There was no point in delaying the acquisition of a mattress, or a sofa for that matter. I was going to need the Austrian equivalent of a white van driver for this job.

Keen as I was to move off a mattress that was barely thicker than a writing notepad, I didn't want to rush into buying the wrong thing. This was a much more serious business than buying a car. If I got it wrong, I'd need *another* man with a van to take it out again. That would be at least double the hassle simply to get back to square one, and I didn't fancy that one bit.

So I spent some time searching online. Were there any second-hand mattress possibilities on Vienna's much-loved *Willhaben* website? Which stores, if any, would deliver me one? If I wanted to go and test out lying on mattresses in the stores first - which seemed a sensible thing to do - then where were such retail wonderlands to be found? And how much did a man with a van cost?

The Internet would have been great for answering these questions, but of course you don't get WiFi installed in a new home overnight. You have to wait for a man to come around, and, in my case, an appointment which I'd managed to line up for mid-December. In the meantime I would have to do my research at work (not something anyone wants to do in their first week), or I'd need to use my mobile data at home. At least the mobile side of things was working for the time being.

What the Internet told me was not just that beds were expensive, but that these Austrians seemed to take them quite seriously. All sorts of fancy grids and slats came as standard issue it seemed. But did I really need a bed at all? What, in all honestly, does a bed do that a floor can't, apart from give you a lot of storage space underneath and a few more nooks you've got to clean? From what I knew of the world, the floor would do a perfectly adequate job of stopping my mattress plunging to the centre of the earth, which is really something you don't want happening in the middle of the night. If I had limited cash to spend, it made sense to spend it on the things I'd actually sleep on.

It was Friday (I was working a four-days-a-week contract) before I could head out to any shops and bounce on their mattresses. It turned out that the places with the most affordable furniture - surprise! - were in huge industrial parks on the edge of town, which were flanked by enormous highways. Terrible for someone without a car, in other words. But I made it to one of them eventually, slogging all the way on public transport. Towering above the whizz and whoosh of the elevated highway, I could once more see those brightly-lit blue signs for Budapest, Bratislava and Brno.

I grumpily added visiting IKEA to my list of new experiences for the year. I was glad to have waited thirty-six years to visit one of these holy shrines, and I have to say I'll gladly wait another thirty-six before I volunteer to go inside one again.

I wasn't at all aware of the famous IKEA store layout, which tries to force you to follow a specified, one-way route through their riot of shopping opportunity, in such a fashion that you're compelled to see so much more than you came for. Such tactics might coax carloads of unplanned purchases from the weak-minded, but they weren't going to work on me. I just wanted the mattress section, which I finally located after several consultations of the store map, sneaking illegally through some doors that had been designated one-way by HQ in Stockholm and knocking over a few garden gnomes as I went against the human tide in the conservatory display. If it had taken much longer, I'd have had to warm myself up some of their famous meatballs in one of their microwaves before I passed out. And at the end of it all, I didn't think much of their mattresses anyway.

In a neighbouring furniture store, which was called Möbelix and allowed customers to navigate for themselves, I found the bed section with far more ease. And, to my delight, a proper double mattress that felt comfortable enough for me to spend €250 on. If only I could have just popped it in my satchel and headed home for a fine night's rest! Too much to ask, of course. As far as I could understand from the sales staff, deliveries would be really expensive or take a really long time. Or, if you were particularly unfortunate, both. (Anybody who says we live in a world of instant gratification clearly hasn't shopped for major items of furniture in Vienna with limited funds and no car.) So I started hatching a van plan.

Meanwhile, in an unexpectedly pleasant development, I'd found somebody on Willhaben who was willing to give away an entire sofa set. Pickup would also require a van, but if I was smart with my timings, I could pick up the mattress at the same time. A van and driver would cost €70 for a couple of hours, and if I was efficient, this would be enough. I decided I would do it all on Saturday, the next evening.

You'd think it would be a simple matter, late in the year 2016, to have ordered and paid for the mattress I wanted online, and then, if delivery was really such a big deal, simply go to some specified place and pick it up. In Vienna the truth wasn't so straightforward.

For reasons I'll never fully understand, I was required to present myself in person at a store that didn't even stock mattresses, and pay there. I would then be given a receipt, a pick-up slip and instructions to proceed to a nearby warehouse, where the goods would be issued. All very lovely if you had a car and knew your way around Vienna, I suppose.

In the interests of efficiency, I planned to go to the payment place, skip to the pickup place and meet the van driver there. It didn't make sense to start his clock ticking before that, so I looked up the address of the pickup place online and texted the van man in pidgin German.

Meet me at 5pm at Windswept Car Park A, Godawfulsheim Industrial Estate.

And that's the loose understanding of the agreement we reached.

Things went just fine at the payment place. They even had a little map which told you how to get to the pickup place. It was only when I enquired how long it would take to walk there that I began to suspect I'd got my timings wrong.

"*Zu Fuss? Das geht nicht!*" said the woman on the till with a surprised look. She was telling me, using that much-favoured German expression, that it wasn't walking distance. I must have misunderstood the scale something horrible when I'd looked this up on Google Maps. I'd convinced myself it was a 15-minute walk, and planned accordingly.

195

"Bus?" I asked tentatively, fairly certain that this most international of words would be understood, especially if I pronounced it *boooss*, the way every other language that wasn't English seemed to prefer it.

"Ich glaube nicht," she said with a shake of the head, which I took to mean there wasn't an easy transport connection. I sighed and headed for the exit. The only good news I could think of by the time I reached the icy car park was that I'd at least noticed my receipt slipping out of my pocket as I'd left the store, and picked it up before someone else did. I *really* needed that thing if I wanted the mattress.

Other people might have flagged a taxi at this point, but this wasn't quite desperate enough a situation for me to want to get ripped off. The clock might be ticking on my van man quite shortly, but what if I *ran*? The woman in Möbelix hadn't looked all that sporty. Maybe she was the kind of person who considered the end of her driveway to be beyond walking distance. There were plenty of those in the world, after all. So, instead of being even halfway sensible, I started to run.

When I paused for breath, I would do so at bus shelters, squinting my eyes at the transport map in the hopes that out-of-shape Möbelix lady had been wrong about the buses. But as far as I could make out, any buses that stopped at any of the bus stops would soon be turning off in the wrong direction. I was somewhere a long way east of the Danube - Brünnerstraße to be precise - and genuinely seemed to be attempting just about the only route not covered by Vienna's transport system.

This really was a sorry part of the world - nothing but darkness, car parks, bright-glowing traffic lights and an endless stream of smug cars driven by smug people. I felt quite alone here; the heartlessness of urban life suddenly seemed most vivid. It was too late to start playing at hitchhiking, or even to wait for a taxi. I'd lose precious time and possibly get nowhere. In this forlorn part of the 22nd district, where all the sensible people were somewhere else, somewhere warm, the only way to really control my destiny was to run like hell.

I didn't have to worry about overheating from the exercise, because I think the temperature had by now dipped below zero. It really was a night for snuggling under a blanket in front of the fire, not for running a half-marathon in completely the wrong shoes and a heavy jacket. And no matter which maps I looked at - on my phone, on the bus shelters, or on the decidedly not-to-scale doodle I'd been given at the checkout - it definitely seemed like I had a number of miles to cover.

But it's amazing how fast you can run when your destination is a man with a van whom you know is already charging you by the minute. For forty minutes I sprinted and sprinted and sprinted, stopping to gulp down some more sub-zero air and text the van guy to tell him not to drive away. I wasn't quite dead when I got there, half an hour late, but I wasn't far off achieving frozen-corpse status. Running's something I just don't do, unless there happens to be a cricket ball that needs chasing. And even then, I'm told, it doesn't look good.

My lungs were burning and freezing at the same time, my every limb ached and I knew it would be a long time before I could feel my nose again. But catching my breath could happen once the van was rolling. I banged on the window of the yellow van I'd been told would be there. It was driven by an Afghani man whose German made mine look like Wittgenstein's. It was clearly his boss I'd been texting, because I could only communicate with this chap by sign language. Anyway, it wasn't hard to get him to reverse up to the pick-up point, help me shove what looked like the right mattress into the back, and leave this spirit-sapping place behind.

It was just as well that there wasn't going to be much chat in the car, because I really was heaving in great servings of oxygen for the first few minutes of our journey back across the river. But I do remember feeling quite pleased with myself. Curve balls might have come my way, but I'd rallied to the cause and dealt with them. My run might have hurt bad, but in a way it made the fact that I was now sitting in a warm van, with a new mattress in the back, even more satisfying.

We were now heading for the 19th district, aka Döbling, on the edge of which I lived and in the middle of which we'd pick up my free sofa. Apparently the 19th was considered a relatively posh part of town, perhaps owing to the fact that it used to be contained within the American quarter of Vienna after the Second World War. Did you know that Vienna, just like headline-hogging Berlin, was divided into different segments by the Allied powers, and quietly stayed like that for a decade? This was something I'd only learned in the previous couple of days.

The navigation system, which I assumed had been pre-programmed by my Afghani friend's boss, brought us to a narrow street that looked like pure hell for parking. No worries, reckoned my driver, he could reverse through the skinny archway into the inner courtyard. He didn't achieve this without losing a little bit of paint and ramming the odd kerb, but the end result was good from my point of view. The two of us were able to haul a three-man sofa and an armchair away from the apartment of a jolly-looking Iranian couple, only once knocking a frame off the wall. I noticed that the Iranian couple had a fine-looking rug or three, which I thought would do a rather nice job of making my living room cosier.

"Say, while we're on the subject of dragging stuff out of your home," I ventured, "are any of your rugs for sale?"

"No," said the wife sweetly. "They're not."

It was worth a shot, I suppose.

From there it was a short hop up the road, past Kahlenbergerdorf with its intriguing onion-dome church and *Winzerhaus* (I didn't know what a *Winzerhaus* was, but I was curious to find out), along the hulking, forested flank of the Leopoldsberg to the left, and then up my epically steep hill.

Just a few minutes later I had sent my van man on his way, still within the two hours I'd budgeted for. My run had been worth it, financially speaking at least. It was an immensely satisfied, exhausted sleep into which I fell that night.

At this point, I suppose you might well be thinking 'why isn't he writing about his new job?' Well, firstly, it's because I still work there as I write these words. You wouldn't, would you? Also work's boring. I try to think about it as little as possible. I work to live, not vice versa. And right now I had an awful lot of living to think about.

Resisting the French

A week or so later, with the absolute essentials for a successful life in Vienna now in place, I found myself back at Gatwick Airport. I was living the English dream: waiting a long time for an unjustifiably expensive bus to arrive.

Under normal circumstances I'd have taken the train straight up to Merstham. But the railway drivers were on strike again. Every minute I waited at this particularly grim bus stop, which sat in the middle of a dual carriageway and was almost impossible to find despite my mastery of the English language, I missed Britain a little less.

It took an age to get back to the house in Merstham, where I'd left my car sitting for the first three weeks I'd been in Vienna. I'd already packed it up, banking on the fact that most of the stuff pressing up against the windows wasn't of much interest to the bored youths of Portland Road. These items included cricket pads, duvets, towels and that bright yellow duck I'd been carrying around since my Witney days.

This was the entire point of driving as opposed to flying: being able to bring oversized and non-essential stuffed animals with you.

The dates had fallen in such a way that all I was going to be able to manage was a quick bite with my hosts, who were back from America and had reclaimed their house, then a few hours' sleep in the spare bed, and a five o'clock wake up call. It had to be so if I wanted to catch my ferry from Dover.

I would take the efficient northern route as opposed to the captivating mountain route, since by pure coincidence I had a friend from Cape Town who happened to be finishing up a conference in Bonn, and who happened to want to visit Vienna. So I would drive through Belgium and scoop Melissa up in Germany, taking full advantage of the paid-for hotel she had that night, before driving on refreshed in the morning.

It was a shame I couldn't stay longer in Merstham, if only to catch my breath before what would be a massive drive. But I needed two full days to make it back to Vienna, and besides, that free hotel in Bonn wouldn't be there if I waited another day.

I barely slept that night. Not so much from the anticipation of the trip (it takes far more than that to keep me awake these days) but the fear that I'd messed up setting my alarm (it happens) and would still be in bed when my ferry to Calais set sail. It was a fair drive to get to the port, and I wanted to stop and fill up the tank in Britain, where I still had money in the bank, rather than Europe, where I was living off my credit card until my first Euros salary came in.

I rose shaky, disoriented and angry that life always had to be a time squeeze that ate into my sleep. I vowed, as I always do when alarm clocks go off, to prioritize getting rich enough not to *ever* have get up early again, apart from to watch live sport transmissions from New Zealand. (People say things like 'you can sleep when you're dead', but to me the pleasure of sleeping isn't the unconscious part that might be interchangeable for death. It's the slow dance of waking up in various stages of consciousness. It's looking at the clock, going '7am? That's interesting...' and then rolling over again. Try doing all that when you're dead.)

My hosts, who'd both had the good fortune to retire, were still enjoying their freedom to stay in bed as long as they liked, and quite understandably so. I boiled the kettle and stumbled outside to let some hot water de-ice the windscreen, which I always find quite a satisfying process to watch. I made a final check for passports, wallets, tickets and keys, splashed another sinkful of water in my face, carefully closed the front door behind me and climbed into my polar-cold Peugeot 306.

And you know what? She started first time. Just like she always did.

I may have said this before, but that car was the one thing that had stayed constant throughout all the madness of my life in the last year and a half. It had always fired up since the day I drove it off that forecourt in Brize Norton, even when temperatures dipped to toe-freezing levels. No heavy load had proven too much to ask, not even that chest of drawers I shoved into the back after I fled Karola's intolerable apartment. This transcontinental trip would be by far the heaviest cargo it had ever carried on my watch - and the longest distance into the bargain. But with the confidence that goes hand in hand with mechanical naivety, I had no choice but to assume it would work out.

It somehow seemed right that the 306 would join me in Vienna, even if that might prove to be her final chapter. The fact that reliability was (or should have been) a question mark would only lend a greater sense of achievement to actually getting there.

And a sense of achievement was exactly what I'd been missing so far. I might have already been living and working in Austria for three weeks, but such had been the rush and scurry that the whole thing still felt a bit like an extended business trip. But a two-day road voyage in a precariously laden car, waiting for that beautiful moment when your final destination first appears on a road sign, and then, hours or days later, finally seeing its skyline loom up on the horizon? That's how you really get a sense that you're moving your life across a continent.

Unsure exactly how the car would react to the pots, bats, duvets and ducks weighing it down, I edged very tentatively out of the driveway in Merstham. I hoped the steering would still work. It did. I really needed to blast some heating, and that worked too. It was absolutely pitch black, but there were still plenty of bad-temperedly polite cars about, playing their strange waiting game on the narrow roads. Thankfully I only had to flash my lights and reverse a couple of times before I reached the highway. A good thing, too, since I couldn't see a thing in my rear-view mirror. There were far too many giant ducks in the back seat for that.

I made a quick stop at a petrol station and did my best impression of a responsible car owner heading on a long trip with a heavy vehicle. Which meant little more than squirting a totally made-up measure of air in the tyres.

In Britain, unlike anywhere else I've been, you have to *pay* for air. (Think about this for a second.) The system at this station was one of my personal favourites, under which you would put a coin in the machine and it would then pump air for something like two minutes. This meant that if you didn't want to put another coin in (and who would?), you had to become a one-man Formula 1 pit crew, with the critical difference that you would be using equipment you'd never tried before and on which you'd had no chance to warm up. As usual, this meant I had tyre smudges all over my hands and jeans before I'd even left Surrey. But at least I didn't put another coin in.

I'd driven the stretch of motorway across southern England a million times. Going over to Calais by ferry had been bed-wettingly exciting the first time I did it, but although there was still a faint *frisson*, I'd done it too often by now to get worked up. I think I'd only ever done this run for work trips, and it had always been at the arse-crack of dawn like this, or else the return stretch in the dead of night, invariably with an early alarm call looming. It had always been about getting somewhere (usually bed or a boat) on time.

Even if you did have time on your side in England, you always feared a mass of brake lights suddenly appearing on the horizon. One of these famous traffic jams could throw even the most conservative travel plans. They usually occurred at predictable times in predictable places ('If you don't get past the M26 turnoff by six, you're done for,' an experienced commuter might tell you) and the fear of missing one of these intermediate deadlines meant you were always racing the clock. Even when you weren't.

With a tank to fill, a ferry to catch and a cheap ticket limited to a specific early sailing (obviously), I wasn't going to take any chances. I'd like to tell you I got glassy-eyed and nostalgic as I watched the turn-offs for Sevenoaks, Wrotham, West Malling, Maidstone, Ashford and Folkestone slip past. But actually I was just holding my breath, waiting for any whiff of brake lights up ahead. Sure, I'd flown past all the usual flashpoints by seven in the morning, and I was going against the rat race heading for London, but still, you never knew.

I made it onto my ferry in the end, despite doing my best to eat up ample spare time by cruising around looking for an off-highway petrol station, which I assumed might prove to be cheaper than the last couple before Dover port. It would perhaps have been easier if I'd consulted my Google Maps, but I simply didn't have the patience to fiddle around with my phone. I reckoned that by the time I'd pulled over and my fat fingers had zoomed in on a hardware store in Folkestone rather than a gas station outside Dover, I'd be just as well off driving about hoping to find something.

But I filled my tank in the end, making it onto the ferry just in time to tackle the next bit of strife that had come to mind. A truly last-minute affair, this one hinged upon what was becoming my new favourite annoyance: the rules about cars in Europe.

I'll say one thing for Britain: there are a lot fewer irritating regulations than on the mainland. All over the continent they expect you to carry high-visibility jackets, first aid kits and those little reflective triangles truck drivers put on the road to tell you they've broken down. As far as I could understand, this now applied to all cars at all times. Even British ones that weren't accustomed to such interference in their boot space.

But all this fiddlesomeness was nothing compared the rule the French had just brought in. I had to Google this one multiple times just to make sure it wasn't an April Fool's Day joke. But apparently it was straight-faced truth: every car on French roads now needed to contain a *breathalyser kit*.

While I could see some argument for the triangles and yellow jackets and the first aid kits I wouldn't know how to use, this bit of legislation made me nothing but militant and defiant. Were the French seriously asking people to bring along a piece of equipment traditionally found in a policeman's bag of tricks? What was coming next? Would everyone have to lug handcuffs around just in case the local constable might want to arrest you and he'd forgotten his pair back at the station? Bring a fully-qualified judge with you just in case they wanted to press charges and couldn't find anyone to preside over a court? My mind fried and boggled in equal measure.

I have no problem with policing drunk drivers. But if I were French, I'd strongly question where my tax money was going if it couldn't be used to pay for basic law enforcement tools. Bring your own bloody breathalyser, *Monsieur Gendarme*!

I didn't know what other crazy laws lay in wait on my journey. Would Germany have an injunction against ducks on back seats? One really couldn't say for sure, but I was quite certain I wasn't going to jump through the morally objectionable hoops made up by the French. They might have had a state of emergency going on, but I wasn't going to supply my own alcohol testing kit. Especially when I only needed about half an hour's driving in their stupid country before I reached the relative sanity (I hoped) of Belgium.

I was also planning to take a chance on the triangles and jackets and person-fixing kits. If I was going to keep the car in Europe, then I would begrudgingly oblige, but I was by no means sure that holding onto the vehicle would work out. I refused to shell out on all that rubbish for a one-off trip. I simply wouldn't do it.

Granted, breaking all these life-threatening rules was a riskier game in December 2016 than it had been in the carefree days before Charlie Hebdo and the Syrian influx. Border checks were all the rage again. The French were a bit pissed off about attackers planning their evil games as day trips from Brussels. Germany, whatever Angela Merkel might have been saying to the contrary, didn't want every single asylum seeker in Europe diving gleefully into their welfare system. Chances were good that somebody in a uniform might pull me over on any of the three frontiers I had to cross. But I was still going to wing it.

One thing I did at least have to my name - something which I'd discovered was considered much more important in Europe than in South Africa - was an insurance policy. And in contrast to England, where the lack of a need to run around with your passport at all times was apparently quite exceptional, I'd read that they rather liked you to be able to produce papers in Europe.

And it was somewhere along the road to Dover that I realised I didn't have the actual papers. I was quite certain that I had a policy. But that might not convince a pig-headed officer.

The reason I didn't have papers was entirely down to the Axa Insurance Company being annoying in the way that most Internet-age companies seem to think is their true calling. Instead of just emailing me the papers when I'd signed on - way back in Witney, that was - they'd lumbered me with an online account and password I really, *really* didn't want, and told me I could download them papers from there. Of course I'd never got round to doing that (is it *really* that surprising, Axa and all the rest of you morons who've forgotten that the customer is supposed to be king, that your paying clients don't want to be given homework assignments?) and the password long forgotten. And as always happened in these cases, I didn't even know which of my email addresses I'd used to conduct business with them.

With my Peugeot safely stashed on the decidedly unromantic hulk of metal that was going to ship us to Calais, it was now dawning on me that I really needed my papers - in digital format at the very least. And preferably in the ten minutes before I lost my UK mobile signal. You didn't want to be paying roaming charges while kept on the line for twenty minutes listening to *Mull of Kintyre*.

I looked up a number for Axa and got through to them way faster than I expected. The boat was just being de-moored, or whatever it is they do to boats nowadays.

"What can I do for you, Mr Dalkey?" asked the lady.

"I'll tell you very clearly," I said as politely, yet urgently, as I could. "I need you to email me my insurance policy documents as a matter of absolute priority."

"No problem, Mr Dalkey," she purred. "I'll just need your dog's mobile telephone number, the email address on your account, and…"

"Please, please, *please*," I interrupted. "I have searched all my emails and everything to do with this account is not to be found. I am in an urgent hurry and don't have time for jumping sideways through hoops or talking about my pets. Can we please just have an old-fashioned human conversation where I give you my name and you look me up? The way I know you can?"

She hesitated.

"I'm on a boat and about to lose signal and email access on my phone," I pressed, before playing my trump card. "If you don't send me this, I will shortly be driving a car *illegally* in Europe."

When I used the i-word she sprang into life. She discovered that she could, much as I had suspected, quickly look up my policy and email it to the address I proceeded to read out to her over the phone.

"That should be with you in the next couple of minutes, Mr Dalkey," she said, much to her credit.

"Thank you," I said. "That was actually quite refreshing."

Now, why can't phoning up your insurance company always be like that? Why must one tell these people that there's a pending police situation before common sense can prevail?

Heaven be praised, I had a PDF of my European car insurance policy safely on my phone before we left British waters. At least that was *one* thing they couldn't lock me up for. (Although I supposed the new French regime couldn't possibly lock me up if I hadn't thought to bring along a few bricks to build my own prison cell.)

Oh, and I still don't have a clue what my dog's mobile phone number is.

Wrong Turns in Belgium

People seemed to love saying bad things about Belgium, but I'd never understood the reason. And it wasn't just because I was a fan of Tintin (or, to be precise, his far funnier friends Captain Haddock and Professor Calculus), who, along with Hercule Poirot, was perhaps the country's best-known son. There were many more reasons why I was looking forward to the few hours I'd spend crossing Belgium on my road trip to Vienna.

Belgium may not have been very good at having famous people who weren't fictional sleuths, and it may have had a higher-than-average number of miserable bastards, but it was a winner when it came to food and drink.

Yet beer lovers were about the only people who appreciated the country. Even people who didn't much care for beer, like myself, could find a nice brew. My saving grace was the cherry- and raspberry-infused ones that the Belgians invented. It was clever stuff: enough sweet flavours to disguise the awfulness of beer flavour, and actually taste nice. I had long been a big fan.

But there had always been so much more than that. The waffles, the chocolate, the mussels and the *frites*. It's very nice to travel to the country where stuffing your face with chips is not considered some kind of cheat against the culture you're supposed to be experiencing through your connoisseur taste buds.

Hot chips and mayonnaise really *was* what Belgians ate as a staple, or at least so it seemed. Moreover they were cheap and never in short supply. Even tiny towns had a *friterie* or two in the high street, where they would fry up your not-too-thick, but not McDonald's-skinny, potato strips in a double or triple helping of special oil that I'm led to believe might rob the meal of the slightest vegetarian credential it might otherwise have. Whatever they do, it's seriously tasty.

Not only was Belgium a fine place to eat and drink, but the oft-levelled accusation that it was boring wasn't fair. Places like France and Germany were the unimaginative ones if you asked me, insofar as they did nothing much besides speaking French and German. In Belgium, there were pockets where you didn't need to do much more than cross the street for the language to change. French and Flemish (which is like Dutch, at least on paper) jostled for position throughout Brussels and along a linguistic border that streaked across

206

the middle of the nation. I always found it quite invigorating to walk into a chip shop and find myself unsure whether to say *Bonjour* or *Goedemorgen*. As long as I got my chips, of course.

Then there were the curious dialects, particularly on the Flemish side of the country. And some of the smaller villages - Pepinster, Huppaye, Trooz and Xhos - bore names that didn't appear to derive from any European language at all. In these little settlements, one could easily mistake the local lingo for the barks of a drunken baboon troop. Which was only fitting, really, if you were going to give your towns names like that.

Belgium had its grim side, though: I'll be first to admit that. While the *Grande Place*, and Antwerp's *Grote Markt*, were among the most ornate and uplifting squares in Europe, things deteriorated quickly after that.

The Flemish didn't have canals in quite the same quantities as the Dutch do, so maybe they never felt much like copying the skinny waterside houses from across the border. Meanwhile the French-speaking Walloons had no architectural inspiration to draw on but the misery of Northern France, where quite frankly I'm surprised everybody hadn't killed themselves long ago.

All in all this added up to not very much, giving Belgium its own distinct look. A look which consisted mainly of flat red bricks, often covered with the grime left by derelict industry and the many millions of vehicles that continued to cross the country on their way to getting somewhere else as fast as possible.

But Belgium's pros comprehensively outweighed its cons, even without considering that it didn't have stupid rules about breathalyzers. I had every reason to want to reach Tintin-land as quickly as possible after the boat docked in France.

After the ferry crossing, winding the clocks an hour forwards and giving thanks that I didn't live anywhere near Calais - whose image had been done no good at all by the ongoing reports that people from war zones were risking their lives all over again to get away from the place, even though it was supposed to be perfectly possible to claim asylum in France - it was late morning by the time I crossed the border into Belgium.

I heaved a sigh of relief as I whizzed past the windswept and bleak row of former duty-free shops at De Panne without having gotten pulled over for a do-it-yourself breath test in France. Despite a stuffed car that might have attracted attention, I'd managed to give the French authorities the slip. And there's not much more satisfying than that, let me tell you.

Now, despite the grand distance between the Belgian Riviera and Vienna, there were just two more border crossings to go.

I felt a lot more comfortable at this point, because Belgium wasn't generally known to be among the strictest of countries. I'd travelled there plenty, but wasn't sure I'd ever seen a policeman. I'd always had the impression they were either too busy running Europe, or fighting about what language in which to write the word *police*, to do much actual law enforcement. It wasn't that long since the country had apparently functioned without any government at all, which somehow made it an agreeable sort of a place for a motorist with a car of dubious legal status.

While I had indeed done the drive across Belgium many times, usually heading for the circuits of Spa-Francorchamps or Zolder during my days as a motor-racing journalist, it was admittedly the better part of a decade since I'd done so. But I recalled it being as easy as eating chips: Belgium only really had about two main highways. As long as you made sure you were pointing east after the Brussels ring road - which was actually only half a ring, because the Walloons still didn't seem to have completed their side of the bargain south of town - then you couldn't help but end up in Germany.

Of course, Germany is a big place, and Bonn, where I needed to be, was quite a specific part of it. While my driving experience anywhere east of Belgium's two motor racing circuits was severely limited, Google's original route proposal had said I just needed to go past Hasselt (where one would drive if heading for the Zolder track), through the funny little appendix that hangs down at the bottom of the Netherlands and onwards into Europe's economic and industrial powerhouse. Once there, I would manage just fine with highway signs until I got to Bonn.

I *did* know that I was supposed to just programme a route into my phone's navigation system. I *did* know that's what everyone else in my position was doing. But I didn't like moronically following a blue arrow when crossing Europe any more than I did on a wander through Vienna. It took something away from the travel experience, and would lead to a scary phone bill.

Moreover, I came from the old school. The 'I know how to read a bloody map' school. And if I was driving through places I'd been before, I got even more stubborn about this. I saw every car journey as a geography test; one that would give me a certain satisfaction to pass. What, after all, was the point of having travelled through Belgium so many times before if I hadn't memorized the way? I might as well have stayed on the sofa all those years ago, right?

Given my digital navigation allergy, you'd think I might have bothered to print out some goodish maps, or at least buy one. Not on your nellie. All I had was a scrappy A4 overview of the route printed from Google. It didn't show much more than about three cities and a blue worm connecting them.

I'd half-planned to buy a proper map on the road, but I'd gotten preoccupied with more pressing matters as usual. 'I can always pick one up at the roadside,' I'd thought to myself on the way to Dover, before proceeding not to do so when the chances came along. Shopping, you see. Never my strong point.

Anyway, a map isn't always much use when you're driving solo. You've got far too much looking-at-the-road to do. And the moments when you most need to give the map closest attention - massive highway interchanges with hundreds of signs, rammed with cars and trucks changing lanes with the annoying, impatient ease of people who know where they need to be - are the moments when you most need your eyes on the road.

(Once, in Australia, I crashed into the back of a Holden, simply because I was too busy trying to figure out a map to notice things like red lights. Since then, I'd always been curious about the legal status of map-reading. Lawmakers had excitedly clamped down on mobile phone usage, but was this much more mature source of driving distraction still a legal Wild West? If reading a paper map on your lap wasn't a crime, then it seemed odd that reading a digital map on your lap could be so.)

But I made my mapless way across the first half of Belgium just fine. There was really nowhere else you could go, unless you deliberately turned off into small villages. You just followed the signs for Brussels, and snickered as you pass Jabbeke. The stretch of highway near this amusingly-named (it's only a few letters short of a jabberwocky, you see) town was apparently once quite popular for car manufacturers testing out how fast their cars could go. And there were plenty more long, flat, straight sections on the run from the French border to Brussels. The biggest challenge *en route* to the Belgian capital, really, was preventing yourself from driving at 180 kilometres per hour.

Not that the road was empty. It was as international as I remembered Belgium to be. Polish trucks, Dutch station wagons and German Audis. Sometimes there were so many vehicles from other places that you could barely spot the distinctive red-and-white stumpy licence plate of a Belgian-registered car at all. And when you did, you couldn't resist pitying them a little. Everyone else was on some elaborate trans-continental journey, and they were just on their way to the supermarket.

As always it got much busier near the capital, but on this day Brussels had more traffic than I ever remembered seeing before. The ring road was largely at a standstill, despite being only a little past lunchtime. I guessed it was already weekend for the good folk of Brussels and Antwerp, which are so close together that the ring skirting north of Brussels was more like a corridor between the two cities. So this was where actual Belgian cars finally joined the fray in significant numbers, mingling with the ones heading from or to Britain or Germany or Poland. The airport was also there, just where all the biggest roads meet, adding to the mess of it all.

Although I was becalmed for several lengthy periods of time, in truth there wasn't much panic. This wasn't the *big* day of driving: Bonn was only supposed to be a couple of hours past Brussels. All mapless me needed to do was follow signs to somewhere east, like Liège, and then look out for the big split in the road, where I would turn off towards Hasselt and Maastricht.

It would surely be easy, even given Belgium's unique system of putting unexpected sub-turnoffs in the very middle of turnoffs. Typically found halfway along one of those ever-tightening spiral turns that slip roads so often are, these little stings in the tail could come as a nasty surprise to the motorist performing a fist-pump for having successfully found what they *thought* was the definitive highway exit. Still, I had no problem escaping Brussels in the direction of Liège.

(Even though Liège was sometimes signposted as Luik, which is what Flemish people call the city. These curveballs are just something you have to know about when you drive around in Belgium. They won't signpost destinations in both official languages, only in the tongue that prevails wherever you happen to be. This being so, you might think that Gent and Genk are another trick of the signposting authorities, but these are actually distinct towns in opposite ends of the country. Ghent is Gand in French, while Genk doesn't seem to have a French name at all.

So watch out, in Belgium, even if you're using one of those new-fangled navigation systems. One slip of the finger, or a slight mis-grasp of Flemish-Walloon relations, and you can end up sailing in entirely the wrong direction. And if that happens, please don't take it personally if you find me cackling insanely at your misfortune. That'll just be me assuming you've been dumbed down by technology, and don't actually *know* where anything is. Just ignore me.)

So I shot merrily in the direction of Liège. The more kilometres slipped by, the more concerned I became that this wasn't quite right. By the time Liège was just forty kilometres away - which happens surprisingly fast in Belgium - I was sure I'd somehow missed the northern route. So sure, in fact, that I even pulled over and switched on the navigation.

I peered at my not-very-good digital map, looking at where I lay in relation to Hasselt and Maastricht. Much as I'd feared, it revealed that Hasselt was basically behind me already. Somehow, somewhere, I'd missed what constituted one of the most important intersections east of Brussels. One that I'd managed to take as recently as 2007.

Naturally enough, I harangued and berated myself not for failing to have any navigation plan, but for failing to spot a turning that I should have remembered from a decade earlier.

It didn't look as though there was any point in turning back. Taking a more southerly route, past Verviers and the turnoff towards my old friend Spa-Francorchamps, and then crossing the border near Aachen, wouldn't constitute any major time loss. At least not in comparison to the traffic that had snagged me in Brussels.

Less than an hour after that, I was fist-pumping once more. I had driven unmolested into Germany. There were no border checks, even though the Germans were supposed to be getting snarky about policing their frontiers. Nobody wanted to cast a beady eye over car, papers or passports.

More than a year went by before I discovered that I'd been lucky. That's when I learned that you were supposed to have specialist winter tyres to drive in Germany. Oops.

How Do You Ask For Tap Water In German?

How do I begin to describe my friend Melissa? About eight years earlier, she'd hired me to help her edit a golf magazine in Cape Town. Not long after settling into the lovely offices not far from where I'd grown up, I discovered that she didn't actually care for golf very much. Environmental stuff was more her thing, and the water sins of the golf industry didn't sit well with her at all. But we all need to pay the rent somehow, don't we?

We'd kept in touch ever since our year or so as colleagues, even though I'd subsequently moved to England, and then Australia, and then back to England again. Whenever I was in Cape Town I would visit her country house (well, 'cottage in much need of repair' would be more accurate) in Riviersonderend, a little town a couple of hours out of the city known to most travellers as nothing more than a refuelling stop and the home of a pie shop with a cult following.

With a rather beautiful Afrikaans name that translated to 'never-ending river,' Riviersonderend was the kind of place where property was cheap, but jobs were non-existent. The latter point meant Melissa couldn't be there full-time, and that was a shame. Because watching the birds flit amongst the fruit trees in the back garden, and the subtly changing hues of the moody mountains beyond, was very much her thing too.

With her devotion to vegetarianism, enthusiasm for talking to plants and tendency to operate on the brink of discombobulation almost all of the time, Melissa always provided me ample opportunity to crack a joke or two. Such as when her principles melted at the sight of a good salami and she would make (extremely) satisfied noises upon consuming it, which validated my carnivorous lifestyle choices no end. Even if nothing particularly funny was happening, the chance to use the word 'discombobulated' - it became a running joke between us - was never far away. And that is reason enough to make anybody feel jolly.

And now Melissa had gotten the kind of job *I* really wanted. One which involved being able to work from pretty much anywhere she pleased, including pink cottages in one-horse South African towns. Every now and then she would be flown to Europe for a meeting or two, such as this one in Bonn. After which she had the freedom to join the second half of my road trip and work in Vienna for a few days.

I was still going to have to drive the entire distance on the second day, of course, despite Melissa's possession of a driving licence and regular use of a car in South Africa. We were talking almost 900 kilometres, but I decided to shrug and get on with it rather than insist. I'd long since given up trying to figure out why women never wanted to drive in foreign countries, particularly if it involved using the other side of the road. Just when you thought it was unacceptably old school to assume that you, as a man, were going to be the driver, you couldn't help noticing that any women in your party were scrambling to get as far away from the steering wheel as possible. I didn't know what to think anymore.

Bonn was completely dark by the time I arrived, and I reluctantly switched on one of my phones for navigation purposes as I came into the city. Still, finding the hotel and somewhere to park long enough to run in and say 'let me into your parking garage' was the usual barrel of laughs. One-way roads kept slipping me curve balls, and a non-stop flow of impatient locals charging up behind me with their lights ablaze meant even finding a moment to pull over and look at my digital map was too much to ask. (Next time you impatiently roar up somebody's exhaust pipe, consider for a moment that they might not know the roads as well as you do. A registration plate from outside your country is often a *very* good indicator that this might be the case.)

But I got there in the end, and found Melissa's room in a breathless hurry. I'd parked somewhere nearby, unsure - as usual - of whether I was really allowed to do so. I had visions of a slick German *Polizei* officer pouncing on my car mere seconds after I had left it, and arranging for it to be towed away. This being so I had positively sprinted from my car to the hotel. I needed Melissa to get reception to open up the garage in a hurry, so I failed completely on delivering an emotional greeting to one of my most hug-happy friends.

A few minutes later I found myself in the tight confines of the hotel courtyard, watching the guy from reception press buttons and pull levers as he operated one of those weird double-deck European garages in which cars can cleverly sit one on top of the other by means of a system of dynamic platforms. It's all very confusing, and far from the most reassuring of parking experiences.

After quite a performance, front desk guy beckoned me onto a metal ramp of sorts. My tyres enjoyed about half a millimetre of clearance on either side.

After being chased about the streets by unsympathetic Bonn-ites (what do you call someone from Bonn, anyway?), sprinting to beat imaginary police officers and edging into impossibly tight garages, I was drenched with sweat by the time I finally got out of the driving seat. The hotel guy watched on patiently as I rummaged about to try and find my toothbrush and other goods I might need for the night. Bearing in mind that my car might disappear three storeys underground at any moment during the night, and that a massive performance would be needed to gain access, it seemed advisable to grab everything in one go.

Then, after a lie down to catch my breath, the time was ripe to plunge into the streets of Bonn. I'd have been delighted to stretch my legs anywhere - even Birmingham - after a day hunched in the driver's seat of a Peugeot 306, but it was a bonus that I found myself somewhere new, intriguing and heaving with Christmas cheer.

Bonn was just an odd case. I remembered hearing its name on news bulletins whilst growing up in the 1980s, when it was capital of West Germany and a man called Helmut Kohl ran the country. But since the Berlin Wall came down, I'd barely heard a peep out of the place. It seemed surreal, now, to think that this had ever been the capital of a quite major nation. Now that politicians no longer had reason to visit, did *anyone* actually come here? I'd certainly never seen 'two-night city break in Bonn' in the windows of any travel agents.

With less than half a million inhabitants, Bonn barely cracked the top 20 of German cities by population size. Even in its own state, North Rhine-Westphalia, several settlements outranked it. I'm sure there must have been good reasons to put the capital in such a piffling place after the Second World War, but they're not immediately obvious to me. Perhaps they decided Munich was too Bavarian, Frankfurt too boring and Cologne smelled too nice.

Or maybe Bonn got the nod simply because it could claim to be the birthplace of Ludwig van Beethoven. I hadn't known this pre-arrival, but it became immediately apparent when we stumbled across a huge bust of the composer in the middle of a park near the river. It was a magnificent thing, all wavy-haired and wild-eyed and maniacal, and Melissa was rather taken with it. I was rather impressed too: I hadn't seen such an enormous head since the foreboding and remarkable Lenin statue they've got in Ulan Ude, half a world away in Siberia.

Although I hadn't planned it this way, the next day's journey was going to be rather poetic from a Beethovenian point of view. The composer died in Vienna, you see. At one point he'd lived in Grinzing - which I now knew to be a marvellous source of free sofas - at some point during his very frequent residential switches. Apparently the good Ludwig had rather a bad run with landlords: something with which I could sympathise entirely. I wondered what *he* would have made of being told where he had to store his shower gel? I bet it wouldn't have ended well.

After our encounter with one of music's greatest names, we went down to the riverside. The Rhine was as unspectacular in low-rise Bonn as the Danube was in Vienna - it didn't even have an island to offer - and it didn't take long for us to conclude that the Christmas markets, slightly inland in the old town, would be a more interesting bet.

People were forever flying to Germany to experience the Christmas vibe: one heard much about the magic of Dresden, Cologne and Munich, to name but three. Bonn's market, on the other hand, wasn't one you'd expect to find in the next *Ten Christmas Markets You Absolutely Have to Visit This Year and Which Will Blow Your Mind* story you stumbled across while procrastinating at work. The only top ten list Bonn was likely to make, I think, was *Ten Cities You Haven't Heard From for a While*. (I think this would make quite a fun article, come to think of it. I'd like to nominate Palermo, Kinshasa, Ottawa and Belfast for immediate inclusion.)

Anyway, the surprising point I mean to make is that Bonn's *Weihnachtsmarkt* was, in spite of its total lack of fame, genuinely mind-blowing. It crept all over the city like oil coursing through an engine, its colourful little stalls splaying out every which way in the streets of the historic centre. They sold all kinds of remarkable things, from curious smoked fish to hot white wine with whipped cream on top. One of the busier stalls had a grinning, mechanized moose's head shaking its antlers this way and that, while hulks of meat and bread and confectionary were gaily traded below.

Huge crowds of merry-makers swarmed the streets, making it an entertaining business to move about at all, never mind while you were trying not to spill your goblet of steaming *Glühwein*. I didn't think any of these people were tourists - the Internet hadn't sent them here, you see - which made me like the Bonn market even more. It was all quite positively jolly, and even after ten o'clock the festivities showed no signs of letting up.

That probably sounds unremarkable for a weekend evening, but I'd already had a glimpse of the markets in Vienna, and noted that they loved to bang down the shutters and tell you to go home well before ten o'clock. You had to be on the ball if you wanted to reclaim the deposit every Teutonic market took off you for your *Glühwein* mug. And unlike the pleasing, cramped chaos of Bonn, most of the Viennese markets were laid out in decidedly orderly rows on spacious public areas. It was all far too organized to be as fun as it might be. I concluded that if Bonn was anything to go by, then the Germans did Christmas markets far better than the Austrians did.

I was warming to the opinion that smaller was definitely better where the markets were concerned. It was a bit like London versus Oxford - how many stalls do you actually need to sell you warm alcohol, really? You're never going to visit them all. I'd seen a giant market in Vienna - the *Christkindlmarkt* in front of the *Rathaus* - and hadn't liked it much.

The *Christkindlmarkt* usually made any travel-website lists willing to include parts of the German-speaking realm that weren't in Germany, but I suspect that was mainly down to the gorgeous backdrop of City Hall. Editors couldn't help but want to use the photograph. But a pretty building doesn't automatically make for a great market, especially if said market's main drawbacks include not being able to actually buy anything. In my experience there were so many people between yourself and the wares that you wanted to give up and go home long before you got near a *Glühwein*.

Sure, there was a limit when it came to size: three lonely stalls and four rickety tables would be depressing. But Bonn struck a nice balance. There might have been a little wait to get served, and yes, progress in the vicinity of crowded stands could be slow, but it never got to the point that you needed to head-butt people in order to take a step forward. This was about right in my book, and I decided I would think very carefully about planning Yuletide visits to the likes of Cologne. I could only imagine what the jostling there might be like, not to mention the chances of getting mown down by some grinch with a van or a gun. Berlin had just had a sad experience with this. The grim truth of the times was that having your fun in a major city did jack up the risk factor.

(If you're reading this twenty years from now, I sincerely hope that humanity has moved on from barbarianism, you have no idea what I'm talking about, and the world is once again an innocent place that has forgotten all about large-scale terrorist killings. Sadly I fear this may be optimistic...)

We called it a night after a couple of drinks and a good wander. I had a massive drive ahead of me the next day, and we had to be up extra-early to re-arrange the cargo in the Peugeot. She'd been an absolute trooper on day one, but now she would have to carry an extra person and their luggage. Also, the front seat would have to be freed up. It was going to be a tight squeeze, that was for sure.

After a six o'clock alarm call and quick shower, I watched in dismay as the full extent of Melissa's baggage dawned on me.

"You *do* remember me saying you'd have to pack light?" I grumbled. I was the one moving to a new home. She was only over in Europe for a few days, yet somehow she had a suitcase big enough to fill the boot. And I could barely even lift the thing. "What *is* all this stuff? Have you got bricks in here?"

We may have laughed, but I was getting genuinely concerned that I was asking too much of a car designed to ship four people and a little shopping. The Peugeot 306 was never meant to be a heavy-duty removals van, and I felt a glum certainty that this time it would finally refuse to move. What if I had to leave my giant yellow duck in Bonn? Or my cricket gear? I'd have a sense of humour failure about that.

But after a traditional German hotel breakfast of bread, jam, cheese and eggs, followed by another virtuoso performance as the staff defied physics to bring my car back up to street level, some fastidious repacking and a couple of attempts at getting certain doors to close, the bulging car did fire into life and proceed to move. With the temperature hovering around zero into the bargain, I swelled with pride on her behalf.

After a stop for fuel and more token maintenance, we hit the road south. Getting out of a city is always a lot easier than looking for a specific address within it, I find. You can usually rely on signposts to get you to the nearest highway. But, whether through incompetence on our part or that of Bonn, this day proved an exception.

Sure, we found ourselves pointing in the direction of Frankfurt easily enough, but we'd somehow bumbled onto a regional road that sailed along the banks of the Rhine. It was ages before we got anywhere near *Autobahn* access again, but we didn't mind too much, because the snowy scenery was pretty memorable. And a nice way to ease into things: there wasn't going to be much opportunity to look at pretty things today.

217

Once we finally made the highway, things got dull. Very dull. It may come as no surprise if I tell you that the Germans built their highway network with efficiency, rather than nice views, in mind. Either that, or the fat belly of the *Bundesrepublik* just doesn't offer much of interest to look at. Even when we passed through forests, they looked as uniform and sad as the concrete all around us. Even the green leaves had an edge of grey to them.

The whole day was an education in just how flipping *big* the country is. I drove for hours, and hours, and hours, and barely seemed to go near any major cities at all. The only places I'd heard of were Frankfurt and Nuremberg. The road just went on and on. And on. Not even the navigation was a challenge - my Google Maps printout was now more than sufficient for a day that involved pretty much only one or two junctions where we could possibly go wrong. Not that I was going to complain about that part.

Meanwhile my butt complained louder and louder, despite the occasional roadside break for a chilly runaround and a donut. Progress was slow, since I wasn't keen to do more than about 110 kilometres per hour. The car was a laden beast of burden, after all, and I didn't think it would respond well to sudden braking or changes of direction, much less a slide of any description.

The icy roads made me wary, as did the galloping Audis (why are Audi drivers always such dickheads?) that could speed from the horizon to your rear bumper in the time it took to glance at your mirror. I preferred to stay well away from the fast lane, where I would only raise the ire of impatient people with unlimited petrol budgets, and keep to the inside, where I would instead annoy the never-ending stream of truck drivers. I was just about the only pipsqueak car on their territory, but considering I was carrying about as much weight as some of the 16-wheelers were, I didn't particularly rate my engine's chances of accelerating past this multinational parade of diesel monsters.

I barely recognized the risk-averse person I had become. Not all that many years ago I'd spent many an hour hurtling around my neighbourhood streets on my bicycle, shooting out of my driveway with no idea if any cars might be coming. I would descend mountains on two wheels without hesitation. I broke arms and grazed knees. Now, it occured to me that I spent most of my cycling life on the brakes.

At the wheel of a car, I'd made a habit of hurtling round corners at the fastest possible speed, never giving a thought to the vehicle falling to bits. Only five years earlier, I'd taken a Bentley Continental to something like 250 kilometres per hour on a straight but bumpy stretch of South African tarmac between Bredasdorp and Cape Agulhas, the continent's southernmost point. And now, here I was, plodding along at a constant speed, always thinking of the worst-case scenario.

I had truly become a sad, sorry shadow of my former self. In fact, teenagers on bicycles now irritated me. I suppose this is normal life development for all but a few of us, but I didn't like it. When did I sign up to be a grown-up? It's a constant bugbear.

Being the safe, boring old goat I'd become, I had also insisted on completing as many kilometres in daylight as possible. That meant it was after four o'clock before we had a proper lunch stop, in a frozen, pitch-black little town that had exactly one of those depressing, three-stall Christmas markets that can really kill a party. The name of the place escapes me, but I know it was somewhere in the depths of Bavaria, perhaps not too far past Regensburg. The bar we found did have a perfectly acceptable jacket potato with sour cream and chives to offer, however. It paired nicely with a glass of tap water, which I only managed to order with some difficulty.

"*Leitungswasser?*" enquired the girl as I waved my hands in the direction of the tap behind the bar.

"Probably," I said with a vigorous nod. I knew *Wasser* was water, so her suggestion sounded plausible. And when she proceeded to fill up a glass and hand it to me, I knew I'd learned a useful word.

"*Ah, gut,*" I said with a happy face that hopefully told her she'd got it right. "*Leitungswasser*, right?"

"*Ja,*" she said with a sweet smile, understanding perfectly that I was trying to develop my language skills here. "*Leitungswasser!*"

"*Dankeschön,*" I thanked her, before wandering off to await my potato, feeling satisfied with today's German progress. It's a critical thing to learn in any country, isn't it? Get it wrong, and nine times out of ten you'll be confronted with a giant bottle of horrible sparkling water - I'm highly suspicious of anybody who insists on putting gas in perfectly good water, and I'm sorry if that's you - and expected to pay for it into the bargain.

Back in the car for the last three hours of the journey, there was nothing much to do but count down the miles and keep on praying that the 306 would go on running as smoothly as it had done all the way from far-off Merstham. It was pitch-dark and slippery-damp, which took any remaining pleasure out of driving. I had to fight the post-lunch impulse to sleep, kept awake only by the growing ache in my posterior, which despite eating my potato standing up, returned mere minutes after we resumed the journey.

I was so fed up by the time we crossed the Austrian border that I forgot I was supposed to be worried about crossing the Austrian border. But, again, there were no checks going on. I'd made it back to my new homeland!

Getting from Surrey all the way back to my adopted Austria ought to have been a cork-popping moment, but in truth I was too tired by then to care. The most exciting thing about it was that the last major opportunity to have any papers or tyres or breathalysers or ducks checked out by nit-picking officials with nothing better to do was probably behind us.

We entered the fifth and final country of the road trip somewhere west of Linz, which was big enough for me to have heard of it but small enough for me to know precisely nothing else about it. And with such numb fingers and bleary eyes, I wasn't about to ask Melissa to start reading its Wikipedia page out loud to me right now. After almost an entire day of travelling south-east, our course turned due east shortly after crossing the border. From there, the map showed a dead-straight run towards Vienna.

It was no more interesting than you would expect a major highway to be in the dark. By the time we got past Sankt Pölten, I was so desperate to reach home that I might even have started nudging 120 kilometres per hour. I managed to figure out the northern route into Vienna, which would bring me past Krems an der Donau and into my neck of the woods (my house was quite literally in a neck, in the woods, come to think of it) without having to negotiate navigating the city. That meant I could avoid the infamous *Gürtel* road that sucks in nearly every motorist at some point.

The final part of the route plan worked perfectly. With the clock fast ticking towards nine, we were whizzing past Korneuburg, along the highway directly across the Danube from my house. I had my doubts about getting the turnoff right - was it the one at Floridsdorf or some place else? - but I got it in one. Thank God.

Then we were on the bridge over the Danube, and I saw just what I'd been hoping to see: a sign to Klosterneuburg. And that meant home. From here, it couldn't possibly go wrong. I'd done this part before. Come off the slip road, take an impatient toddle along the side of my forested hill and towards city limits. Look out for the petrol station and the gambling place, and the job's pretty much done.

I was just about home and I was delirious. It was a mere 50 hours since I'd flown out of Vienna: what an effort! I could scarcely believe I'd returned so soon, by car, all the way from England. And here I was, indicating left to pull onto my dead-end road. I was about to turn up my steep, steep hill.

Of all the challenges my Peugeot had faced on the adventure, this was the one I had thought about the most. There had been nothing like this at any point on the route. Although I knew I could walk the last three hundred yards to my house from here, it would be cruel beyond measure if my car failed at the last.

But I did have my doubts. Because this was the kind of hill that Tour de France winners get off and push their bikes up. The kind of incline you shouldn't try to wheel your suitcase down, either, unless you want to end up in a crumpled heap at the bottom of it. The kind of hill you think of climbing in first gear, even on a good day. We're talking *steep*.

But I was underestimating my Peugeot 306. As ever. I was ready to grab the handbrake in a panic, but the car was having none of that. I had to put my foot down, but she sailed up without a hitch. I even found an easy parking spot that didn't call for parallel parking.

We'd made it. Yellow duck and all.

Hungarian Dentists, Thai Masseuses and Wild Beasts

While I gave my car a much-deserved rest, I went about making my apartment actually look like a home of sorts. My rental contract was set for three whole years, and entirely in my name. That meant I expected to stay in one place long-term. I wasn't at the mercy of other house-mates deciding to wrap up the lease, or obsessive people driving me out with their madness. Within reason, I could do with the flat as I wished. Hence bringing things like ducks and posters all the way to Austria.

Where previous houses had obliged me to use a range of wobbly pots and warped pans passed down from the landlady's great aunt, and a few baking trays you'd hesitate to use as a pig trough, the kitchen here was completely empty. For the first time in my life, I would actually have to go shopping for household essentials. And as much as I loathed shopping, I was at least looking forward to making my own choices on quality: bitter house-sharing experience had repeatedly taught me the value of non-stick pans.

(Equally, house-sharing experience had also told me there wasn't much point having quality stuff. It would only get ruined. I had to sympathize with landlords offering no more than the junk they could find in the attic.)

The biggest shopping trip of my life was called for. And what a stroke of luck that I had a car! I could go to where things were cheap, and bring everything back with room to spare. In my mind, 'cheap' meant somewhere like Slovakia or Hungary. I settled on the latter, on the basis that they used Forints, not Euros, so they'd be the cheapest of the lot.

To this day I'm not really sure if Hungary or Slovakia really *were* any cheaper than Austria. You'd have had to be quite scientific about doing a proper comparison, really, and I couldn't claim to have done that. I was, as most of us did, working on an assumption that was born in my primary school days, when globalization was far less of a thing and post-Soviet economies were in a bit of a mess.

A lot of the reason this perception had survived was that people like beer so much. And that they loved to shout about it even more when it was

222

cheap. A pint was a very simple thing to compare with the equivalent back home - better even than a Big Mac Index, when you considered that having actual beef in your burger wasn't really a thing in places like India - and Eastern European pints usually *were* a giveaway compared to those of say, England.

"Budapest was mega, mate," a lad returned from a stag weekend might say. "Four lagers for two quid!"

"But how much was the fish and chips you ordered while watching the Arsenal game?" I would often ask. "What's the going rate for a lap dance? And did you by any chance go to a supermarket and check what they're charging for a block of cheddar?"

This thing with alcohol prices is perhaps nothing more than a stroke of genius from the local tourist industries. Make the beer cheap, and they will come. Make the beer cheap, and they will tell everybody the whole country is cheap. It works every time.

As enthusiastic as I'd always been about the idea of being able to travel for weeks in places with appallingly weak currencies, I was beginning to accept that I was born too late to enjoy the halcyon days of massive price inequalities. I was no economist, but I reckoned that developments like the Euro, the emergence of strong middle classes everywhere and the fact that we now bought all the same Chinese junk whether we lived in Mexico or Manila, had probably spoiled it all for the backpacker on a shoestring.

Nonetheless, I liked the idea of going to another country to do my shopping. I hadn't brought my car all the way here to do something as dull as pootling down to the industrial park half a mile away, had I? So I settled on spending the early December *Maria Empfängnis* public holiday in the Hungarian border town of Sopron. With Melissa having jetted back to South Africa, I now roped in Rebecca, a new friend from my new job, to join me on the adventure.

"There's a small chance we'll get the car impounded and have to walk back," I admitted to her once we hit the road. "But I *think* I'm allowed to drive a UK car around in Europe for a certain period of time, so we should be fine."

"Haven't you looked on Google?" she asked.

"Of course I did," I shrugged. "But I found three different answers. Then one of my neighbours told me it was six months. Another said he'd been driving his German car here for twenty years, and that nobody cares."

"I see," she said. "Do you have insurance, though?"

"Yes!" I answered brightly. "My UK policy only expires in April, actually."

"I didn't know it was that simple," she remarked. "I thought you had to pay extra for Europe."

"Well, okay, it's a grey area," I admitted. "My policy says something about covering me for 60 days in Europe. It's not clear if means 60 days full stop, or if only the days when I fire up the car count..."

She gave me a look.

"I'm going with 60 days on which I use it," I said haughtily. "I've only got the car for weekends and Hungarian shopping trips, you know?"

"Hmm," she said.

"I'm okay until April," I said firmly. "We're going with that. I nearly died of tiredness to get it here, you know. And besides, what official here can say how long I've been in Europe when they look at my papers?"

Rebecca said nothing, and took another sip of coffee.

"One other thing," I told her as I glanced in the rear-view mirror, hoping not to find any police cars. "We're going to come off the highway as quick as we can, and use the back roads to the border."

"Why's that?" she asked suspiciously.

"Well," I coughed. "One thing I *do* know for sure is that you're supposed to have a toll sticker that lets you use the highways in this country."

"So you're not meant to be on this road? The one we're driving on right now?"

"Not technically," I confessed. "But buying a day pass is kind of a rip-off, you know? I'd buy a long-term one, but I'm not sure how long to buy it for. It all comes down to the thing that I don't know if I can keep the car long-term. Still got to find that out, but right now buying a wok's more important."

"So you're chancing it..."

"Fortune favours the brave, I always think. And I really *am* going to keep car use to a minimum while I find out what the story is. It's just that driving is kind of essential if I'm going to buy a trunkful of shopping."

It might have been madness to push my luck with another border crossing, but fortune did indeed continue to smile on me. Hungary, despite having erected a razor-wire fence to keep refugees from crossing its southern frontiers, offered no resistance to a car travelling in from Austria. We trundled slowly through the concrete canopy that must have appeared so foreboding back when it was a gateway to the Eastern Bloc, but which now looked totally abandoned.

I should have guessed that I wasn't the only 'Austrian' with the idea of coming shopping in Sopron. Pronounced 'shop-ron' in Hungarian, I guess we shouldn't have been surprised that the western outskirts were entirely dedicated to serving day-trippers hell-bent on stocking up at the cheapest possible prices. It was border awfulness at its sickening worst, and possibly no more than a throwback to a time when Hungary really *was* cheaper. Certainly the stark, angular buildings smacked of another era.

Sopron was skin-piercingly cold and frankly not a fun place to be. The spirit was perhaps best exemplified by a once-inflated Santa Claus lying face-down on a pavement outside an odd pentangular construction full of small traders peddling Xiamen City's finest.

"Look, even Father Christmas curled up and died here," I observed glumly.

"And I don't blame him," said Rebecca, looking around the neighbourhood with understandable disdain. There were more grim-faced Austrian motorists than anything else, and retail as far as the eye could see in any given direction.

"Still, can't really complain," I said. "People like me are the reason it's like this, I suppose. Say, have you noticed how many dentists there are?"

"Yeah, that's meant to be a thing, isn't it? All the Austrians come here to get cheap dental work done."

"I wonder if it really *is* cheaper," I remarked. "Or just a habit they've gotten into. Like coming here for a Thai massage."

I had at least hoped for an authentic Hungarian supermarket in between the dentists and massage parlours, but the most sensible option for a one-stop-shop appeared to be an enormous EUROSPAR branch. I had one of those down the road in Vienna, and couldn't think of anything less interesting than patronizing the same shop, to buy the same stuff, in the next country over.

"I bet it's not even going to be cheaper," I grumbled. "This was literally pointless. I'm probably spending more, when you consider petrol."

"But wait, Google says there is a town centre," said Rebecca, showing me her phone. "Look, it has churches and old buildings!"

"Excellent," I said. "Let's get this shopping out of the way and then go there for a spot of lunch. It's colder outside than it is in my fridge, so I think the milk will be safe."

Shopping went reasonably well, although one thing I hadn't considered was that all the labels on products would be in Hungarian, which has to be one of the most impenetrable languages of them all. This isn't a problem when you pick up a courgette or a toaster, but it was a heck of a challenge to tell a bag of sugar from a bag of salt. To this day I still get the odd surprise when I open containers up in the kitchen.

I managed to locate Heinz baked beans, which, as any Englishman will tell you, are the only baked beans worth mentioning. No matter how cultural and integrated one intends to be, there's simply nothing that can rival a tin of beans for convenience. You can store them forever, and they will always be there to rescue you when the shops are closed and you've got nothing fresh to cook with. I picked up a few cans. Interestingly, by way of another like-for-like comparison, they were actually more expensive than they would be in Britain.

Along with non-stick pans, pristine baking trays and all that food, I bought two FM radios. My plan was to have German radio in earshot at all times whilst in the house, and to use it as my alarm call too. This way, I would subconsciously absorb the language, taking in loads whilst in the semi-hypnotic state that typifies the first few minutes of each day. I would learn it like a child does, and never have to touch a textbook.

(I later discovered that this plan was deeply flawed. Nobody actually talks for longer than two minutes on any radio station in Austria. Before you know it, you're being blasted with the latest English-language hip hop, or, worse still, Italian opera. I could, however, pick up some very nice Slovak talk radio being beamed in from Bratislava. If only I was trying to learn Slovak.)

Eventually we got the hell out of the EUROSPAR, walked to the centre and discovered that the rest of Sopron was, indeed, not so bad at all. But we weren't tempted to hang around after lunch, partly because it was too freezing to mooch about, and partly because we intended to visit a *Perchtenlauf* on the way home.

Now I was mightily excited about seeing this peculiarly Austrian tradition, which has its roots in the Alpine villages but could be observed throughout the country at this time of year. All based on some kind of you-better-be-good-or-else Catholic twist on the build-up to Christmas that I can't claim to understand, a *Perchtenlauf* involves people dressed up as terrifying monsters running about the town and whipping people. These vaguely anthropomorphic creatures, a scary cocktail of masks, horns, cowbells and sheepskin that have frightened Austrian kids witless for generations, are known as *Perchten*. And I really wanted to see them with my own eyes.

After we crossed the border back into Austria, we made our way to Perchtoldsdorf, on Vienna's southern skirts. We parked up and followed the crowds to a hillside park, where a course had been laid out on the downslope. This, apparently, was where the *Perchtenlauf* would take place.

We bought *Glühwein* from one of those mobile vendors carrying his wares in a tank on his back, and waited for the antics to begin. And it really was the oddest thing.

Percht after *Percht* came storming down the hill, flicking whips at front-row members of the audience. Their bells jingled ominously, their eyes glowed red, and thanks to some perfume that wouldn't sell very well at your local chemist, they smelled like farmyards at the end of a hot summer's day. It was quite the sensory assault, to which the darkness only added a certain *je ne sais quoi*.

Every so often the wild beasts took breaks from lashing at the crowd to wrestle each other, which I thought was fabulous. I imagined that under the huge, heavy and intimidating costumes, these were just pairs of scrapping lads from the local football team. I resolved to sign up to be a *Percht* in time for the following season.

Over the next few days I stocked up on more essentials I'd forgotten - bed sheets, for example - as lunch breaks permitted. I got into the rhythm of work, went to more Christmas markets and cooked my very first meals in the new apartment. I also got to know my neighbours a little better. Right next door were Hans and Zita, German and Hungarian respectively, who'd taken a friendly interest from the moment I moved in. They'd saved me from having to eat off the floor, too, by lending me a couple of plates and eating utensils before I'd gone off on the elaborate shopping trip to Sopron.

I also made the acquaintance of Roman and Magda, a fine Polish couple who lived downstairs and had an adorable chocolate labrador named Tilda. They were forever walking the dog, so we would often bump into each other on the way in and out of the building. They'd been living in Austria a long time, and while they didn't know quite what the rules were for cars from outside the country, they seemed to have an encyclopedic knowledge of the regulations that applied to just about everything else.

We talked about my car a lot. After all, people were always noticing it. The yellow British licence plate was a colourful addition to a street full of predominantly white and red Viennese ones. And the car hardly moved, what with my numerous doubts about its legal status to be driven.

One day in the middle of December, Roman raised a car-related question that I'd never considered. One that gave me yet another car-related thing to worry about.

"Do you have winter tyres?" he asked.

"Winter tyres? Um, no. I don't think they have those in England."

"Ooh," he said, shaking his head. *Es ist Pflicht in Österreich. Pflicht!*

I got the gist of that quickly enough. Winter tyres were *compulsory* in this country.

Damn.

Driving On Thin Ice

It was already starting to look like the Peugeot was going to be nothing but a headache here in Austria. But, with a Festive Season holiday in South Africa coming up, I decided to worry about my car's dubious legal status after I returned. The Peugeot was only going to sit on the street, after all, and I didn't *think* there was anything illegal about that. I presumed it was only if I started actually driving it that people could ask questions.

Even if my stationary car *did* have potential to upset the authorities, there was no better place to bury it away than a single-lane dead end road reaching up into the forest. I couldn't imagine any traffic officer huffing and puffing his bulky frame up the steepest, quietest hill in the city to check on parked cars, especially when the parking rules throughout that area were officially free-for-all anyway.

My only real worry was that the engine might not like sitting in the cold for three weeks without being given a run. Even at around zero degrees, the temperatures were below what was typical for England's mediocre winters, and I'd been warned that much colder was possible.

"Minus fifteen!" the incredibly Viennese man from the Internet company had gleefully told me whilst setting up my wireless router. After which he'd proceeded to examine my thin winter jacket and said, "Man, you need to go shopping…"

I doubted the 306 had ever known temperatures of minus fifteen. Trying to avoid adding any unnecessary grief to my existing catalogue of car worries, I gave the key to Roman and asked him if he'd mind turning the engine over every now and then while I was away.

Three weeks back home in South Africa came and went in a flurry of live cricket-watching, catch-ups with old friends who now had kids, and, of course, cooking large quantities of meat on open fires. I caught up with Melissa just days after seeing her in Austria, in the very different surrounds of the tranquil Overberg, the rural district where one found Riviersonderend.

Unable to source a car or a lift from a friend, I even hitch-hiked back from Riviersonderend to Cape Town. In the context of 21st-century South Africa, this made me feel like I was still young and brave after all. Melissa, who likes to try and see the best in people, was the only one of my friends who didn't think it was a completely loopy idea in our not-so-safe country.

The trip to South Africa could fill a book. Perhaps, one day, it will do so. But this is a European story, so I'll skip on to mid-January and my return to Vienna. At which point I found that things had changed.

I got home to the fascinating sight of icicles on my windows: it had indeed been down to minus fifteen while I was away, and not just for a day or two. The Danube's side channel was completely frozen over. It had been regular water when I left, but now people were walking their poodles on it. Some brave souls were even skating, although the newspapers reported a couple of them falling through unexpectedly thin patches of ice. Which must have rather ruined their outings.

While the Danube itself was frozen only at the edges in front of my house, it was apparently semi-solid downstream in Budapest. And it might have set completely had they not been thuggishly smashing the ice further along the river in Belgrade, apparently in order to free up shipping traffic. I was disappointed in the Serbs for undoing nature's work: by all accounts this level of protracted freeze was something to be savoured nowadays.

But something far more important than the temperature had also changed. When I went down to buy some milk at Spar - that one nearby store that had played a key role in my decision to take this flat, you will recall - I couldn't find a single carton. Nor a loaf of bread. Nor a block of cheese. I couldn't even get in the front door, in fact. The whole bloody store was gone!

What had looked like a thriving, well-stocked outlet when I got on the plane to South Africa had apparently closed down without warning during the three weeks I was gone. The insides were well and truly gutted, all branding gone; had there really been a shop here at all? Apparently my handy local Spar was now going to be turned into a megastore specializing in pet food. I couldn't believe it.

The sudden closure of the only store in walking-distance meant I now had another compelling reason to try to legally register my car in Austria. Because, when it came down to it, I didn't much fancy dog biscuits for dinner.

My Spar might have been destroyed and the Christmas markets dismantled, but at least the 306 fired up first time when I got the key back from Roman. It was time, I thought, to finally start thinking about sorting out its Austrian paperwork. I couldn't go on living like some kind of automotive outlaw. They would catch me in the end.

My German was still very rudimentary, to the point that I didn't even try to tackle the problem of figuring out where to start by reading the Internet. Nor was phoning anybody going to get me far. I needed someone who could speak English and answer all my questions. Like, for example, whether I needed to get insurance before registering, or needed to register before getting insured.

(I guarantee you Google wouldn't have given me a straight answer on this, because no competent authority would have put all the information in one place, and in such a way that I'd be sure it wasn't out-of-date or hadn't moved into the hands of some different authority. And even if they had, it wouldn't be in English. And even if they'd done it in English, the FAQ's would never have featured any of *my* Q's, which never seemed to be very F. People really needed to stop sarcastically saying 'Just let me Google that for you' until they'd tried solving challenges like mine. Search wasn't as good as they reckoned.)

I found just what I was looking for in the main street in Döbling, the political epicentre of the 19th district. I spotted the office of a local car insurance chain, and supposed they ought to be familiar with the regulations.

And heaven be praised, the people inside spoke English. I carefully explained that I had brought a *right-hand drive* car all the way from the United Kingdom, and now wanted to register and insure it in Austria. And what would insurance cost, by the way?

The man turned out to be more clued-up than I could possibly dream. He was like a kind of super-Google. "Let me write down the steps for you," he said. "First you must get your car in the Austrian car database. Then you must get your roadworthy test. Then you must go to the city and you pay your car tax. Then you must go and pay for your registration plate. *Then* you come to us, and show us proof of all these things. After this, we can give you insurance. Which, I think will cost...hold on...Horst, come here and help me work this out!"

Three colleagues crowded around a computer screen, trying to key in things they'd never keyed in before. Right-hand drive. British. Pretty damn old by Austrian standards. Even the burgundy colour was kind of unusual here, from what I'd seen. But finally the first guy straightened up and dismissed the others.

"Okay, this would be €86 per month," he declared. "I'll print you a quote."

"Per *month*?" I cried. It was more than double what I had been paying in England. "Does this country really hate cars so much?"

"It's quite a normal sort of premium here," he said smoothly.

"I see," I said, still reeling. "Let's just take a step back for a minute. And just assume for a minute I want to actually go through all of this. How do I get my car into this 'Austrian car database'?"

"You need to get it from your manufacturer. I think the main Peugeot dealership is the one just over the tracks in Heiligenstadt. They should be able to help you."

I thanked him for being wonderful and giving me all the straight answers my laptop couldn't. Though the cost of insurance was a shock - and registration and tax would be another €300 - at least I was beginning to get a clear picture of what would be involved in registering and running a car here. Then, just maybe, I would be able to make an informed decision. I was excited by my step-by-step instructions and had the wind in my sails. I whizzed straight over to Peugeot to address step one of getting my car decked out with one of the coveted black-and-red Vienna licence plates every other car on my street so effortlessly sported.

I walked into the dealership, up to the first desk I saw, and said: "I have a Peugeot 306 outside. Apparently I need to put my car in the national database. Apparently you guys are the ones who do that. Am I in the right place?"

In a perfect world, the lady would have nodded, smiled, tapped a few keys on the computer, printed out a beautiful certificate for my car and said, "Here you go, son. You're on the list. Go get yourself a roadworthy!"

But that, of course, would have been far too easy. It wouldn't be *my* life if it weren't fantabulously, splendiferously complicated.

"Sorry, you're in the wrong place for that," she said. "The main dealership is in Wienerberg. It's on the other side of Vienna."

I didn't know how to say 'of course it bloody is' in German, so I just banged my head briefly on the counter, sighed dramatically and went on my way.

Now I was on a mission. I wasn't going to let this rest at all. I wouldn't sleep until I knew *the deal* once and for all. I was carrying every car-related paper, licence and technical document I owned, plus my passport, *Meldezettel* and, just in case, my squash club membership. I didn't think to telephone, partly because my German was even more crap on the phone than it was face-to-face, and partly because I assumed these people would want to see the car with their own eyes. So I just drove the Peugeot across town.

This was the kind of running around I *really* didn't like spending my precious Fridays doing. But dropping the quest now would be the most annoying thing of all: I was in dog-with-bone mode again. I didn't even think about eating or drinking. These would have to wait until I had *answers*. Fool that I was, thinking I could get them.

I arrived at the Peugeot dealership in Wienerberg at about five minutes past one. I went to the front desk and repeated the question I'd asked an hour or so earlier in Heiligenstadt. Who could help me with this Austrian car database business?

"Ah," said the lady in brusquely Viennese style. "There's only one man in that department. And he stops at one o'clock on Fridays."

I tried to suppress the rage building up inside me. "Okay, but can't someone else at least tell me whether it's actually *possible*? Like, whether this database is even a thing at all? And how long it takes, and how much it costs? What I need to do?"

"Nein," she said, before writing something on a piece of paper. "You can email him on this address. He is the only one who knows."

I went and stood in the corner, furious and unhappy, and took a few deep breaths. Only one man in Austria could answer my database question. *One man*. What if he got run over by a bus (or me...) tomorrow?

I had absolutely no more wind in the sails. I was well and truly becalmed until Monday. All I could do was trudge off home. I could have been the Grand Pollack of Wallachia for all anyone cared, and I wasn't going to get an answer until the new week.

When Monday morning dawned, I got a polite reply from this uniquely informed individual at Peugeot. Based on the information I'd given him, and the assumption that I would send him every paper barring the squash club card, he reckoned he could get me in the database within a few days, for the princely sum of €200.

"Your email says €200," I wrote back. "Did you mean €20? Was that a slip of the keyboard?"

He emailed once again and confirmed that it wasn't a typo. I reeled and spluttered and fumed. Peugeot actually wanted *three figures* to punch a few things into a computer. I was certain this job couldn't be more than a few minutes of actual work for them. This was pure monopolistic money-making.

I wish I could let these things rest and accept them as a feature of the world. Many people do. I can't manage it. The whole thing made me seethe. I was truly appalled. Peugeot were the only people authorized to give me this certificate, and they were totally cashing in on the fact that I legally couldn't go elsewhere. There ought to have been a law against this kind of thing. A worldwide law, ratified by the United Nations and enforceable by its troops. Made-up, opportunistic 'fees' for nothing were the scourge of the twenty-first century. When would companies go back to expecting to do some actual *work* to earn their keep?

Once I'd calmed down, I reflected on my options more rationally. Even if I were able to find €200 (I can't even *type* it without wanting to scream ballistically at Peugeot Austria and pummel someone in senior management), there was no guarantee I would pass my roadworthy test. I had no idea what the parameters were in Austria, and with my non-mechanical mind there was no point in pretending I could work them out. The only person who could tell me if I might pass my test would be the guy who would carry out the test.

And that test was the big remaining question mark. Peugeot's paperwork was a cheeky rip-off, but seemingly a formality as long as I was happy to let an automotive giant rob me of my hard-earned money in broad daylight. If the car examination was the most likely stumbling block, it would make sense to do the test *before* the expensive paperwork. Did I really have to do things in exactly the order the insurance guy had said? It was worth double-checking on that. Again, this was a question for a guy who worked at a test centre. His opinion was quite literally the only one that counted.

So I drove down to the industrial park at the bottom of my hill, where there were a couple of places advertising that they did these *Pickerl* tests. I already knew the German was going to be particularly challenging here. Wherever you go in the world, you can usually count on mechanics, bin men, bus drivers and other salt-of-the-earth types to offer up the thickest dialects and accents. And in my early experience, Vienna was no exception.

I battled through a strained conversation with a large, mustached Viennese man whose *Wienerisch* drawl would have had him kicked out of your high school German class on the first morning. Instead of the High German '*haben wir?*' he would likely say the unrecognizable '*Hamma?*' He would pronounce *da* a bit like an English person would say 'door'. And instead of the '*gut*' or '*toll*' you may find in your textbook, he would use peculiarly Viennese words like *leiwand*, starting the word with a sunken-tongue letter '*l*' that would immediately mark him out as being from this part of the world.

Not that I knew many of these details at the time: I could barely make out standard German, never mind anything leaning towards *Dialekt*. This was a challenge I was ready for, however, and perhaps even relished. A bit like learning English in Newcastle, I guess. Although for my money Austrian dialects changed their words far more regularly and substantially than even the most extreme British variants did.

I quite liked the increasingly rare sound of authentic Viennese, although Austrians from other parts of the country, not to mention Germans, said it was one of the most dreadful takes on the language to listen to. But take that with a pinch of salt: people were jealous of Vienna's award-winning quality of life and reputation for enjoying it. And jealousy, as we all know, makes folks nasty.

For someone who has just moved to a place and is trying to make a life there, you would be unlikely to hate the local lingo. As long as you like where you're living, then hearing the accent is going to give a cozy sense of place. And if one day you leave - and provided the memories are good - then hearing that dialect will always make you smile. Just like *that* song from your youth.

As for this particular conversation with the guy at the testing centre, I got the general gist. And the gist wasn't good. I needed to have this €200 paper from Peugeot before he could perform the test.

I didn't know if that was a legal requirement or just something they usually did, but equally didn't know how to phrase the question. I stopped off at another *Pickerl* (another Austrian word I love - it literally means 'sticker') testing centre and got much the same answer. I tried my best to explain that this innocuous-looking paper was going to cost *zwei Hundert Euro*, and couldn't we do the test first? Just this once? Nothing doing.

Well, at least I knew the deal now. If I wanted to run my car after April, I would have to do things in precisely the wrong order - or *arse about face*, as British dialect would have it. I would have to submit to Peugeot extortion, then pay another €60 to probably fail the test. All in, €260 for nothing. And if I somehow achieved roadworthy status, there were registration fees, taxes and that juicy €86 monthly insurance fee. And petrol. And maintenance.

So it was official, then: trying to register the car was going to involve money, luck, guesswork and lots of nervous waiting to find out if I'd wasted a ton of cash on nothing. It didn't sound all that appealing.

Resolving to bury my head deep in the sand, I decided simply to enjoy the car until April, when my UK insurance ran out. And *then* I would reassess the situation. Maybe the Peugeot would have broken by then, which would make my decision for me.

Although I was insured (depending on how you read my policy), I was pretty sure I was supposed to have registered the car in Austria by now. But registration was a huge deal, as I had just discovered. If I got pulled over between now and April, I banked on getting away with saying I was just passing through on holiday. My one concession to the law was to have winter tyres fitted (€220) and buy the stupid first aid kit and safety jacket (€10 total) I was meant to have had all those weeks ago in France. Checking these boxes at least meant there wouldn't be anything visibly illegal about the car if someone started sniffing about. And I could always sell tyres and first aid kits in due course, surely?

Cars aside, life in Vienna was proceeding very nicely. I was loving everything about it, save perhaps for the fierce winds that could rip through its streets in the winter time. I started to try out sitting in cafes and drinking coffee, which proved to be every bit as pleasant as it had looked from outside the window of Cafe Ritter on that first night.

This is one of the last places on earth where it's socially acceptable - even normal - to take a book to a cafe, order a coffee, and sit there on your own for the entire day. I'm not kidding: the waiters will not bug you for so much as a refill.

But they more than make up for this when you first come in. You'll still be struggling with your coat and yet to sit down, and they'll leap upon you, asking if you have '*einen Wunsch*'. To which the answer is usually that 'my wish' is to be allowed to actually take my seat and look at the menu before being hassled. And the funny thing is that after all the excitement and urgency of your initial order, you get more than just left alone. You get studiously ignored. You become invisible. If you *do* decide you want that second coffee, you virtually have to throw yourself at the feet of a passing waiter to get any attention. It's a very odd system.

But it was a decidedly unglamorous spot that became my favourite and my local. Cafe Baumeister, technically outside of Vienna in Klosterneuburg, the next town along if you drove past my house, was a friendly little place where nobody would dream of wearing a suit. You'd be served by down-to-earth ladies who would greet you with a *Grüß Gott* and salute you with a *Wiederschau'n*.

Baumeister had a little book library, the daily newspapers and all the same cakes you'd find in the fancy city place. It was the sort of place where they actually got to know you just a little. After I introduced myself as a newbie in the area, they gave me a sweet, pink, rum-soaked *Punschkrapfen* as a welcome present. And the second time I came back, the landlady remembered me, and asked me how my *Einleben* was going. I didn't know what that meant, but she explained it as something akin to 'settling in'. I loved the German version though: 'getting into living' might be a literal translation. A fine example of the power this language gave you to construct words.

And considering I had discovered a local that gave you confectionary to welcome you to town, I had to admit that my *Einleben* was going pretty well. I guess I'm just easily pleased.

One last thing about Baumeister: it had a smoking section. And this was nothing unusual in Austria. In fact, you may be staggered to learn that the cafes with smoking sections were actually considered the progressive ones. There were plenty of establishments that were one hundred percent smoker-friendly. Yes, right in the middle of Europe! In 2017! Never mind what Brussels said, nor what the rest of the continent had accepted as standard, Austria's smoking culture still persisted and resisted.

I hate second-hand smoke and I hate the smell it leaves on my clothes. But you know what? I liked Austria's stubborn adherence to the old ways. We had more than enough standardization and streamlining in the world. Enough health, safety, regulation and identikit chains. Why not let the experience of walking into a smoky cafe be Austria's little thing? Something the rest of us could travel to Vienna and marvel at.

Because hey, if you didn't want to sit in a smoky bar, nobody was forcing you to go into one.

A Little Bit Of *Einleben*

As the countdown to spring and the deadline to make a final decision about my car approached, I continued to do a bunch more *einleben*-ing.

One of the first things I had to do was find a doctor. I signed on with one on the fringes of Klosterneuburg. He came recommended and turned out to be good. The only curiosity was that he had an evident fetish for frogs.

We're not just talking a subtle logo on the guy's business card: the entire surgery was devoted to the little green critters. The kids toys in the waiting room? Frogs. The motif on the doormat? Frog. And the garden gnomes on the back balcony? Well, they were garden frogs. You could, if you felt inclined, count over three hundred instances of frog on any given visit to this doctor. And I think the world needs more of such playfulness.

I got round to guzzling down my very first Wiener Schnitzel in Vienna, and rather than doing it in a restaurant, it was actually one of those pizza-style deliveries. As a new cultural experience, this was hard to fault. Nor was the *quantity* of food that a schnitzel entailed. It was perfectly normal for one to take up an entire plate.

And I found this to be a good policy. Size definitely mattered when it came to my meals. Somewhere after university it had stopped being the fashion for my generation to rave about how *much* one ate. People had become sophisticated. They'd started to earn real money, and begun to frequent establishments where portions were small. They went to pop-up eateries and cooked hipster dishes for dinner parties, where it was presumably now uncouth to pile one's plate sky-high with mashed potatoes or arrange the hot dog eating contests that had been perfectly acceptable in primary school. I never could understand why stuffing one's face had had to go away. I liked good food, but if a meal didn't fill my belly then it had failed. I rather enjoyed taking huge helpings when surrounded by grown-up friends. It made me feel a little bit younger.

To my immense pleasure, I also discovered that there was a cricket scene in Vienna. Despite the sport being about as known on mainland Europe as spotted dick and scones, it seemed there were enough Commonwealth ex-pats living in Vienna who wanted to swing a bat. There were several clubs, actually: enough to form a league.

So in February I joined my first indoor practice sessions with the Vienna Cricket Club, the only one I had been able to trace on the Internet. Icy as it was outside, April and the outdoor season would no doubt roll around fast. I was excited to get out on the field at Seebarn (Austria's main cricket venue, just beyond the edge of Vienna) and give a few balls a wallop.

Even while awaiting the thaw, I couldn't see much that would sway me from the opinion that Vienna's regular awards for being the most Amazing Place on Earth to Live were pretty well justified. By no means would you call it the most *exciting* place in the world - under no circumstances could I imagine its inhabitants exuberantly dancing the *samba* in the middle of the stately Ringstraße - but if you wanted to live well and safely then Vienna came into its own. The public transport was as reliable as any place I'd ever lived, the cycling lanes were excellent and the people selling things on Willhaben were almost unnervingly polite and pleasant.

Sensational news of murders, bombings and rapes was in such short supply that one of the local *S-Bahn* railways getting a new colour on the city transport map made all the Vienna papers. There was even a photo call, in which Viennese transport dignitaries gathered for the unveiling of the new pink signs for the S45. That a place could be so innocent in this day and age could only be a testament to its quality of life.

If there were enough developments on the city signage front to keep the local press busy during the week, Sundays were surely a nightmare for any journalist. Vienna came to a complete, total and state-enforced shutdown.

It was a day of rest as strict as you would find anywhere in Europe. Thou Shalt Not Go Shopping on a Sunday. Petrol stations aside, only four grocery stores stayed open in the entire city, and then only because they'd apparently exploited some loophole in the law. But once I'd gotten used to the fact that I had to buy provisions by Saturday evening, before 'the Shutdown' kicked in, I decided I quite liked the idea of us all being forced to chill for a day. It was an institution here; no more or less than a fact of life.

What I didn't so much enjoy about Austrian shopping hours was how curtailed they were on the *other* days of the week. Close everything on Sunday by all means, but slamming the doors shut at six o'clock on Saturday evenings? That's very limiting. What if I were out on a long bike ride in the twilight? Even on regular weekdays, you wouldn't find shops open past eight o'clock. On busy days I might still be in the office at that time, with barely a thought given to dinner before I emerged. The message was quickly learned: one had to plan one's meals in advance in Vienna.

(It's no use telling me I ought to have done my shopping at lunchtime. I tried that, but soon realised that no amount of pushing and shoving was going to fit salmon fillets, cabbages and tubs of fresh yoghurt into the miniature fridge at work so that they could survive until I went home.)

It was little wonder that the cafes - and kebab stands - did so well here. The kebab kiosks, run by Muslim gentlemen from a broad swathe of the planet ranging from Ankara to Casablanca, were seemingly as good a business idea in Vienna as anywhere else, even if you did need to add the *Käsekrainer* and *Schnitzelsemmel* to your repertoire.

What you really didn't want to do was try to open a McDonald's or a Starbucks. While branches of these mega-chains did exist, it was fair to say they did so on the fringes of society. The Viennese were as suspicious of these global monsters as they were loyal to their local cafes, to the point that *Mäci* and Starbucks seemed to have been pushed underground. Quite literally so, in the case of the metro hub at Karlsplatz. I suppose there may have been a law forbidding these companies from appearing anywhere too conspicuous. And if there was, then that was perfectly reasonable to me. One of the reasons the Ringstraße looked such a postcard was that commercial activity was understated or non-existent along its best stretch. If you gave Burger King half a chance, I'm sure they'd have thrown open a branch on the steps of the *Rathaus*.

We really were very lucky to have an office where we did. If I chose to take the tram to work, the last mile or two would take in the University, Parliament, the *Burgtheater*, the *Rathaus*, the *Volksgarten*, the National Library and the twin Museums, between which a portly Maria Theresia statue kept watch on proceedings.

If you ever needed a reminder of just what a big deal Vienna was for a few hundred years before World War One, you only had to stand next to the much-admired empress and look across the Ringstraße, where a positively imperial gate guarded the entrance to the *Heldenplatz*, upon which you'll find both the library and the Hofburg, the palace from where those Habsburgs used to rule. Above the gate's five arches, Franz I was remembered as the Emperor of Austria - which was a much bigger and more powerful place, easily a rival to Germany, back when they built it. In 2017 it was easy to forget that Austria's modern incarnation was only about a century old.

I took to working some afternoons in the National Library, where anybody could come along and use the reading rooms for an annual fee of just ten Euros. No way could any office be as quiet as this place, which was teeming with the students that make up so much of the city's population. Many of them seemed to spend a majority of their time on Facebook and flicking through their phones, rather than doing anything scholarly, but they were jolly quiet and respectful about it all the same.

While the modern reading rooms, with all the conveniences you would expect, were perfectly fine for working, I was rather puzzled that I couldn't see any actual books about, save for a sorry handful of shelves containing things like Slovak-German dictionaries, the 2016 bound volume of *Angora Goat Husbandry Quarterly* and that day's morning newspaper. There had to be more! This was supposed to be a library, after all.

I had had visions of strolling quietly amongst the dusty wooden shelves, leafing through whatever tome took my fancy. But, like some kind of modern take on the *The Name of the Rose*, these were fiercely guarded by librarians with computers. The dusty books, I could only assume, lived in the curved wing of the building adjacent to the Hofburg. Unless you were a terribly important scholar - and the library did have its share of members-only areas, where I was quite sure I didn't belong - you weren't going to be leafing through anything you pleased willy-nilly. You had to look it up in the database and make a formal request for it. Which is absolutely no fun at all.

Speaking of that Umberto Eco novel about a secret monastery library run by homicidal monks, the movie which I'd first seen at the far-too-young age of ten in faraway Cape Town, I got the shock of my life when I picked up a dropped wallet on a walk next to the Danube one Sunday afternoon. The cards revealed that the purse belonged to a certain Mr Qualtinger. Who upon coming round to pick it up and enjoy a whiskey, admitted to being none other than the son of Helmut Qualtinger. The same man who'd played quite a significant role (Remigio di Varagine, the corrupt cellarer, if you're wondering) in the film. And also, as I discovered, one of Vienna's most celebrated actors and singers. It was one of those small-world moments of synchronicity that had you shaking your head for an explanation.

In the second half of that winter - and only because I had visitors who insisted on doing so - I took in a couple of operas. While going to the elegant *Staatsoper* might have been the quintessential Viennese experience, the fact remained that I don't care much for this particular art form. What's the point in singing something in pleading, ear-piercing, pompous fashion when you might just as well, oh, I don't know, *say* it?

How is one supposed to take these strutting buffoons seriously? I didn't mind hearing a good singer, but the distinctly persuasive style of opera songs has a jarring effect on me. It's the same with musicals: breaking into 'spontaneous' dance isn't going to dispose me favourably to whatever it is you want. All it will do is make me laugh. Come to think of it, if operas and musicals actually *admitted* how ridiculous they are, and marketed themselves as comedy, I'd probably be first in line for a ticket.

With all of that said, going to the many opera, classical music and theatre productions on offer in this arts-crazed city was just something you had to do. One feels ever so sophisticated when one says "I'm going to the opera this evening," a feeling which stays with you only as long as it takes for some mean colleague, who knows perfectly well what they are doing, to throw you under the bus by asking exactly what performance it is that you're going to see.

What I saw, for the record, was *L'Elisir d'Amore* at the *Staatsoper* and *Hansel and Gretel* at the *Volksoper*. I much preferred the latter. There was no soppy love story and no fat guy in leather boots wailing about getting his hands on a love potion. Instead there was a witch, who got thrown into a furnace just before the curtain went down. If I go to any more operas, I think I'll once again stick to children's productions.

One thing both of the primary Viennese opera houses had in common was a dedication to obsessive injunctions regarding jackets in the auditorium. They had people employed for the express purpose of enforcing these regulations. At the *Staatsoper*, for instance, while we stood innocently waiting in the cheap *Parkett* standing area, a bad-tempered old Viennese lady appeared from nowhere, rearing up like a spitting cobra ready to strike. Her height seemed to double as her eyes flashed with fire and fury. She proceeded to jab a bony finger into a friend's winter coat as she issued the singular command that apparently gave full meaning to her existence: "This...must go out! To the cloakroom!"

At the *Volksoper*, it was an anorak under my seat that qualified as an outrage. The usher there was somewhat younger and less aggressive. She approached my seat with the same sort of terrified look most people reserve for the words 'Sir, we've just been informed that a family member of yours has been taken ill,' but whose *actual* fear was that I might dare to sit through the entire performance with my jacket rolled up beneath my chair.

It's at moments like those that I'm quite sure the sheep and the birds and the fish are merrily laughing away at us. I sure hope they are, anyway, because what's the point in us humans over-complicating our world to such a ridiculous degree if it doesn't at least provide some entertainment for our animal brethren?

Speaking of complicated, learning German was proving to be frustrating beyond measure. Although it had little to do with mastering relative pronouns or the devilish dative case. Nor even the constant bugbear that stalks every European language, which is the continent's obsession with ascribing gender to nouns, something English has quite successfully proven to be completely unnecessary and which makes putting together a sentence infinitely tougher than it needs to be. German's particularly brutal in this regard, thanks to its insistence on having a third gender, the neutral. (Into which category, by the way, the word for 'girl' falls. Go figure.) Not even the Italians or the French expect you to deal with more than a masculine and a feminine gender.

But none of this was the real problem. I was a language geek, and although I'd rather not have to learn some sex-related article to go with every single word in the dictionary, I can and did battle through. What I really couldn't handle was trying to practice German with people who kept on speaking English back to me.

Given the almost obscene level of English ability that plagues northern Europe, I'd arrived in Austria with concerns that this would be an issue. But I'd never thought the problem would exist on such an epic scale. My attempts at immersion were proving to be a total failure. Because immersion, I quickly understood, only really works if people around you *don't* speak your language.

And if English happens to be your mother tongue, well, you've got a heck of a disadvantage if you want to practice another language through daily use. Because everyone else already speaks yours. Thanks for nothing, Hollywood.

Immersion might work in Japan or Brazil or the Central African Republic, where they might not speak English so well and there's nothing for it but to bumble through and learn the local vernacular as fast as you can. But if you think you're going to get fluent in German by moving to Berlin or Vienna, master Swedish by shipping your life to Stockholm, or learn Dutch by emigrating to Amsterdam, be prepared for a long, hard battle. It sounds dramatic and overstated, but trust me, practicing a language in these places really is a test of character. The moment anyone clocks you're not a local - which is obviously going to happen quite soon, no matter how impeccable your grammar is - they'll switch to English.

I found this an odd phenomenon, to say the least. If an Ethiopian came up to me in Cape Town and addressed me in English I could understand perfectly well, I doubt I would automatically switch to Amharic. Partly because I don't speak a word of it, sure. But that aside, he's making the effort to speak my mother tongue, and we are on my territory after all. Equally, if I went to Addis Ababa, I wouldn't expect any Ethiopians to do *me* any favours. This seems the natural order of things.

Not so in Austria, where people seemed to jump at the chance to speak a foreign language. English was a special case - I got that - but to me it still comes across as a strange and almost subconscious tic.

Even when people got the message that you wanted to speak German to them, it seemed to magically be forgotten the next day. You could have an entire evening speaking about Newtonian physics in German, but the next time the sun came up and your foreign face walked into the room, they'd greet you with a hearty 'Top of the morning, mate!' or some such. It's like that whole conversation you had just vanished from memory, and you have to remind them all over again. And it wasn't just one, or two, or three people - it was almost everyone. I couldn't begin to understand.

I tried to think of reasons why it was such a battle, and came up with four. The first was that they were trying to be polite and make it easy for me. The second was that, English proficiency being the status symbol it was, they thought you were insulting them by suggesting they couldn't manage in English. ('Of course!' was the tepidly irritated response I got used to getting after trying to be decent enough to ask people if they speak English, rather than just assuming they did.) Theory three was that they simply found my patchy German irritating to listen to. And finally, that people's English was so good that they were genuinely unaware they were even speaking it to me. (I wish my German could get to that level.) Probably it was a mix of all of the above.

With some people, you just couldn't win. But if you worked hard, trained people and were insistent, you could eventually find your fair share of conversation partners. I would also strongly recommend telling people you're from, say, Armenia, and don't speak English at all. That way, they'll simply *have* to let you practice and learn.

Here, I would like to take a moment to publicly thank everyone who patiently helped me improve my German by letting me speak it. To those who were being polite: I appreciate the thought, but you have my express permission to be rude. And to those who might have felt insulted or impatient, please remember how it was that you came to speak English as well as you do. It's because you never had any problem getting the practice you needed.

A Pickle About a *Pickerl*

While settling into general life was going as well as I had dared hope, the head-burying was going to have to stop soon. D-Day for the Peugeot was fast coming up.

Now that the thrill of the road trip had worn off, and I was confronted by a mountain of question marks and bureaucracy, a part of me was starting to regret having brought the Peugeot here. It wasn't a decision you could really undo, and she was beginning to look like the problem that wouldn't go away.

Still, the less responsible part of me wanted to squeeze as much as I could from the pleasures of car ownership. As the expiration date on my open-to-interpretation insurance policy approached, I tried to use the 306 as creatively as possible before perhaps being forced to give it up. I eschewed visiting the likes of Budapest, Brno and Bratislava, which would easily be accessible any time by buses and trains, and instead made a point of visiting the out-of-the-way places you needed a car to reach.

This was a fun new experience. I would go onto the Airbnb website and zoom the map onto rural-looking corners of Southern Moravia or the Tatra Mountains. If the accommodation was anywhere near a train station, it was out. I wanted tiny villages offering no obvious transport links.

It's fair to say these places usually had no points of interest whatsoever. But, on the other hand, they were spots I'd never otherwise get to. And they offered whole flats rented out by poor old grannies who probably only got one or two guests a year.

(In keeping with standard Eastern European Airbnb practice, you only discovered your landlady was a granny the day before you arrived, when the glamorous-looking granddaughter who posted the Airbnb advert texted to tell you that she's actually studying in Prague and that grandma, who doesn't speak English, will be the one letting you into your lodgings.)

It was thus that during the spring I got to visit little Křepice in the Czech Republic. The grandmother there cooked me marvellous mountains of hearty Mittel European food while I wrote up a storm without the slightest distraction. Apart, that is, from the Orwellian street broadcast that lit up the village with marching-band music and various local announcements on the Friday afternoon. Apparently this communist-era relic is still quite common in the Czech countryside.

On another weekend I stayed in the village of Liptovská Kokava on the mountainous Slovak-Polish border, where I'm convinced drunken men jumped on the bonnet of my obviously foreign car at the end of a long night of beer intake. Being dent-blind and scratch-blind, I only noticed the indentations when I got home to Vienna, at which point the connection with the otherworldly shrieks and metallic banging that had awoken me at five o'clock that Sunday morning quickly became clear. (Actually, calling it merely a *night* of drinking may be an understatement, considering I'd seen several of the villagemen already at it in the local cafe at nine o'clock that morning. I hoped their dentists earned handsome wages for having to peer amongst their teeth.)

I was no longer much afraid of borders, since I'd had my safety jacket and first-aid kit (though I'd dug my heels in about the triangle) and even winter tyres duly installed in and on the Peugeot. In fact I felt much safer driving outside of Austria, where any half-decent sleuth could figure out I'd been living for some time without having registered the car. In Hungary, Slovenia or any other neighbouring country, on the other hand, I could quite legitimately say I was just passing through with my insured and roadworthy British car. Which was perfectly allowed, to the best of my knowledge.

But as my car got closer to achieving uninsured status in April, I could clearly feel the net beginning to tighten. It didn't help, either, that my parents received a speeding fine dating back to December in Vienna, which meant the authorities now had a very clear record of how long I'd been in the country. I drove like a tortoise after that, convinced I'd be in trouble for more than just speeding if I got flashed again.

But ironically, it was driving ultra-slow and trying to avoid trouble that got me pulled over by the police three days before my insurance expired. After a day spent exploring the *Weinviertel* country between Vienna and the Czech border, I found myself pootling about after dark just a kilometre from the frontier at Laa an der Thaya. Following my new policy of extreme caution, I must have barely been doing 60km/h on a road with a 100km/h speed limit.

With hindsight, I realized that old, foreign cars going extremely slowly are even more suspicious to Austrian police than old, foreign cars going at normal speed. Especially when the registration in question doesn't even have that reassuring collection of gold stars on a blue background that indicate some kind of EU affiliation. Britain doesn't bother with all that European stuff, you see.

When I noticed a pair of bright headlights bearing down on me from behind, I thought the same thing I always do when that happens, which is, 'Oh joy, another Audi-driving show-off.' When the lights pulled out and overtook me at what seemed like the speed of sound, but was probably still well under the limit, I thought the same thing I always do when *that* happens, which is, 'Why must people always be in such a hurry?'

I assumed the car would disappear over the horizon in a matter of seconds, but what happened next really threw me. Once it was in front of me, it slowed down substantially. Then someone started waving a lollipop-shaped light, flashing an angry red, out of the window. I'd never seen anything like it before.

At this point, largely due to the fact that my tormentors had no markings and lacked any of the traditional blue lights, it still didn't cross my mind that this might be a police vehicle. So I thought the same thing I always do when someone's fooling around in a nearby car, which is, 'Must be some teenage idiot jerks trying to bait me. And I'm not rising to it!'

Thus it came to pass that when the car pulled over in a lay-by in front of me, still frantically taunting me with its lollipop, I cruised right past it and threw a superior look in its general direction. It was the darkest of nights, but still I hoped they got the vibe I was trying to project.

The occupants didn't seem to like me ignoring their lollipop. They pulled out of the layby like scalded cats after I swept past, and then - only then - found the switch for some blue lights too. 'Cripes,' I thought. 'These might actually be police.' But I still couldn't fathom the lollipop.

The next time they pulled off the road, I thought I'd better do the same. A tall Austrian policewoman emerged from the car, accompanied by a male colleague and a silent third officer, who judging by the *Policija* on his uniform, was on some kind of work exchange program from Slovenia.

The policewoman addressed me in German. Though by now I could have gotten by, I thought this was a particularly good time to play the dumb new arrival in Austria, shrug and tell her I could only speak English.

She was fluent, of course. Damn Western European education systems. Damn Hollywood. Damn it all. "Why didn't you pull over the first time?" she asked.

"Sorry," I gulped, "I've never seen that device before...I thought it was somebody playing a joke. And it didn't say 'police' on the car. I'm from South Africa, you see, and over there you really don't let unmarked cars pull you over in the dead of the night."

She seemed satisfied enough with this not to continue debating the point, countering instead with "Do you have your driving licence?"

"Oh, yes, absolutely!" I gushed. I really wanted to leave a good impression with this positive answer - I wasn't sure how many more I was going to be able to give. My mind was racing: would I go with telling them I was just passing through Austria on holiday, or come clean about living here and hope for the best? If the limit for registering locally really *was* six months (and I still hadn't quite gotten round to confirming) then I was safe anyway.

But there was only ever one answer to the question of fibbing. I'm an appallingly bad liar. Seriously, I'd be the worst cheat ever. I just can't do it. On the other hand, I'm quite good at coming across as confused and stupid even when telling the truth, probably because these qualities come so naturally to me. And that's usually an asset when it comes to dealing with police, who tend to be on the lookout for maliciousness rather than innocent simpletons.

So when she asked me if I lived in Austria, I truthfully told her that I lived in Vienna and that I'd 'recently arrived from England.' I prayed she wouldn't ask me what 'recently' meant, and, heaven be praised, she didn't. I was rather banking on the hope that proper police like these (it was a multinational operation, after all) were after slave smugglers and drug runners, and wouldn't be all that interested in car registration issues.

I was requested to open the boot, and although I think they were hoping to find a stash of illegal stimulants, I proudly displayed my first aid kit and high-visibility jacket. They didn't say anything about the fact that I still hadn't got a triangle: perhaps roadside geometry was beyond their remit too.

At this point I was rather more worried about the second Austrian police officer, who had taken my licence off to his car and was now doing things on a laptop computer. He was looking up my speeding fine, no doubt, and was going to emerge triumphantly any moment, crowing, "Aha! This car has been driving around Austria for weeks! And still with a British registration! And no European insurance cover! Away to the cells with him! The cells, I say!"

For a while I stood around with the Austrian policewoman and the escaped Slovenian policeman, who looked every bit like you'd expect someone who'd turned up to the wrong country for work to look: confused,

249

embarrassed and bashful. Then, neither triumphantly nor dejectedly, the man with my licence got out of their weird unmarked car and came towards us. He nodded at his colleagues and handed me my licence.

"*Passt,*" was all he said.

Now this was a word I'd already heard a lot in Austria. It usually signified agreement. Like if you suggested you would meet somebody at seven-thirty, they might respond with *passt*. It was kind of an all-purpose 'okay' as I understood it, but I still wasn't entirely sure what it meant in the context of a policeman giving you back your driving licence. I got that I was free to go, but was it 'okay' as in 'Okay, we've found out all the dirt, so now you can drive off and wait for your court summons,' or 'okay' as in 'Okay, you're a fine and upstanding person, young man, and we're sorry to have troubled you this evening."

I was dying to know what he'd pulled up on his computer, but thought the better of asking. It would only make me look like I had something to hide. Not wanting to seem too eager to get away, either, I waited respectfully while the police trudged back to their car and departed.

Then I got in my increasingly troublesome Peugeot and drove back to the city with my heart pounding. I felt like I'd *probably* survived this grey zone until my insurance gave out - but only just. And in two days, even I had to concede that the grey was going to turn definitively red.

The next day I popped down the hill for one last massive shopping run. I'd be limited to what I could carry by hand the next time, so made sure to buy potatoes and toilet rolls. Then I parked the car outside the front of my house. Indefinitely. After that freak-out with the police, I wasn't touching it again until it was fully legal.

A trifle annoyingly, the car was still firing on all cylinders. Steadfastly refusing to break down and make my decision for me. Instead it was being far too good, taking me to remote corners of central Europe, and also to our out-of-town cricket ground that had no public transport links worthy of the name. There were so many reasons to fight on. So many reasons to hand over a risky 200 Euros in a bid to get it registered.

Looking back now, it's clear that what I should have done was to very nicely ask a mechanic to at least *look* at the car and tell me if there was anything obvious that would make it fail the test. If I'd done that, I would have found out straight away that in Austria you could be failed for having a *scratch* on the paint. Or for having a chip in your windshield. Since neither had been an issue for the British roadworthy test, my car had both in abundance. If I'd simply asked the guy at the testing station to glance out of the window, I'd have known the game was up. If I'd done that, I'd be over two hundred and fifty Euros richer today. (To put that in perspective, I'll need to sell about 600 copies of this book to recoup that.)

But no, I didn't think of having an informal chat with a mechanic. I just bit the bullet and signed over a week's worth of wages to have Peugeot print out a piece of paper. Which they couldn't even manage to do quickly. You'd think that paying the world's most outrageous and exorbitant administration fee (It had to be top five, at the very least. Unless they were using saffron-spiced ink, in which case I completely understand), might have earned me some kind of priority in Peugeot's bureaucratic hierarchy. But you'd be wrong.

At least there wasn't any *problem* with the final papers. Nobody whistled in a low tone and said 'good luck with this, sonny' as they handed them over. These expensive sheets were, by and large, just a bunch of technical specifications anybody (sickeningly) could have printed out off the Internet. A standard against which a mechanic - should I pass the scratch test - could measure a few key performance indicators.

Now I needed someone to do the test itself. My mistrust of mechanics had always been sky-high, and the language factor made it trickier than ever to choose one I thought wouldn't go making up issues he could charge me to fix. (The industrial area, as you've probably figured out, was the one place people didn't speak English back to me. It was also the one place I could really have used them doing so.) Then Roman and Magda saved me by recommending a guy they'd been using for years. But there was a catch.

The honest mechanic was obviously *really* good, because he was booked out until July. I would have to wait two months, until the height of summer, to discover my car's fate. I shrugged and booked an appointment: my car couldn't come to any harm sitting there on the street in warm weather, could it? And I could give it the occasional run down to the recycling bins at the bottom of my hill. There wouldn't be much risk in that.

July came. Seven months after driving my car into Vienna that freezing December night, my day of reckoning had finally arrived. I got in the car and drove it to the testing station, which I presumed *had* to be allowable. I took my bike out of the boot, cycled home, and waited until Honest Mechanic could get around to deciding my machine's fate.

251

When the phone rang later that day, Honest Mechanic said a lot of things. In German. Quickly. I didn't get much of it. "Let me come down," I told him. "I'll understand you better in person."

I cycled back to the testing station and saw my car sitting in a different part of the forecourt to where I'd left it. Clearly someone had moved it, looked at it, done things to it. What would be the verdict? Would I, or would I not, get that coveted *Pickerl*?

The End of The Road

One look at Honest Mechanic's face told me everything I needed to know. He looked serious, but couldn't hide a tiny trace of amusement. I thought I had an inkling of what was coming when he handed me the test report. But I was wrong: it was all so much worse than I could have dreaded.

My Peugeot 306 had failed the test on a staggering 26 counts. I reeled as the mechanic calmly, professionally and still-stifling-a-smilingly took me through them one by one, which was a complete waste of time since he was telling me things in German that I wouldn't even understand in English. The one part I did get was the bit about scratches and chips in the windshield. Which is when it dawned on me that I could have had a simple answer to this whole business the day after I arrived.

"It wouldn't make any sense to try and repair all this," he said. "It would be far cheaper to buy a brand new car."

I smiled weakly and nodded, my thoughts churning with all the *waste* of time, money and effort this thankless endeavour had entailed. Actually *waste* didn't even begin to cover it. I'm not sure words ever could.

"So now, that will be sixty-seven Euros please," he said. "Will you pay by card?"

I handed over more money for nothing, cursing the system, the rules, Austria's pickiness, Google's uselessness and above all myself for failing to have a two-minute chat to this guy months ago. After all he clearly *was* honest, since he wasn't trying to sell me hope in the form of repair work. I reckon he could have eyed up the car on any number of times I'd driven past his workshop, probably without me even needing to slow down, and said 'You're wasting your time, mate.'

Hindsight is a fabulous thing, isn't it?

Understandably, I think, I fell into a deep and dark depression. My car's fate was sealed, I was considerably poorer for nothing.

The path forward, if such it could be called, was clear enough. There was nothing for it but to try and sell the car. To a *very* small market of people who might want a car that had no prayer of ever being road-legal in Austria. The only thing it had going for my Peugeot, really, was the virtually new set of tyres that still adorned the wheel hubs.

Despite the odds being against me, I was quite keen to get some money for it after the financial bleeding the whole performance had cost me. I'd pulled in at a couple of dodgy scrap dealers on the way home from the testing station, and they'd offered me a hundred Euros. A hundred Euros! This was less than half of what I'd spent on the tyres alone. I'd be giving away a chassis, an engine and two new tyres for free. *Surely* I could get more than that for it?

I picked up one of the advertising slips one found lying around all over Vienna, which offer to give cash for cars - even ones without a *Pickerl*. This sounded like exactly the sort of thing I wanted. I phoned up a charming Ghanaian gentleman, who sounded decidedly disinterested after I told him the car was right-hand drive, and then begrudgingly offered me 150 Euros. I told him about the new tyres that were worth more than that, but he wouldn't budge. I declined the offer to give him some discounted tyres and a free car.

After all, there was no need to rush into anything now. The car was well and truly parked once again, and not doing any harm to anyone. Much as I wanted to be rid of the thing, I didn't feel like now was the time to cave to the first offer I could get. Not after all the work I'd put in to get this far. (Which was nowhere, evidently, but still, it *had* been a lot of effort.)

Over the next few days, I pondered what the used-car landscape might be like in Austria's many neighbouring countries. Sure, my car might never be declared legal *here*, but Bratislava was less than an hour away. The Czech Republic and Hungary lay barely much further. Surely there was reason to hope that outdated stereotypes might still have a grain of truth to them when it came to cars, and that belchy rust-buckets could still be legally driven in at least some of these places?

After all if the same car could pass a roadworthy test in Britain, and fail it miserably in Austria, then it was clear there wasn't a lot of EU standardization going on in such matters. From that point of view, there was every reason to hope that a Slovak or Hungarian might be able to enjoy it for many years to come. Which might, I reasoned, make it a much more valuable asset on the other side of Austria's borders. In Slovakia they even used Euros, and I could compare apples with apples.

Of course, there was the question of how to *get* it to all those keen buyers in next-door lands. I was out of valid excuses for any police I might meet between home and Austria's borders. Could I advertise it on websites in neighbouring countries and hope that somebody with a tow truck would come and pick it up? If I'd tried hard enough, and enlisted regular help from native speakers, then probably yes. But by now, more romantic plans were taking root in my brain.

I was starting to feel a need to go out in style. Why not do an exciting and highly illegal dash to the frontier at four o'clock on a Saturday morning, that would get me to Gyor in Hungary in time for the car dealerships to open? Or should I just forget about selling it, and rather just have some fun? By which I mean a similar dash to the Czech Republic, followed by thrashing the last bit of pleasure out of the car in a track day on the city's Grand Prix-standard racetrack. If I could completely destroy the car with a good crash, it would solve the one nagging doubt I had about selling it anywhere, which was that I'd sign some dodgy contract and fail to get the car out of my name. And that some Slovak speed freak would then keep on racking up speeding fines on my behalf.

Or, if I couldn't crash it or sell it in some neighbouring ex-communist country, then I could always just park it with the keys in the ignition and the door unlocked. Then I'd jump on the bus home and report it stolen. That way, nobody could pin any speeding fines on me. I mean, if someone *did* drive it, then I wouldn't be lying to say they'd stolen it, right? I might have made it very *easy* for them to take it...but facts would still be facts.

Then something happened that made me have to shelve all of these fanciful ideas in a hurry. After my careful efforts to make sure the battery didn't go dead in the depths of winter, I now forgot to fire it up regularly enough as it awaited its final fate on my sun-drenched doorstep. The battery went completely dead.

'No problem,' I thought to myself. 'I'll just find a neighbour with some jump leads.'

In South Africa, every self-respecting male has a set of jump leads. Even *I* had a set when I lived there, for the love of all that's holy! But in Austria, apparently, not a soul could lay claim to a pair. I asked friends, colleagues and my entire street. And they all said the same thing, 'Call the ÖAMTC!'

This body is the Austrian equivalent of the Automobile Association, and quite frankly people seemed to be head-over-heels in love with it. Mechanical self-reliance most definitely did not seem to be a thing here. All I'd gotten from a week of asking around was the chance to learn the German word for jump leads (it's *Starterkabel*, by the way.) into my memory. Oh well,

255

at least I could use my new-found vocabulary to get in with the guys down at the industrial park.

So there I was, with a becalmed car that wasn't going anywhere near Slovakia any time soon. The only thing in its favour was that it was pointing downhill. Down a *very* steep hill, come to that. I could use that to bump-start the car! Couldn't I?

There were certain considerations when it came to implementing this plan, of course. Not least of which was the fact that halfway down the hill was an incredibly tight hairpin bend for which brakes and steering were both critical. And while I didn't know much about cars, I did know this: if the engine didn't take, I'd have very little stopping or turning power as I careered towards the sharp bend.

I surveyed the route and noted the little escape path that lay beyond the hairpin. It was no more than a patch of gravel between the edge of the road and the entrance to the forest footpath. But up to a point, it was a place into which an out-of-control car could be directed and hopefully stopped.

My attempt at a bump-start proved to be a frightful cockup. Wary of the potential catastrophe awaiting if I didn't get the thing fired up within a hundred and fifty metres, I was probably just too careful after dropping the handbrake and beginning to roll. Old age, risk aversion and all that. Perhaps I never allowed the car to build up enough speed before my repeated attempts to get the clutch to bite. Or maybe it was just never going to happen.

Whatever the mechanical truth, I ended up coasting rather gently, and without even a hint of engine power, into the gravel outside the hairpin. It was at this point that I noticed that thanks to the hairpin taking the incline in another direction at this point, I was now on a substantial *uphill*. And that only my front wheels had made it to my impromptu gravel trap. My back wheels, far from reassuringly, were still on the actual road. And I'd need an army of people to push it any further on from where it was.

It was all just so *lame*. At least I hadn't gone all the way to Brno Autodrome to have an accident as pathetic as this.

It wasn't a catastrophe, being a particularly quiet dead end and given that there was still plenty of room for people to get by. But it was the kind of thing that grumpy neighbours tell the police about. And if there was one thing I wanted to avoid with all my heart and soul, it was the police visiting my car again.

Now, all of a sudden, the time for caving to the first and fastest purchase offer had indeed come. I was stressed out, tired and couldn't take much more of this car. Now that it was stuck halfway down my road with its nose in a forest, I needed the Peugeot out of my hair once and for all. I'd have to let pretty much anyone who could fire the thing up and put it on a tow truck take it away.

I put two advertisements on *Willhaben* right away. One was for the car at €200. The other, for good measure, was for a set of brand new winter tyres at the same price, with the text containing the small caveat that the tyres were attached to wheels, which were attached to an unroadworthy Peugeot, and that any buyer would need to take the lot.

Within a couple of days, during which I inevitably did have to explain to neighbours that the car was basically stuck and that no, I wasn't going to buy an ÖAMTC membership just to fire up a car I was about to sell, I got a call from a mechanic in Wiener Neustadt. He'd spotted my clever tyre advertisement, but was actually interested in the car itself.

"You're welcome to it," I told him glumly, expecting him to flee as I broke the news of its current status. "But there's one more thing. The battery's dead. You'd need to have a way of firing it up, because I'm sure as hell not paying a penny more towards this drama."

"That's fine, I've got one of those," he replied.

"And you've got a tow truck?" I asked, feeling slightly more hopeful.

"Of course!" It was as though I'd just asked him if he spoke English. (Even though he didn't.) I should have known, really, that the sort of people who own tow trucks are the same sort of people who own *Starterkabel.*

The next day he came over and met me at the gravel patch, taking the car's obviously difficult circumstances very much in his stride. He asked if he could take it for a test drive.

"Well, I don't think so," I said. "It's not registered or road-legal, you see. I *did* write that on the advert, didn't I?"

"You did," he smiled. "But don't worry, I'm allowed to do it."

I watched on in awe as he produced some special blue licence plates from the boot of his car. He then fixed them over my number plate, made some meticulous notes in a log-book and assured me that with these, mechanics were allowed to take cars in every imaginable state of disrepair for test drives.

I shook my head, wondering at the world. Here this strange man was, hanging some strange plates over the top of mine, which apparently made any questions about my car's legality vanish. He then proceeded to jump-start the car and drive us down the nearby autobahn at a solid 160km/h.

This only succeeded in making me sad, because the engine was singing along the highway like a bird in the treetops. With my careful efforts to avoid attracting attention in recent weeks, it had been a long time since the car had been stretched to such lengths. But the engine was clearly still in very good shape. Why was I having to sell my faithful Peugeot again?

It all seemed so unfair. I'd spent untold time and money, jumped backwards through hoops to try and be allowed to use my car in Austria long-term. But the only one to benefit was this grinning mechanic, who was, considering he was getting the new tyres and no doubt had a way of prising them off and selling them, getting an effectively free and perfectly sound 1600cc Peugeot engine. No wonder he seemed so happy.

We went back to my road, where he was able to park the car in its proper spot once more. We walked upstairs and signed a simple deed of sale he'd brought with him. I didn't doubt his integrity, to be honest, and liked the guy to the point that I even gave him a beer. He sipped it as we did the paperwork, and I explained what a catastrophic experience bringing my car to Austria had been. He nodded sympathetically.

I knew he was going to tear the car apart and put the engine in some other chassis. But for what it was worth, I was glad I'd at least sold it to a decent bloke. I didn't think I'd ever say this about a car mechanic, but if anyone was going to get the bargain of a free engine, then I'm glad it was a guy like him. I'd watched the careful way he filled out that log book with the correct date and time: it seemed I'd found a second honest mechanic in less than a year. I felt quite sure this man wasn't going to run up speeding tickets in my name.

He gave me four fifty Euro notes. It didn't feel like very much reward for everything, but it was something at least.

I gave him the keys and we drank a toast to the Peugeot. He would come back the next day, while I was at work, and put the car on his tow truck.

When I walked down the hill to the bus stop the next morning, it was the last time I ever saw my faithful Peugeot 306 from Brize Norton, Oxfordshire.

Did I shed a tear? Did I think to take a goodbye photo? Both would have been nice, but such was my relief that I forgot to do either.

And how do I get to my cricket matches in Vienna nowadays? I rely on other people with cars. And when all's said and done, that's not so bad after all.

Epilogue

In the days following the sale, I was plagued by recurring nightmares involving daily speeding fines being sent to my parents in England. In all of them, the mechanic to whom I'd sold the car, cackling maniacally, was boy-racing around the streets of Wiener Neustadt in the middle of the night.

I had no idea if that thing we signed in my house had any legal status in any country. I wasn't a bloody lawyer, and the basics of contracting was another thing school hadn't prepared me for. And how would the British authorities know about the sale? They would just keep telling the Austrian traffic police that any fines should be assigned to me.

Even if the mechanic changed the plates before going off and crashing into things, I felt sure cars had serial numbers or similar that could be traced to me. God, I was sure to be ruined!

After a few minutes on the Driver and Vehicle Licensing Agency (DVLA) website in the UK, I concluded (as I *always* seemed to have to do with everything) that my case was a special one. Nobody, it seemed, had ever bought a car in Britain before and then sold it outside Britain. All the forms, like the hardcopy V5C that lived with the car, were set up for domestic sales. I'd got the mechanic to fill that out too, but parts of it made no sense in foreign context.

You could declare the car exported, sure, but the form for that didn't seem to free me of the burden of ownership and resulting speeding fines. Once again, it looked like I was making some kind of history with my strange requests.

So, in the absence of any forms and *extremely* low on patience for the whole thing, I did the only thing I could think of: write a letter. Wanting it to be as quick and easy as possible, and wanting to appear so moronic and technically-challenged that they would give up any attempts at dialogue, I hand-wrote it and put it in an envelope.

I'd had experience with this kind of letter doing the job. Because handwritten letters couldn't be processed very well by their automated systems, yet surely still have legal standing in a world that couldn't actually *force* you to own a printer or even have Internet access, authorities generally found it easiest to just say yes to whatever you've written. Such letters had worked a treat with the UK tax office before.

This one worked equally well. Within a few days I received a written confirmation (by post) that the Peugeot was no longer registered in my name. For amusement and the record, then, let's conclude this saga with the full text of my hand-written letter to the DVLA.

26/7/17

Dear DVLA,

I moved to Austria and have just sold my Peugeot 306 (reg W398RGJ) here. I am not sure if there is any form for that kind of sale in Europe, but I thought I had better write and tell you. I enclose the V5C - I got the Austrian guy to fill out the new keeper part.

This is declaration that the car is no longer in my name and no longer lives in the UK. Please do not send any speeding fines to my UK address if they come from Austria or anywhere else, as the car is no longer in my possession.

Yours Sincerely,

R.A. Dalkey

Your Thoughts?

If you liked this paperback, would you mind taking a moment to review it online? It would be a great help!

If you ordered it online, you'll already know exactly where to go to leave a review. But if you got yours in a bookshop, or you borrowed it from your library or book club, then just pop on over to **books2read.com/Austria**. There you'll see the links to my book in all your favourite online outlets. You could leave a review on Apple Books, in the Kindle Store, or wherever else you prefer.

Should you be interested in ordering a truckload of signed copies for all your neighbours, or even just want to give me some constructive criticism (bring it on!), then mail me on rasher05@gmail.com.

About the Author

R.A.Dalkey *(nom de plume)* was born in Cape Town, holds British citizenship and now lives halfway up a steep, wooded incline on the edge of Vienna. Since growing up amidst the euphoria and disappointments of post-Apartheid South Africa and settling (Brexit-permitting...) in Austria at 35, he's lived in the USA, Australia and the UK.

An incorrigible dreamer, he's driven outback trucks in Australia, spent two years trying to be a professional golfer and slept rough everywhere from Monte Carlo to Siberia, visiting over 70 countries along the way. Including Ireland, where he cracked up every time he rode the DART train past a town called Dalkey, and an author name was born.

As for the occasional bout of work, he's known to do his fair share of editing magazines and writing. Under his own name, his words have been published by *GQ, Reader's Digest, The Sunday Times, Australian International Traveller, Die Presse, Autosport, Sports Illustrated* and Reuters, to name just a handful.

You can follow him on Instagram @worldsleeper

Printed in Great Britain
by Amazon